Rights and Wrongs of
Children's Work

The Rutgers Series in Childhood Studies

The Rutgers Series in Childhood Studies is dedicated to increasing our understanding of children and childhoods, past and present, throughout the world. Children's voices and experiences are central. Authors come from a variety of fields, including anthropology, criminal justice, history, literature, psychology, religion, and sociology. The books in this series are intended for students, scholars, practitioners, and those who formulate policies that affect children's everyday lives and futures.

Edited by Myra Bluebond-Langner, Distinguished Professor of Anthropology, Rutgers University, Camden, and founding director of the Rutgers University Center for Children and Childhood Studies

Advisory Board

Joan Jacobs Brumberg, Cornell University
Perri Klass, New York University
Jill Korbin, Case Western Reserve University
Bambi Schiefflin, New York University
Enid Schildkraut, American Museum of Natural History and Museum for
  African Art

Rights and Wrongs of Children's Work

MICHAEL BOURDILLON
DEBORAH LEVISON
WILLIAM MYERS
BEN WHITE

RUTGERS UNIVERSITY PRESS

NEW BRUNSWICK, NEW JERSEY, AND LONDON

LIBRARY OF CONGRESS CATALOGING-IN-PUBLICATION DATA

Rights and wrongs of children's work : new perspectives from research and
action / Michael Bourdillon . . . [et al.].
     p. cm. — (The Rutgers series in childhood studies)
  Includes bibliographical references and index.
  ISBN 978-0-8135-4888-3 (hbk. : alk. paper) — ISBN 978-0-8135-4889-0
(pbk. : alk. paper)
  I. Child labor.   I. Bourdillon, M. F. C.
  HD6231.R54   2011
  331.3′1—dc22   2010003039

A British Cataloging-in-Publication record for this book is available
from the British Library.

Visit our Web site: http://rutgerspress.rutgers.edu

Manufactured in the United States of America

CONTENTS

PREFACE

Even if it is not your habit to read book prefaces, please read this one. Before starting to read this book, it is important to understand what it is, and why, and what it is not, and why. And that involves knowing how it got this way.

We are four widely published specialists on "child labor" who share a concern that much current thinking and policy regarding children's work is wrongheaded and out of kilter with recent social science research and the lessons of experience. We decided to write a book that would express these concerns based on a thorough exploration of available research that would present its findings, critique its methods, and discuss its implications for policy. Below the surface of the wealth of new research that has poured into the field in recent years we find an interesting pattern: the gradual emergence of a critique of the conventional wisdom of "child labor." This was not necessarily new—a precursor book to this one (Boyden, *et al.*, 1998) and some articles have challenged aspects of the conventional wisdom—but what has not been available is up-to-date exposition of research and experience driving these new ideas, and sustained discussion of their implications for policy and practice.

In preparing this book we have consulted many hundreds of sources—many more, in fact, than the 500-plus sources that readers will find in the bibliography—but we have tried to avoid the intimidating and boring reference work that might have resulted, and to keep the book short and readable. This has meant, first, that we have privileged information that we expect to be new to most readers and, second, have reluctantly sacrificed in-depth discussion of some important issues that some readers may have wished to see included. So, what is this book? It is an investigation into the place of work in children's lives and development, and also into the kinds of policies and interventions that are (and are not) appropriate for ensuring their work is safe and suitable. It is not a book about "child labor." The following explanation will illustrate why. In his introduction to a large international, comprehensive encyclopedia of child labor, *The World of Child Labor* (to which all of us have contributed and which is being published as we write), the editor Hugh Hindman posits two general approaches to the topic. The first is a "mainstream" view that regards child labor as harmful, that "entraps whole populations, regions, and nations in cycles of poverty and underdevelopment—so that its abolition is sought, and the sooner the better"; and a "minority view," which "holds that there are many things worse than premature labor that can happen to children . . . and that as long as children's economic contributions remain essential for family and child survival, rather than seeking to abolish child labor, we should support children and enable them to find 'decent work'" (Hindman, 2009, xxvii). We do not subscribe to either of these positions, and the reason is that we have come to think that "child labor" frames the subject far too narrowly, which is problematic both for thinking logically about the issues and for intervening to protect children. We therefore have expanded the field of vision to "children's work," including much not usually considered "child labor." That expanded view provides valuable research and action perspectives that escape Hindman's categories and allow us to consider information and ideas that correct many of the disadvantages of a "child labor" focus. The reasons will become clear in the text.

Work is part of the lives of almost all the world's children—in the USA and Britain, as much as in Uganda and Bangladesh. Some kinds of work are extremely harmful to children; other kinds are relatively harmless; still others are beneficial, a positive element in child development and growing up. How can children find protection from the harm that some kinds of work may involve, without being deprived of the advantages and benefits that other kinds of work may offer?

The "rights" and "wrongs" in the title of this book are intended to carry double meanings. "Rights" should be understood to refer both to the human rights of children, especially as set forth in international documents such as the Universal Declaration of Human Rights and the UN Convention on the Rights of the Child (UNCRC), and to what is correct and valuable not only in children's work but also in the way we understand and govern it. We argue that work in proper circumstances can be "right" for children, and that they may have a "right" to engage in such work. We discuss what we consider "right," or at least better, ways to think about children's work in the light of evidence from research and experience, and we challenge some prevailing assumptions and stereotypes that we find to be unjustified by evidence—and therefore "wrong." "Wrongs" refers also to what is abusive and inappropriate in children's work, as well as to mistaken interventions in child work. Children can be "wronged" not only by harmful work, but also by misguided policies and interventions that, despite good intentions to protect children, may actually leave them worse off.

A further word about children's human rights is in order. Human rights as articulated through international law are so new that the world is still in the process of working out how to conceptualize and apply them. And so are we; we all subscribe to children's human rights but do not always agree on what that means in practice. The texts of international law and legal discussion around them are of limited help for facing real-world situations. We have minimized legal discussion of children's rights in regards to work, which is in any case well covered elsewhere (e.g., see Weston, 2005). Moving from text to action is fraught with controversy, and that is where we focus this book. Despite our diversity of opinion on the details, we do agree that rights texts should be flexibly interpreted and applied with common sense as necessary to fit them to real-world contexts. Often that means looking more to the spirit and objectives of rights texts than to their letter. That is the approach taken in this book.

Children often suffer discrimination or abuse in work relations. This problem is shared by other social groups: women, migrants, minorities, and the disabled. But it is only in the case of children that societies aim to resolve the problem by protecting them from work itself, rather than protecting them in work relations and promoting their rights as workers. Why do we think about child work situations differently than about adult work situations? How did the idea arise that children should be protected from work itself? What particular image or model of childhood do these ideas reflect? And where do these ideas come from?

There is a need to rethink both current policies and the assumptions that underlie them about children, work, and school; we cannot rely on "conventional wisdom" if it is faulty. Instead, we look at other ways of understanding what is bad and what is good when children spend time working and learning. To do this, we need to hear and respect the views of Moroccan factory girls, Guatemalan shoe-shine boys, Indonesian farming children, and American school children—we cannot figure out what harms and what helps girls and boys without including in the discussion their experiences of work and school, and their understandings and views.

As authors, we are not isolated in these concerns, which are shared by many others. Indeed, we rely heavily on the research and insights of others. But we hope in this book to have raised the issues in a systematic way, to provoke and give form to further debate. We hope that the book will be useful for people planning policies and programs relating to children's development and the role of their work in their lives, by providing frameworks to assess situations and intervention. We also hope that it will be useful to students and academics, in presenting systematically issues for research and debate, suggesting theoretical tools, and indicating where to find further information and ideas.

The mistreatment of children is a moral and political issue, and rightly arouses passions. If responses are reliably to improve the situation of mistreated children, passions need to be tempered by information and reason. Much has been written about children, work, and education. Not all of it is based on good information or solid research. We have chosen in this book to present enough information to indicate what people concerned with child protection need to think about, keeping the chapters short and based on a careful selection of available, reliable research. We have made frequent use of illustrative case materials, both qualitative and quantitative, and particularly research that attends to the views and perspectives of children.

We want to provide understanding that leads to principles for practice. We do not claim to have detailed solutions to all practical problems. Although we recognize the importance of law in reflecting, setting, and enforcing standards, our concern in this book lies elsewhere. Our discussion of rights and standards is concerned not so much with their legal interpretation and enforcement as with an understanding of how they impinge on the lives of children. In addressing this question, it is useful also to ask who has the authority to determine rights. Are rights properly granted by the powerful or claimed by the powerless? By what authority does the United Nations, rather than children or their families and communities, determine what children's rights should be? The issue becomes pertinent when one thinks, as we will in later chapters, about the participation of working children in defining their own best interest and the actions that serve it.

In chapter 1, "Raising questions, questioning the answers," we show how British assumptions of what is appropriate and inappropriate activity for young people damaged the opportunities of girls in Morocco. This example upsets some common assumptions and attitudes about child work and leads to reflections on how children's interests relate to adult interests, on the ways we understand childhood, on children's rights, and on the information needed to understand children's work.

Chapter 2, "Work That Children Do," indicates the sorts of work undertaken by children and adolescents in poor and rich countries and the realistic alternatives open to them. We start by discussing problems of defining and classifying work, and point out that no classification coincides well with whether the work is harmful or benign. There is a wide range of kinds of work that children do at different ages, and a range of reasons behind their choices of work. We pay particular attention to what children themselves say about their work, how they perceive the alternatives realistically open to them, and how they make decisions about their work.

In chapter 3, "Children's Work in Historical and Comparative Perspective," we compare the history of children's work, and ideas and interventions about it, in countries with different economic and social histories. We first take the case of Britain, where the concept of "child labor" as a social problem first appeared, and where the first attempts at its regulation were developed during the Industrial Revolution. We then present contrasting brief histories of children's work in two low-income countries (Zimbabwe and Indonesia). As further contrast, we look at the quite different experience of children's work in societies that attempted to follow "noncapitalist" roads to industrialization and modernization, using the examples of China and the former Soviet Union. These contrasting cases show the importance of state policies and of larger political and economic forces in shaping the life course of children and young people, including their involvement in work. Finally, we indicate how the "British model" influenced the development of international standards during the twentieth century.

The relationship between poverty and children's labor-force involvement is complex. Some children work when it is not necessary for basic survival. Also, some children from very poor families work a lot, while children from other very poor families do not. Is child work more a cultural phenomenon than a matter of economic necessity? In chapter 4, "Child Work and Poverty—A Tangled Relationship," we draw on the growing research literature on these issues to untangle the complex and varied connections between poverty and children's work. We also examine interventions that address the relationship between children's work, their schooling, and poverty. Although poverty may affect household work as well as paid and unpaid work in the labor market, this chapter focuses mainly on labor-market work.

In chapter 5, "The Role of Work in Child Development," we consider difficulties of defining and thinking about children's development in practical ways that facilitate determining whether work supports or undermines it, and then turn to social science for ideas and tools that can be helpful. We review the implications of research on child work from psychology and anthropology/sociology, and consider the negative impact of Euro-American ethnocentric constructions of work and universal policies based on them. Finally, we suggest how to regard work as a positive influence on children's development while monitoring it to prevent abuse.

Chapter 6, "Education, School, and Work," addresses what is perhaps the most heated and widespread debate regarding child work; the relationships between children's work and their education. Are work and education compatible? While most societies agree that school should be the main and indispensable non-home activity of children, there is disagreement about whether that implies school-age children should not take on work outside school. In this chapter, we consider evidence for and against the idea that stopping children from working will improve their attendance and performance. This leads to the methodological question of whether failure of the school system encourages children to take on other kinds of work, or whether work outside school hinders school attendance and performance. We look at a study that resolved the question by following a panel of children over time, assessing the effects of different kinds of work on their subsequent lives. Finally, we consider ways of combining school work with other kinds of work, and of learning through productive work, such as through apprenticeship.

In chapter 7, "Children Acting for Themselves," we consider ways in which children can and do manage their lives and their affairs, including their productive work. Many young people—among them orphans, street children, and young migrant workers—live with little or no adult support and work to support themselves and sometimes others as well. In the first part of this chapter, we explore ways in which such children manage their lives and affairs, including productive work. The second part of the chapter explores another example of children's agency in the emergence of organizations of working children. These organizations provide a further example of children acting, in partnership with adults, to control and improve their own lives. Finally we consider how children can exercise agency by participating in decision making.

Assessing the harm and benefits of different forms and conditions of children's work is a key to developing strategies and interventions that serve children's best interests. In chapter 8, "Assessing Harm Against Benefits," we start with the example of child domestic work to show the problems of dichotomizing work too crudely into "good" and "bad" categories. Situational factors such as conditions of work, the social context surrounding children, and alternatives realistically available are all relevant to the effects of work on the children, as are the perspectives of children themselves. We discuss the particular importance of the relations of work, both inside and outside the home. Since assessing the effects of work on children is rarely straightforward, we provide some practical suggestions for how to go about such an evaluation. We indicate the importance of taking seriously the perceptions and decisions of children, even when they enter harmful forms of work.

Chapter 9, "The Politics of International Intervention" presents two cases, one in Bangladesh and the other in Pakistan, in which foreign interventions in children's work in export industries followed recommended international child labor policies and ended up harming working children they had intended to protect. The viability of current international policies removing children from their work is challenged, and questions are raised regarding the relative unaccountability of powerful political and economic interests intervening in child work issues. In contrast to the problematic cases that left children worse off, we present a positive example from Egypt that worked in accord with child rights principles, leaving children in their work but making improvements in their working conditions.

Chapter 10, "Policies and Interventions: What Should They Achieve, and How?," outlines what policies are for and what they should be trying to achieve. Our approach recognizes that children are members of communities, with rights and responsibilities in society, and takes seriously the responsibility to make "the best interests of the child" a main priority in intervention. We argue that minimum-age strategies are effective neither in removing children from the "worst forms" of work, nor as a tool for getting children into school: rather, they greatly reduce opportunities for work to have a dynamic place in child development. Alternative approaches are available. Policies for children should protect them from harmful work, universalize children's access to education of the highest quality that society can provide, protect children's access to work that doesn't impede their access to education, and link work more closely to education by treating work as an educational tool in a positive sense.

Since this book is about children and work, we should explain how we use these terms. We consider "work" in a broad sense of activities performed to achieve a purpose, usually to satisfy a need and often under some kind of necessity, whether or not they are performed for payment or other rewards. As explained in later chapters we do not find the common distinction between "child work" and "child labor" helpful, and we avoid the term "child labor" unless quoting from sources that do use it. We also recognize the truth of arguments that school work is a form of work. In our use of the term "children" we follow current international conventions to include all persons below the age of eighteen; because this broad age group comprises people of widely different competence, needs, and interests, we refer to the specific ages of those we are discussing where this is relevant, and generally distinguish between "adolescents" and "younger children" (in chapter 5, we argue that it is not possible to precisely define stages in child development that can be applied across societies and cultures).

Finally, to prevent any possible misunderstanding we want to clarify our standpoint at the outset. We condemn the exploitation and abuse of child workers: this requires more urgency than it presently holds on national and international agendas. We support the right of all children to free education, of as good quality as society can afford, and consider this also a matter requiring greater priority than it presently receives. We support the UN Convention on the Rights of the Child, including the right of all children under eighteen to "protection from economic exploitation and from any work which, by its nature or the way in which it is carried out, is likely to harm the health, safety or morals of children" (article 32). But we also recognize the value, and in some cases the necessity, of work as part of growing up, and the reality that a "workless" childhood free of all responsibilities may not be a good preparation for adult life for children in any society and any social class.

ACKNOWLEDGMENTS

The book is the result of much research and discussion. We are indebted to the many people—from working children and their communities to researchers, advocates, and policy makers—who have challenged our preconceptions and shaped our observations and ideas over many years. To achieve the broad view that we take in this book, we stand on the shoulders of countless giants.

We are grateful to The Institute of Social Studies, The Hague, and to the Netherlands Institute of Advanced Studies for fellowships (in the former case financed by Plan Netherlands) that enabled Michael Bourdillon to do much of the groundwork and drafting.

In May 2009, Plan Canada arranged a colloquium (financed by CIDA) at which we received feedback on our drafts from academics and practitioners, helping us to focus on presentation and issues that are likely to prove useful, and after which we were able to stay together for a week to decide how to incorporate the ideas into our book. We are grateful to all of these institutions.

We would like to thank the following people who took part in the colloquium: Senator Landon Pearson, Michael Montgomery, Frances Cosstick, Janine Cocker, Tara Painter, Bianca Gucciardi Gonsalves, Andrea Khan, Robyn Chomyshyn, Richard Carothers, Will Postma, Ilana Alice, Anne-Marie Bourgeois, Jennifer Shorthall, Natasha Cassinath, and Sarah Stevenson. We also thank others who have looked at and commented on our drafts at various times, and discussed various issues with us, including Jo Boyden, Susan Bissell, Martha Nelems, and Victoria Rialp.

We would like to take this occasion to express our appreciation to the Canadian International Development Agency (CIDA) and to Senator Landon Pearson for their uniquely constant and long-standing moral support for approaches to children's work that are more sensitive to children's rights and well-being. We admire CIDA's patient and skilled donor support of the innovative PPIC-W project we cite in chapter 9 as a positive example. CIDA personnel expressed enthusiasm for this book project at an early stage when they first heard about it, and their collegial encouragement has helped us see the project through to completion.

Thanks to Hugh Hindman for having made a complete pre-publication text of his edited book, *The World of Child Labor*, available to us so that we could make use of and cite valuable information and insights from its articles. Thanks also to Richard Carothers for providing access to unpublished information used in chapter 9.

Ben White would like to thank his students at the Institute of Social Studies for their feedback and the often heated exchanges on these topics that they have enjoyed in recent years. Deborah Levison is similarly indebted to her students at the University of Minnesota's Humphrey Institute of Public Affairs.

All four of us thank our families for their patience and support.

LIST OF FIGURES AND TABLES

LIST OF ACRONYMS

AMWCY	African Movement of Working Children and Youth
BGMEA	Bangladesh Garments Manufacturers and Exporters Association
CCT	Conditional cash transfer
CDW	Child domestic worker
CWC	Concerned for Working Children
EFA	Education for All
EACID	Egyptian Association for Community Initiatives and Development
GDP	Gross Domestic Product
ILO	International Labour Organisation
IPEC	International Programme for the Elimination of Child Labour
MANTHOC	Movimiento de Adolescentes y Niños Trabajadores Hijos de Obreros Cristianos
MFI	Micro-finance institutions
MOU	Memorandum of Understanding (signed by UNICEF, ILO, and BGMEA)
NGO	Nongovernment organization
PPIC-W	Promoting and Protecting the Interests of Children Who Work
PROGRESA	Programa de Educación, Salud y Alimentación
UN	United Nations
UNCRC	United Nations Convention on the Rights of the Child
UNESCO	United Nations Educational, Scientific and Cultural Organization
UNICEF	United Nations Children's Fund

Rights and Wrongs of Children's Work

1

Raising Questions,
Questioning the Answers

In Europe and North America it is widely assumed that factory work is bad for children, a clear case of harmful "child labor." In this chapter we introduce an example of working children in Morocco which disturbs such common assumptions and attitudes about child work. This example leads to reflection and questions on how children's interests relate to adult interests, on the way we understand childhood, on children's rights, and on the kinds of information needed to understand children's work.

"When I was fired, I cried for two weeks": How Intervention Went Wrong in Morocco's Garment Industry

Toward the end of 1995, a team from British Granada TV's *World in Action* investigated the labeling of garments made in the Sicome factory in Méknès, Morocco, and found that many girls between the ages of twelve and fifteen were working in the factory.[1] Representatives from Marks and Spencer, the well-known chain that retailed the garments in Britain, quickly visited the factory. At the end of 1995, many of the girls were summarily dismissed, allowing Marks and Spencer to announce in January 1996, two days before the Granada program was aired on British television, "Marks and Spencer has conducted a full investigation . . . and absolutely no evidence has been found to support this claim . . . no young person under the age of 15 years is currently employed there" (Zalami, et al., 1998, 32). Superficially, the matter appeared resolved; there were no longer any under-age girls working in the factory.

The girls and their families, however, saw things differently. This is how Amal, a girl in Méknès, described her experience of finding a job at

the age of thirteen in the Sicome clothing factory, and losing it the following
year.

> I started to work at Sicome in 1994 and was fired in December 1995. My
> starting salary was 210 dirham ($21). My job consisted of trimming threads
> with scissors from finished garments. Sometimes I used to draw the lines
> on fabrics. . . .
>
> We used to begin work at 7.30 A.M. (the company bus picked us up
> from the neighborhoods at 6.30 A.M. and brought us back in the evening).
> We had a lunch break from 1 to 2 P.M. and we worked very often until 8 P.M.,
> but we were never paid for overtime. The working conditions were
> extremely tiresome and our supervisors used to insult us and tell us, "If
> you don't like it, leave: there are plenty of other girls waiting at the gate to
> be hired for less money." When the Europeans came to visit, one of the
> supervisors used to ask me and other young girls to hide.
>
> One day, as I was leaving at the end of the day, they called me into the
> office and one of the accountants, Shadia, asked me to sign a paper.
> When I signed it, she told me that I had just signed my resignation
> papers. They gave me severance pay ($90). I told her that I did not know
> what I had signed, but she told me that I was the one who wanted to quit.
> Then she said to come back in a year and we will probably hire you. . . .
>
> I wanted to study but I did not have money to buy school supplies and
> books. Now it's too late for me to go to school. I would not mind learning
> a skill in order to get a job. I need to work to help my family. The only per-
> son working now is my elder sister, who is a maid living in a home in the
> city . . . (Zalami, et al., 1998, 44: paragraphs have been re-ordered.)

Amal's account raises a number of questions. Why were she and other girls
working in the factory, and why were they fired? The action of the Granada team
was based on the assumption that factory work was bad for Amal and her
friends, and that their proper place was at home or in school. Were these
assumptions valid? Was the girls' employment illegal? And what were the consequences of their dismissal?

A Moroccan researcher, Fatima Badri Zalami, met Amal and eleven other
girls who had been dismissed from Sicome, and heard their stories. Her report
reveals the complexities of the situation and helps us understand the importance of knowing about the contexts of children's work.

In the mid-1990s, Morocco's textile and garment industries accounted for
about 40 percent of Morocco's export revenues and employed mainly young
female workers from poor rural and urban families. Work was nothing new for
Moroccan girls in low-income households, who traditionally started to take on
household chores from the age of five. They were usually confined to the house
or its immediate surroundings, while boys were free to roam. In the 1990s,

however, increasing numbers of young women joined the paid work force. Girls no longer wanted to stay at home, doing household chores and waiting for a husband. They found paid work outside the home a liberating experience, boosting their self-esteem and freeing them from the total control of the family. Their contributions to family income improved their status in the family. Work gave girls access to a world that they could not experience at home, including friendships and entry to the labor market. This experience would provide a chance to postpone marriage and improve their standing with their husbands when they married.

Unemployment among high school graduates was high, and the girls saw that extended schooling did not guarantee access to good jobs. So, with their parents' encouragement, they tried to enter the job market early. The Moroccan government encouraged young people to opt for vocational training. As in many other societies, young people had traditionally learned their trades and made themselves employable by working as apprentices. Morocco's laws allowed young people between the ages of twelve and eighteen years to take two-year apprenticeships (extendable sometimes to a third year), and offered them some legal protection. The laws specified that the employer should teach the apprentices a trade, that this training should not be longer than eight hours per day, that the apprentices should be allowed to attend professional classes, and that they should be paid according to regulations.

The girls gave many reasons for seeking paid factory employment. Some of them had been victims of gender discrimination, pulled out of school to help at home while their brothers were able to pursue their studies. One girl had dropped out of school because she was failing, and others had also been doing badly in the formal education system, which they saw as inadequate, irrelevant, rigid, and failing to provide sure access to a job. Economic pressures and family debts obliged families to seek extra income, and household heads—especially women—relied on their children to share responsibility for the family livelihood. Although it was not always dire necessity that drove the girls to work, their income made important contributions to family welfare.

Amal and about 100 other young girls worked under apprenticeship contracts in the factory alongside several hundred adult workers, producing pajamas and other garments on contract to one of the suppliers to Marks and Spencer. When they started to work at Sicome, all the girls had reached both the legal minimum age for apprenticeship in Morocco and the age for employment in light work in developing countries permitted by the ILO Minimum Age Convention (no. 138 of 1973).[2] They were therefore legally employed.

On the other hand, the girls' accounts make it clear that they had been systematically exploited in the factory. Sicome regularly contravened the provisions of the apprenticeship law: the girls received little professional training, they worked standing up for long hours, they were usually paid wages lower than those specified in their contracts, they were not paid for overtime work, and they did not receive adequate health benefits. Some young girls left the factory of their own accord because of the way they were treated.

Most girls nevertheless saw advantages in factory employment. Their main alternative were jobs in the informal sector, such as street vending, or in domestic service where pay was worse and conditions of work may be very harmful (discussed in chapter 8). Many young people worked in home-based or cottage industries, where they had no legal protection and sometimes suffered permanent damage (for example, from inhaling fumes from the glue they used). An apprenticeship in a garment factory offered a rare opportunity for formal-sector employment, which the education system no longer guaranteed. Conditions in factories producing for export were certainly not ideal, but they were better than in enterprises producing for the local market. Employment in the export sector was consequently relatively prestigious work. The girls' earnings, though small, gave them some financial independence. In spite of bad treatment at Sicome, it was the preferred employer in Méknès by both girls and their parents, providing the girls with a relatively safe work environment and safe free transport to and from work. Viewed from this perspective, the textile industry represented the best among available options, providing girls with work that was considered culturally appropriate.

When their employment was suddenly terminated without any period of notice, the girls lost all these advantages. For Amal and her friends, dismissal meant a reduction in family incomes. The employer, not the children, was responsible for violating the regulations on working conditions for apprentices, but it was the children, not the employer, who suffered the consequences of dismissal. It is widely assumed that if children are stopped from working, they will go to school,[3] but these girls could not and did not return to school, for reasons they were not in school in the first place, and because it was difficult once out of school to obtain re-admission. They were effectively robbed of a relatively secure, formal-sector job, in what was considered the most desirable form of employment for low-income women. All were desperate to find alternative employment. Some of the girls formerly apprenticed at Sicome remained at home, helping with household chores and making buttons, a time-consuming and poorly paid task, which the girls say damages their eyesight. Others found less attractive jobs, while at least one became involved in prostitution. Some may eventually have been re-employed at Sicome, but with the same poor working conditions as they suffered before they were dismissed. The intervention by the TV team and foreign corporation affected only work for the export market, which in the eyes of the local community was the best and most sought after work. Outsiders had no influence over, nor any apparent interest in, the less advantageous forms of work to which the girls were driven.

How should we view the employment of these girls? Certainly, there are some kinds of children's work that are clearly so harmful that they should be stopped. An example is the glass factories of Ferozabad, India, where children work long hours in intense heat and at high risk of injury, in such conditions that adults often cannot continue beyond their mid thirties (Wal, 2006, 52–62). But work in the Sicome factory was not like this.

It is too simplistic to try to classify all kinds of child work dichotomously into "good/safe" work that can be permitted and "bad/harmful" work to be abolished, based on ideals prevalent outside the community concerned. In the case we have presented, the situation of the girls could be seen as exploitative and harmful, but it is not necessarily factory work as such that is harmful: the problem lay in the working conditions and relationships with employers and supervisors. Not all factory workers are mistreated, and poor working conditions can potentially be improved. When compared with alternatives realistically available to the girls (such as drudgery at home, or early marriage, or worse employment elsewhere), even factory work in poor conditions seemed good. When we assess the place of work in the lives of children, we need to ask what alternatives are realistically available.

In the example we have discussed, Amal and her friends were treated by the film crew as objects whose presence in a factory threatened Western ideals of childhood, and corporate images and profits linked to them. Suppose, instead, that they had been approached as people, making choices in an attempt to control the direction of their lives, and with rights and interests to be protected. Might the filmmakers then have given them a chance to talk about their lives and their reasons for working, instead of simply appealing to the moral indignation of viewers at home? As the report by Fatima Zalami and her coauthors concludes, "Given that the employment of apprentices from the age of 12 is legal in Morocco, Marks and Spencer could have approached the allegations of child labour in Sicome in a caring manner which acknowledged the realities of life in a Moroccan slum" (Zalami, et al., 1998, 36). Might the importers then have used their market power, supported by periodic unannounced factory visits, to press for improved working conditions and proper compliance by the employers with the apprenticeship regulations that were supposed to provide adequate protection to these young teenagers?

The Méknès case is not an isolated exception. As recently as June 2008, the BBC presented an "undercover" report in which the reporter misled children and communities into believing that he was interested in buying the clothing they were decorating, when in fact his concern was to stop the British company Primark from selling their products, thus destroying their market and their income: his report did not indicate what the children thought about their work.[4] We present many similar cases in this book. These show that intervention based on good intentions and other people's moral standards can have harmful consequences for the intended beneficiaries.

Whose Interests?

A key question raised by the Méknès case asks whose interests are in fact served by actions that appear to be conducted for the protection of children. There is no indication that the British media team, Marks and Spencer, the Moroccan government, or any other adult actors involved considered what form of intervention would have been in "the best interests of the child," or of "the views of the child being given due weight" in this matter that affected the children so drastically. These awkward phrases, "best interests" and "the views of the child being given due weight," are taken from the United Nations Convention on the Rights of the Child (UNCRC, articles 3, 12), the most widely signed and ratified of all the UN Conventions, which both the United Kingdom (in 1992) and Morocco (in 1993) had ratified. Ratification means that both countries agreed to bring their national laws and regulations into line with the provisions of the Convention.

But what are "best interests?" This simple phrase is problematic in many ways (Archard, 2004, 62–65). First, it may be difficult, even impossible, to be sure about what is best. The issue of interests is partly material. But it can also involve fundamental and conflicting values among adults as well as among children. For example, parents may believe that it is best for their children to be educated in a strictly religious environment that supports their faith, while educationalists believe that children should be provided with a broad range of knowledge and be taught to question values and practices dominant in their environment. How are such differences of opinion to be resolved?

Second, "best" in relation to what? When it is not possible to give to every child a place in a top-rated school, or to provide every sick child with all that modern medicine has to offer, is it enough to consider "best interests" in relation to what is realistically possible or available under specific conditions, or are we bound by some more absolute standards?

One way to ensure that children's interests are not simply subordinated to adult interests is to allow and encourage children to voice their opinions on matters that affect them and to take their views seriously, as the Convention requires. This point leads to a third problem in defining "the best interests of the child": what happens when the views of the child are at variance with what adults judge to be in his or her best interests? Generally, it is in children's interests for adults to respect their opinions, but there may be a conflict between what adults believe to be in the child's interest and giving due weight to the child's opinion, a matter we will discuss in chapter 7.

The interests people serve are related to the kinds of problems they are trying to resolve. People sometimes refer to the "problem of child labor" as if it were a self-evident problem requiring no discussion (e.g. Fyfe, 2007; Hindman, 2009b). But is there a single all-embracing problem? Author Michael Bourdillon faced this kind of issue when trying to help children on the streets of Harare, Zimbabwe. Everyone agrees that children living and working on city streets comprises a problem, but different groups of people perceive the problem in different ways.[5] For the urban educated public, the sight of children living and working on city streets upsets cherished notions of what childhood should be like. These problems are resolved by keeping children off the streets and out of sight. For local and national governments, the presence of street children degrades the city, suggests poor governance, and might keep tourists away. In Harare, the solution of the authorities was regularly to round up children found on the streets, especially just prior to the tourist season, and place them in detention centers (officially designated "places of safety"), or simply dump them far away from the city. Authorities referred to such action as "cleaning up the city" (thus depicting the children as dirt, a point we shall return to later), and it was effective in making street children less visible for a short while.

In contrast, for two adolescent boys living with their mother and two older sisters in a single room in Harare, the main problem concerned privacy and embarrassment at home, both for the women and the boys. The boys resolved this problem by moving onto the streets (Bourdillon, 1994, 520). For other children abused at home by parents, step-parents, or by kin in the absence of parents, the problems were again different, and moving onto the streets was again a solution. For a child who goes hungry in a rural home, living and earning on the city streets can sometimes provide more and better food. A few children came to the city streets under the delusion that they would find freedom and excitement there, but for most of the children, living on the streets was an attempt to find a solution to greater problems although it remained unpleasant and problematic. For them the problems of street life were harassment and assault, obtaining regular food, finding somewhere to wash, the cold in winter, preserving dignity and self-respect, and so on. Problems, to be sure, but quite different from the expectations of outsiders, such as tourists and even uninformed Zimbabweans.

"The problem of street children" thus may comprise very different problems for different people. We will return to consider street children in chapter 7: for the moment we raise two questions. If we accept that society has a responsibility to help street children overcome their problems, how can we find approaches that pay due attention to their specific interests? And when the interests of children do not coincide with those of other groups, which have precedence and who should decide?

Similarly, the "problem of child labor" is not a single and self-evident problem, but comprises different problems for different people. If the girls at Méknès had remained at work, the image of the factory and its retail outlets would have been tarnished and its sales threatened. Removing the girls from the factory allowed retailers to distance themselves from "child labor," and the Moroccan government to confirm its support for international standards. People in Britain with humanitarian concerns were genuinely disturbed by reports of girls working in the Sicome garment factory. To dismiss them from the factories effectively removed from sight the problems that worried British consumers, whose consciences were salved with the assurance that they were purchasing merchandise "free of child labor." Even aid agencies might subordinate the interests of particular children to their fear of scandal. In all these considerations, how important are the problems and interests of the factory girls?

In its submission to the UN Study on Children and Violence, the first point made by Bhima Sangha, a working children's movement in India (see chapter 7), with respect to violence in the workplace is as follows:

> The Government conducts raids on our work places as a part of its Child Labour Eradication Programme and "rounds up" working children like stray dogs. We are pulled out of work, taken away against our wishes and illegally confined. The actual raid experience is very traumatic for us. No one talks to us before hand to ask us if we need to be rescued. No one talks to us after the raid about what the next steps will be. Sometimes we are sent off to the Observations Homes and kept there for days. We are constantly told that we have to stop working and start going to school. But they do not realise that in our given situation of poverty and deprivation, work is a necessity. Even if we try to explain our situation, we are not taken seriously. If we are migrants, we are sent off to our villages. They do not realise that we left our villages because we had no livelihood there. In the raid process we the concerned children are not at all consulted. Our needs are not taken into consideration. The alternatives forced on us by the Government actually make our situations worse than before. These raids are a total violation of our rights and are not a solution to child labour.[6]

Their statement illustrates further the problem of deciding where children's real interests lie. For them, while conditions of work remained a problem, employment was a solution to more fundamental problems. Here, children are pleading for attention to their problems. In this book, we argue that intervention should aim to solve children's real troubles, not create more for them.

Ways of Thinking

"Listen to me"

At an international conference on Urban Childhoods, held in Trondheim in 1997, representatives of working children were invited to speak at the session on "child labor" alongside academics and representatives of international organizations and NGOs. A thirteen-year-old girl from Senegal had this to say, in a short speech which reduced the hall to an awkward silence.

> Do you understand how you insult me, when you talk of "combating" and "abolishing" the work that I do?
>
> I have worked as a domestic servant since I was eight. Because of doing this work, I have been able to go to school (which my parents in the village could not afford); I help my parents with the money I earn. I am very proud of the work I do! I joined the movement of working children, and I know what the Convention says about children's rights: the Convention also says that you should listen to me![7]

This young worker started to work and earn money well below the permitted age according to any contemporary formal standards. Moreover, she was in domestic work, which has been widely reported to leave children open to psychological, social, and physical abuse. If anyone is a child "out of place," surely she is one? Yet five years later, she is proud of what she has achieved for herself and her family through this work. In this case, far from preventing her schooling, employment has enabled her to attend school. She feels insulted by the way people speak negatively about her work, and she is a proud member of an organization of working children. When we pointed to the need to listen to the children in the Méknès case, it was to ensure that their interests were attended to. This young school-going worker from Senegal, however, challenged adults in a more fundamental way, to listen to her in order to consider how they think and speak about her, and about her work.

A similar issue was raised by working children in Peru: "just because we work we are regarded as if we were sick, outlaws, or anti-social delinquents that need to be 'rehabilitated and reincorporated into society'" (MNNATSOP, 1999). When children work hard to improve not only their own lives but also those of their families, is it correct, helpful, or just to speak of them as in need of "rehabilitation"?

How did this way of thinking, that is so objectionable toward working children, arise? We can trace one of its Western roots to Jean Jacques Rousseau's influential polemic on the nature of children and children's development, *Emile*, first published in 1762. Prevailing Christian dogma presented humankind as innately corrupted by "original sin" that must be contained and repressed by society. In contrast, Rousseau argued that people are born naturally good, but are corrupted by society, and that children should be nurtured in such a way as to allow them to retain as much of their natural virtue as is permitted by the need to grow up and adapt to society. This view of children as representing the purest aspect of human nature was popularized in Britain and elsewhere by thinkers and poets of the Romantic Movement, who in the early nineteenth century promoted an ideal of childhood as a blissful period that children should enjoy, close to nature and unencumbered by worldly care and responsibility. They strongly condemned the employment of children, typified in their day by the toil and exploitation of children in factories and mines, for corrupting the natural innocence of children and destroying their potential for moral and intellectual development. They considered children, in their innocence, to be vulnerable and passive victims of exploitation, incompetent to act on their own behalf, and dependent on adults to know what is best for them and come to their rescue.

This vision of childhood, based on religious and philosophical views rather than empirical observation, continues to have a substantial impact on international thinking about child work, including thinking among governing elites in many developing countries. The M. Venkatarangaiya Foundation in Southern India, for example, "believes that every child has a right to childhood and an opportunity to develop to his/her full potential and that every form of work done by a child interferes with this right."[8] In this view, anything more than occasional light work is inimical to a proper childhood, which should be dedicated to school and play, without the burdens of helping earn the family livelihood or, beyond light chores, maintaining the home and taking responsibility for younger children. This sweeping condemnation of work as a serious threat to children's development seems never to have been accepted by most parents in the world, even in rich countries, but it has found a powerful home in labor and associated activist groups focused on the "elimination of child labor."

Among the conclusions of a report on a recent tour examining "child labor" in several African countries was the comment, "One of the major challenges encountered during the tour is to change people's mindsets on the issue of child labour. . . . Child labour is enshrined in the African society because Africans largely believe that children have to work in order to become a responsible adult [sic]" (Strakova and Vondra, 2008, 10). Perhaps the mindset of the campaigners needs adjusting at least as much as the mindsets they met in Africa. In chapter 3, we shall point to very different histories of children's work in different countries. At this stage, we caution against the assumption that the way of life in high-income countries is superior, and that children's economic participation is not part of "good" childhoods.[9]

At an international meeting of working children in Berlin in 2004, the participants, while not claiming that their working and living conditions were ideal, underlined some positive aspects of their work. "In our lives, our work allows us to resist with dignity the economic, political and suppressing model that criminalizes and excludes us and continues to worsen the living conditions of ourselves, our families and our communities" (World Movement of Working Children, 2004).

How seriously are we to take such views of children? Adults often assume that they have a right to decide what is best for children, questioning the young people's awareness of how their work will affect their future.[10] When adults talk about "combating child labor," they speak as if such labor is always something morally reprehensible that callous adults inflict upon children. Children in this view appear to be passive victims to be rescued and rehabilitated. In chapters 7 and 8, we shall discuss the importance and the difficulties of taking children's views seriously. For the moment, we hope to have shown that children's perspectives can be both informative and challenging. To understand any situation involving children, we need to ask how children perceive the situation and how they respond to it.

We also need a lexicon to use for these situations. What precisely is "child labor?" The term, unfortunately, means different things to different people. Some people use it broadly to include all kinds of children's work in a neutral sense: "Not all child labor is bad" (Bass, 2004, 3). When it is used in this way, it is clear that there is no need to eliminate all "child labor." Others use the term specifically to apply to work that is in any way harmful, as opposed to "child work," which is neutral or benign. Apart from the difficulty of translating this distinction into other languages, it can contribute to confusion in English. The term "child labor" also frequently refers to any form of employment below the minimum legal age (whether or not this is shown to be harmful—e.g., Winrock International, 2008, opening statement). Sometimes a single report uses different meanings of the term without discussion, for example defining "child labor" as harmful work and then assuming that this includes any work undertaken below a certain age (e.g., UNICEF, 2005, 7, 10; Lieten, 2009). Several ethical codes imply that any employment below the age of fifteen (whether or not it is legal in the country concerned) is "child labor" to be abolished. Some quantitative studies count as "child labor" any "economic activity" by "under-age" children (as little as an hour in a week—e.g., Hazarika and Bedi, 2003, 33). In India, some activists categorize as a "child laborer" any child of school-going age who is not in school (whether or not they are working—e.g., Sinha, 2003, 341). In spite of its various meanings, the term "child labor" is usually strongly associated in most people's minds with child abuse. In the authors' experience, thinking about the work of children in terms of "child labor" turns out to create more confusion than clarity. In this book, therefore, we prefer the generic term "work" with appropriate qualifiers—harmful, illegal, paid, economic, light, etc.[11]

Children Out of Place

The Romantic ideal of childhood was challenged in the nineteenth century by the plight of poor children, who were perceived as children "without childhood" (Cunningham, 1995, 136). Now people sometimes refer to working children as having their childhood "lost" or "stolen" (e.g., Blanchet, 1996). What are the implications of such discourse? Clearly, everyone has a childhood in the physical sense of a time of growth and in the social sense of a time of not yet being treated as a full member of society. Working children have childhoods in these senses, and they may have many valuable experiences that help them to grow and adapt to later life.

Views that accept children's activities outside this romantic ideal often meet strong condemnation. Why do people react so strongly? To understand this, and to guard against destructive emotional reactions, it is helpful to consider how people defend their cognitive categories. Anthropologist Mary Douglas has pointed out that people and cultures structure their worlds into discrete cognitive categories, which are usually supported by myths or strongly held stories. The system is threatened when something transgresses the boundaries of these categories, and such transgressions are therefore vigorously rejected as moral aberration. A simple example is "dirt," which is something out of place and therefore transgressing categories: mud is fine in the garden but is dirt and taboo in the bedroom (Douglas, 1966, 314–317). Adulthood and childhood are distinct cognitive categories: the question is whether in real life there are clear and dichotomous boundaries between the two that need to be vigorously defended.

Clearly, children are more dependent on others than are most adults, and are in need of care, protection, and guidance. So it is convenient to have markers at which people can be expected to take up different tasks and responsibilities, and can no longer expect things to be done on their behalf. Young people who threaten the validity of such categories, such as street children living on their own (Ennew and Swart-Kruger, 2003) or girls engaging in the sex trade below the age of majority (O'Connell Davidson, 2005, 16–19, 26), often provoke reactions of outrage that may pay little attention to the circumstances or choices of the young people concerned. Similarly, many people assume that waged work, and particularly factory work, is inherently bad for children, and that children who work (especially outside the home) are "out of place" (see Connolly and Ennew, 1996b). The danger of such perspectives is that preserving the "proper place" of children may become a moral issue, more important than understanding the particular conditions and effects of the work children do. In practice, outrage is aroused particularly by work that does not fit middle-class concepts of childhood in rich countries. Delivering newspapers or other goods, or work in food outlets, is commonplace in rich countries. In several rich countries, regular jobs appear to be a majority experience of children by the age of 16, often in defiance of cumbersome regulations (B. White, 1994, 860; Lavalette, et al., 1995; McKechnie, et al., 2005, 5; Mortimer, 2007, 117). This work is taken for granted and assumed to be harmless or beneficial, while outrage is usually directed at the work of children in poor communities, including both relatively light and safe work as well as more arduous and hazardous work.

Our critique of dichotomies does not mean that we have to abandon any notions of difference. People need cognitive categories to structure the world and their responses to it, and children are different from adults. Young children in particular need support and protection that adults often do not need, reflected in the widespread acceptance of the United Nations Convention on the Rights of the Child. It would be dangerous to abandon this distinction: the notion that children should be "liberated" from the restrictions of childhood can easily slide into justification of a liberal free-for-all system that disadvantages marginalized people and attacks the basic social rights of children (see Lavalette, 2005).

Nevertheless, seeing differences in terms of a radical dichotomy does violence to reality and, when translated into policies, can and does harm children. Adults and children live in the same world, and children are not transformed into adults overnight on their eighteenth birthday. Children move gradually toward adulthood, learning behavior and skills over time, increasingly participating in the activities of adults and adopting, questioning, or challenging their values (as we will discuss in chapter 5). They learn, over an extended period, to make their own decisions and to control their own lives. While dichotomies based on a particular age boundary (or, in some cultures, on initiation rites into adulthood) may be helpful for particular purposes such as determining who is allowed to leave school, to vote, or to drive a car, they should be understood for what they are: an artificial contrivance for administrative or legal convenience.

In this book we avoid a restrictive separation of childhood from adulthood, while accepting the difficulties of developing ideas flexible enough to accommodate a diverse world. We allow for different experiences of childhood in different contexts, and changing experience over time. We question claims to a universally valid conception of childhood. Nevertheless, are there not some principles that are universal?

Children's Rights

The young domestic worker from Senegal claimed the right to be heard, based on the UNCRC. The effect was in part to provide her testimony with a sense of added authority and urgency by reason of a document signed by most nations. But her appeal to rights communicated more. What is a right, especially in the case of dependent children, and what is the source of its authority?[12] There are many ways to think about rights, as is revealed by the enormous legal and philosophical literature on the topic. For example, one general viewpoint regards rights primarily as social ends that are ultimate expressions of human dignity and respect for individual worth and autonomy. They stand as goals to which societies should aspire. Rights texts, such as the UNCRC, are in this perspective considered to be more than mere international agreements: they are imbued with moral authority beyond question or challenge. They are treated as categorical mandates whose rules are expected to apply uniformly everywhere. A quite different approach understands rights documents primarily as means rather than ends. In this view, they are helpful but imperfect instruments intended to improve life—in the case of the UNCRC, for children—and they are open to question and evaluation according to how well they meet that objective. Instead of following rules beyond debate, this approach actively assesses the rules and standards of rights according to their consequences. What doesn't work can be modified or discarded. Rights as tools are open to continuous change in order to improve their effectiveness. There is no pretension to absolute moral authority, and international rights documents are valued primarily for their political ability to mobilize broadly based support and promote change.

Both perspectives, and others as well, have honorable histories, enthusiastic advocates, and their own particular lines of argument. There is no compelling justification for preferring one over the other. However, when rights are cited, it is important to be aware of the particular rights concept being employed. In any case, children's rights as articulated in the UNCRC have their effect only through voluntary compliance.

A further limitation is that the rights formally acknowledged in law may not exactly coincide with what individuals or groups accept as rights. People sometimes speak of "moral rights," which are accepted by the society or community concerned but may not be enshrined in or enforced by law. Indeed, such rights are likely to be more significant in daily social life than are the rights acknowledged in law or in international conventions (which, unlike laws, may have no mechanisms for their enforcement). Other rights may be written into law yet may not be generally acknowledged or enforced.

The final version of the UNCRC in 1989 was the culmination of a decade of discussion and negotiation. The precise wording was often the result of compromise, which was necessary to produce a document that had widespread agreement and could form an international basis for policy and discussion. It could be considered as the lowest common denominator of children's rights. To what extent is it a final determinant of these rights in particular contexts?

The UNCRC was compiled by adults, without any inputs from children. In 1994, the founders of the African Movement of Working Children and Youth met in Dakar, Senegal, and identified twelve rights that they claimed and wished to defend, only some of which can be found in the UNCRC.

- The right to be taught a trade
- The right to stay in the village[13]
- The right to work in a safe environment
- The right to light and limited work
- The right to rest when sick
- The right to be listened to
- The right to health care
- The right to learn to read and to write

- The right to play
- The right to self-expression and to form organizations
- The right to equitable legal aid, in case of difficulty.

These rights arise from injustices the young people experienced in their lives. When author William Myers showed these to a high-ranking officer in UNICEF as an example of rights drawn up by children, he was told, "These are not real rights." Are these any less rights than are legal documents formally agreed by adult bodies? Must rights be granted by authorities to be valid? Or can they be claimed, to be recognized by others? In practice, most of the twelve rights can be linked to rights declared in the UNCRC: in what ways does this affect their status as rights?

To what extent does the UNCRC transcend boundaries of time and space and culture, or reflect the values of a particular body of people at a particular time? When ratifying it, several countries placed formal reservations on particular clauses relating to such issues as citizenship, asylum, and freedom of religion.[14] *The African Charter on the Rights and Welfare of the Child* (1990) expresses some divergence from the assumptions behind the Convention with an article (31) on the *responsibilities* of the child to family and community.[15] In some situations, activists give UNCRC reluctant support, concerned that it reflects a Western emphasis on individual rights, and neglects the rights of families and communities (Burr, 2006, 74–78).

Does the Convention support a notion of normality that denigrates other childhoods? Rachel Burr has argued that the Convention reflects ideals of childhood in wealthy societies, and that rights to free education, and to housing, health care, and nutrition are meaningless in societies and communities that cannot afford these (2006, 68–72). It has been argued that the Convention does not cater for such very disadvantaged children as street children (Ennew, 2000b; Burr, 2006, 74, 149). To counter such arguments, the interpretation of the Convention must be flexible enough to accommodate different childhoods and emerging understanding of childhood.

Rights sometimes conflict with each other. At a general level, for example, rights to protection can conflict with freedom and rights of participation, as when an individual's freedom to take dangerous drugs or engage in other "risky behavior" is restricted. Conflicts between rights can be more specific, particularly in communities with very limited resources. At a more specific level, a child's right to education may conflict with the right to sustenance when this requires work. Where a family depends on income from a child (perhaps if a child is head of household), his or her right to education may conflict with the right of younger siblings to sustenance—and perhaps their right to education. Rights acquired through local culture and values may occasionally conflict with rights conferred by the Convention (such as freedom of expression). So, although the Convention treats all rights equally, in particular situations it may be necessary to negotiate priorities or to accept compromises that are sensitive to the social, cultural, and material environment in which the rights are to be applied, and in particular to the specific interests and perceptions of the children concerned.

How are rights applicable to children's work? The 1948 Universal Declaration of Human Rights (article 23, 1) clearly articulates everyone's right, without qualification by age, to work and to join worker associations. In 1966, the International Covenant on Economic, Social, and Cultural Rights and the International Covenant on Civil and Political Rights defined childhood as a state requiring special protection, with rights different from those of adults, an idea that is confirmed by the UNCRC. Children's right to participation in politics, for example, is not translated into a right to vote. It might be argued that their right to special protection overrides their right to work. Yet children have asserted their right to work in Latin America and occasionally in developed countries (Liebel, 2003, 267; 2001a; Leonard, 2004), and working children in Africa, as we have just noted, assert their right to "light and limited work." The problem of balancing the right to protection with the children's choices and claims is a theme that will appear repeatedly throughout this book.

Relating to work, the UNCRC asserts the right of children to education directed at "the development of the child's personality, talents and mental and physical abilities to their fullest potential" (articles 28 & 29), and to leisure (article 31), thus limiting the amount of time that may be given to work outside school. Children must be protected from "economic exploitation," and from "performing any work that is likely to be hazardous or to interfere with the child's education, or to be harmful to the child's health or physical, mental, spiritual, moral or social development" (article 32, 1). It does not define "economic exploitation," a problematic term (discussed in chapter 8), which can be understood as employment that is harmful to employees or for which remuneration is inadequate. The emphasis of the Convention is on preventing harm in work rather than work as such.[16]

We believe in a middle ground between two extreme views on children's rights. One view holds that since children are dependent on adults there are problems in talking about children's rights at all, and that it is more useful to speak of obligations toward children, and of the care and protection that is due to them (for fuller discussion and critique of this point of view, see Freeman, 1997, 23–29; Archard, 2004, 118–124). The view at the other extreme takes and applies the UNCRC as a set of rules to be observed rigidly and without question unless and until they are modified by an international body. This view requires that "duty bearers" be identified as those responsible for fulfillment of every article of the Convention, and taken to task when they fail to do so. We believe that it is important to acknowledge children's rights, and have stated our support for the UNCRC in our Preface. The language of rights is appropriate to a view of young people as continuously and actively developing their lives. Rights provide a framework that allows them to seek redress when they are wronged, or at least allows others to seek redress on their behalf. When the neglect of rights results in children being seriously harmed or their development significantly impaired, those responsible both for the abuse and for the enforcement of rights should be held accountable. Nevertheless, we believe that rights should be applied in a flexible and pragmatic way, sensitive to the cultural values and available resources of particular contexts.

It is particularly problematic when cultural values contradict widely held international norms about what constitutes abuse of children. The ability to make universal statements of value on such issues as child abuse has been questioned (James, et al., 1998, 27). We do not agree with this variety of relativism. A more useful kind of relativism keeps us sensitive to differences as a practical analytical tool, "a way of shaking up and questioning supposed universalist ideas and opening the possibility of others; in other words, a way of opening our eyes to the variety of human ideology and practice, but not a basis for legitimizing whatever we may see when we do this" (White, 1999, 137). When cultures, or indeed individuals, disagree on matters of value, judgments and intervention should be based on clear empirical evidence of harm or benefits to the people concerned.

Widespread acceptance of the UNCRC shows that it is possible through examination and negotiation to come to agreement on many things; the Convention makes a sound base for discussion and action across nations and cultures. Olga Nieuwenhuys argues that, while it reflects thinking at a particular time on issues that could be agreed across nations, the Convention should not foreclose further reflection on, and discussion of, children's rights (1998, 270). We shall return to a discussion of the application of rights in chapter 10. The question to ask, as we meet working children in a variety of situations in this book, is whether and how the situations and cultures in which children find themselves should affect the way rights are applied and exercised. In addressing this question, it is useful to also ask who has the right to determine rights. Are rights properly granted by the powerful or claimed by the powerless? By what authority does the United Nations, rather than children or their families and communities, determine what children's rights should be? The issue becomes pertinent when one thinks, as we will in later chapters, about the participation of working children in defining their own best interest and actions that serve it.

Knowledge, Understanding, and Information

The intervention in Méknès went wrong at least partly because it was not based on a realistic understanding of the situation of the children concerned. How and from where can better information be obtained? In this section we discuss and evaluate a variety of sources of information about children's work.

Much of the most important information needed to make good decisions about the girls in Méknès was available from children, as the later interviews demonstrated. One of the most important and widely recognized lessons learned from experience over the last decade is the critical importance of consulting with working children before making decisions about the nature of their problems and appropriate interventions. Hearing from children is important both to them and to society, and in this book we frequently cite research that has paid attention to what the children say. In brief, field evidence strongly suggests that working children know and understand their situation better than most adults realize, and when their perspectives differ radically from the viewpoints of adults, we need to consider whether the basis for adult viewpoints is justified.

Even in the social sciences, some viewpoints and assumptions seem to be based on surprisingly little evidence, including a number of studies coming out of economics and based on quantitative data. Economics is a relatively influential field, and readers familiar with the large body of econometric research publications on child labor may wonder why they are not more frequently cited in this book. Economics research relies on quantitative data, which often captures only particular dimensions of children's work while neglecting others. Often, the assumptions used to make up for incomplete data are also questionable, and this problem also plagues economics theorizing on children's work.

In our view, however, this is not essentially an issue of disciplinary or quantitative/qualitative divisions. The issue in our view relates more to methodology, and to the need to base assumptions and interpretations on what we actually know, and also an awareness of what we don't know. To take a simple example, Patrick Emerson summarizing "the economic view of child labor" comments, "though almost every theoretical study of child labor posits a fairly rigid relationship between child work and diminished adult human capital, there is very little empirical evidence to support or refute this assumption" (Emerson, 2009, 8).

There are excellent economics studies using quantitative data that we respect and cite; author Deborah Levison is herself an economist working in this field. Some quantitative studies are based on surveys with well-controlled samples and detailed, patient questioning; and some of the best information available comes from this kind of source. However, most quantitative studies of children's work use large-scale national sample survey data designed for other purposes, and with these data they produce statistics on "child labor" and related econometric analyses.

The surveys usually identify whether children are "economically active." If ILO guidelines are followed, children working as little as an hour a week are counted. Because the surveys are adult-oriented, the questions often do not capture well what children are really doing. They typically count some children as workers who arguably should not be counted, while many other working children are not counted. Anybody trying to make use of this kind of country-specific data for practical purposes needs first to investigate and confirm its quality. When international estimates are based on many surveys of this sort, the problems are compounded by definitional, procedural, and quality differences, and the resulting estimates are so problematic that specialists who understand the process seldom use them. The ILO has over the years tried to refine its survey instruments and improve its estimates, resulting in a number of useful country studies.[17] But taken as a whole, the data system is fraught with problems. World "child labor" estimates by the ILO use a large dose of informed judgment to supplement extremely incomplete statistical information. Nobody really knows how many of the world's children (in total) perform what kinds of work, when, and where.

In short, there is a persistent problem of academic studies uncritically using assumptions and concepts that do not reflect real-world situations, or relying too heavily on inadequate data from national surveys. When researchers use data of unknown or suspect quality and pass it through a standard statistical procedure—sometimes without really understanding whether the data meet the demands of the sophisticated analytical procedures being used—the results of the analysis, no matter how impressive looking, may be misleading. While there is also no dearth of questionable studies relying on descriptive and qualitative case material in disciplines other than economics, the tendency of educated adults to find statistics convincing (see Crossen, 1994) is in this case particularly problematic.

Research into child work suffers from a problem of disciplinary fragmentation. For instance, while economists read papers on "child labor" by other economists, many fail to take into account evidence from the ethnographically driven literature produced by anthropologists and sociologists. As a result, they frequently base their analyses on assumptions that studies from a different discipline have challenged. Equally, many ethnographic case studies have failed to understand the influence of larger global and societal economic and other trends that economists have traced in detail. Both economic and ethnographic studies often lack the insights from a longer-term perspective that historians can provide. These disciplinary divisions are especially obvious in discussion of how children's work relates to their education, as will be seen in chapter 6. Different disciplinary perspectives are valuable and complementary in the study of children's lives, especially regarding their work and education. The world still awaits a properly designed major study of child work that is planned and conducted cooperatively by a team of specialists from different disciplines, meshing their skills.

In this as in other fields, much institutionally sponsored research is linked to the promotion of points of view favored by the sponsoring institutions, and has at least a tacit advocacy purpose. The ILO, for instance, is a major sponsor of research on "child labor," and it is more likely to fund studies that promote its political and policy positions linked to Conventions 138 and 182 than those that question them. UNICEF is more likely to sponsor research that furthers child rights objectives laid out in the UNCRC, and so on for other organizations. Only a relatively small fraction of research on child work appears to come from truly disinterested sources. There is no reason to avoid advocacy-oriented research, which when well done can be very helpful. But anybody making use of such studies needs to keep their origin and purpose in mind.

Different types of information-gathering have their own biases in coverage. Analysis of media coverage of child labor issues between 1996 and 2003 shows a large and increasing proportion of media attention to the extreme forms of child exploitation such as trafficking, prostitution, and child soldiers; the academic literature, in contrast, and particularly the economics literature, has relatively neglected these "worst" forms, which cannot typically be discerned using quantitative data (Fyfe, 2007, 61, 66–67).

In this book, we use many illustrative examples or "cases." We rely heavily on detailed studies that explore issues of children's work in a broader, holistic context. This method is particularly developed in the discipline of anthropology but is also found in related disciplines. We find especially useful studies that pay attention to children's perceptions and what children say about the issues we are interested in, rather than relying only on what adults say and observe.

We believe that the stories we use are typical of widespread phenomena, but since we have selected cases that illustrate the points we wish to make, the stories in themselves do not tell us how widespread or typical they are. Zalami collected information about the economic situation and laws of Morocco, but this does not tell us about the situation in other countries.

Because people readily identify with a live example, illustrations may be persuasive. A danger is that authors choose cases or anecdotes that illustrate and support the point they are making, and leave out cases that might point in other directions—especially when information is collected precisely to support particular agenda. While the public is dependent on quality reporting for information on a variety of issues, when reporters collect information to raise awareness of the way children are abused, they are drawn to the most sensational cases, which may represent only a small minority. Journalists need to satisfy editors with a good story, focusing on sensational material obtained in minimum time, often having little opportunity to collect necessary background information (see, e.g., Khan, 2007, 38–46). Amanda Berlan (2009, 144–146) shows how reporting on cocoa farms in West Africa, while stirring emotions on the trafficking and treatment of children, misled the public on the real nature of the majority of child work on family farms, and paid no attention to views of the children concerned. Such reporting, together with some reporting by watchdog organizations, aims to stir the feelings of readers or viewers, which are governed by lifestyles and values often very different from those of the people in the cases described. These accounts can be reinforced with moving images, occasionally taken misleadingly out of context (an example is presented by Offit, 2008, 20–22). Such reporting has an important function in raising awareness, but more detailed and systematic information is required to plan effective intervention.

2

Work That Children Do

The most important thing to understand about children's work is its enormous variety. As this chapter will detail, children are engaged in many different kinds of work. However, the vast majority of what they do is part time or seasonal, unpaid, involved in agriculture or homemaking, and is connected to their family. Relatively few children work full time, in paid jobs, away from family, or in factories, brickyards, mines or other situations that most people tend to think of as "child labor." The reasons children work also differ greatly between individuals, families, societies, and situations. It is important to understand this diversity because, as reflected in chapter 1, most public discussion of children's work has been couched in terms of "child labor," and that term and the stereotypes it calls up don't actually describe most work that children do. The result is that children's work and working children end up being defined as a group by sweeping assumptions and judgments that in fact apply to only a limited number of them. This can result in misguided policies and interventions that are disasters for children they are intended to protect, as the Méknès case illustrated. Therefore, the appropriate place to begin a book-long exploration of the realities of child work is with a consideration of the diversity of the work that children do, and why.

The variety of children's work and working situations can be glimpsed in the following examples:

1. P. Kattaraman started work at a silk twisting unit in Magadi, India, around the age of six, obliged to do so by his parents, who took an advance from the employer to pay for his sister's marriage. He worked for five or six years and complained that child workers got beaten if the thread broke and that they were given no time for eating (Human Rights Watch, 2003, 26).
2. Umesh left school at the age of twelve after receiving several beatings from both parents and teachers. To avoid the constant parental pressure to keep

up his schooling, he left his Indian village to find employment with the help of his uncle in Bangalore (Whitehead, et al., 2007, 29: see chapter 7).

3. In Ghana, Amina completed primary school and would have liked to continue to high school and college. She was withdrawn from junior secondary school at the age of fourteen, to marry and to help in her mother's business of selling food. While waiting for marriage she was responsible for much housework (Obeng, 2002, 63–67). Her work was not harmful in itself, but it made further schooling impossible.

4. Seniman, a fifteen-year-old boy in the Javanese village of Kali Loro, the son of a poor landless widow, told one of the authors with pride how he had supported himself from the age of thirteen with part-time farm and other work, paying his own school fees and buying his own uniform and other clothes. His life would have changed for the worse if he had been forbidden to work, or to earn money, at age thirteen.

5. Eva, a nine-year-old in Los Angeles, U.S.A., regularly and proudly helped her working mother washing dishes, folding laundry, cleaning the house on weekends, and bathing, feeding, and reading to younger siblings (Orellana, 2001, 370–372).

6. Stacey, a fourteen-year-old girl living in Patna, Scotland, looked after the house and cared for her father, who was chronically ill, and her mother, who had almost daily epileptic seizures. She was worried about her mother and did not like going out: she stopped seeing her friends and had not attended school full time for three years (*The Sunday Times Magazine* (London) November 25, 2007, 37).

These vignettes illustrate the range of situations in which children can be found working, from intolerable to beneficial, compelled to freely chosen, inside and outside the home, paid and unpaid. They also suggest that not all work that escapes stereotypes of "child labor" is unproblematic for children.

Tarring all child work with the brush of "child labor," which many believe the rich countries mostly eliminated many years ago, leads to a popular misconception that child work is rare in the modern developed world and a problem only of poorer countries thought to be at an earlier stage of social and economic development.[1] That view is wrong. Not only do many children in rich countries work in their own homes and family enterprises, but regular part-time paid employment before the age of 16 is a majority youthful experience in many high-income countries, often in open breach of regulations (B. White, 1994, 860; Lavalette, et al., 1995; Mortimer, 2007, 117; Hindman, 2002, 294–295).[2] While it is true that there are many more working children in developing than rich countries, that is due partly to the fact that developing countries contain the vast majority of the world's population. India and China alone count for over a third of the world population, and Europe and North America for but a fifth.

Although the nature and conditions of children's work differ considerably between rich and poor countries, at least some rich countries have child economic participation rates roughly comparable to those of poor countries.

What Is Children's Work?

"Work" in its broadest sense is the application of physical or mental effort to some purpose. For instance, one may "work hard" to develop knowledge, or an artistic or athletic skill. Work may comprise or include unpleasant drudgery, but it can also be interesting and enjoyable. However, most discourse about children's work employs the term in more restricted senses. For example, when adults ask if a child works, they usually are inquiring about a job for pay or some other economic activity; they are not thinking of schoolwork or domestic work in the child's own home, still less training for an art or sport. Children themselves tend to speak of "work" as distinct from study or help in the home (Hungerland, et al., 2007, 262–264; Nilsen, 2002, 110). However, "work" in most global discussion about "child labor" is considered the rough equivalent of children's "economic activity," which can be thought of as work that contributes goods and services of monetary value to society. This includes almost all productive activity, whether full time or part time, paid or not. It specifically excludes schooling and chores in one's own household.[3] More in line with popular usage, in this book we will consider "work" to cover a wide range of activities, including household chores, but not including schoolwork unless specifically stated. When we speak of "economic activity," it should be understood as that subset of "work" meeting ILO definitions.[4]

How Many Children Work, and Doing What?

Despite vexing problems of data discontinuity, incompatibility, and unreliability, we agree with most specialists that virtually all the available evidence suggests that, globally, "child labor," defined as economically active children, is in steady decline, and has been for at least fifty years. Claims that it is increasing carry a very heavy burden of proof. Although we harbor doubts about the accuracy of ILO estimates of the numbers of working children, we accept as probably real the downward movement in children's economic participation that they show for recent years (SIMPOC, 2006). The proportions and distribution of child work are in constant change, especially as increasing urbanization reduces the preponderance of children in farming, expanding school attendance reduces full-time work, rising incomes relieve household economic pressures, and technology changes the nature of labor demand for children. Global and local cycles of economic boom and bust affect all of these.

While routine official statistics are especially weak in identifying patterns of child work today (we mention some difficulties in chapter 4), some special studies are informative. An analysis of child work patterns conducted by Edmonds and Pavcnik used data on children from thirty-six developing countries in 2000. They estimated that over two thirds (68 percent) of children aged five to fourteen in these countries were currently engaged in some sort of work. Of those, only a small minority was engaged in "productive" economic activity— 20.8 percent within the family, such as in farming or other family enterprises, and only 2.4 percent in paid work outside the family (see chapter 4). All the rest, the vast majority, were in non-economic household maintenance tasks. These figures suggest that the children most at the center of international debate and discourse about "child labor"—those working outside the family circle for pay or keep—are in fact but a tiny portion (under 5 percent) of all working children.

Edmonds and Pavcnik found that the large majority of children were working moderate hours, less than twenty hours per week. Work at that level leaves time for school, play, and other activities. Only about a fifth of children worked over twenty hours a week, and 6.4 percent for over forty hours a week (2005a, 203, table 1). If children work over twenty hours, or even full time, but only occasionally and for short periods—such as during a peak season harvest—there may be little reason for concern. But if children under fourteen work more than twenty hours per week on a regular basis, there is reason to ask whether their educational and other needs are being met. If not, intervention may be called for. Concern that work not preempt other important aspects of children's lives demands that the work of children be treated specially, because they are children: what is acceptable for adults is not necessarily appropriate for children.

The amount of work undertaken by particular children depends on a variety of factors. Children in poor families generally have more of all kinds of work than those of rich families. Girls generally have more housework, while boys may have more work outside the home (though not usually making up for the extra housework that girls do). The pressure on younger siblings to work may be lessened or removed by the contributions of older siblings, and vice versa (Punch, 2001, 816).

What Is Special about Children's Work?

The work of pre-teen children everywhere is for the most part specially conditioned to the facts of their young age, including school attendance. Accordingly, nearly all work done by young children is part-time. While we distrust global statistics on child work for reasons pointed out in the last chapter, we nevertheless believe, on the basis of more restricted in-depth studies, that the percentage of pre-teen children regularly working full time has been steadily falling for a long time and is now so small that it probably stands in low single digits. This is connected to the fact that the vast majority of children in the world now receive at least some primary schooling. The struggle to ensure that young children are freed from work for enough time to attend school is now concentrated primarily on particular populations, pockets, and cases. Where pre-adolescent children work at all, it is today mostly a secondary activity, and is regarded as such by both adults and children, even when the children's work makes an important contribution to family livelihoods.

Most cultures think differently about the work of children and that of adults. One of the most common concerns about working children is that work may deprive children of sufficient chance to play, and we agree that is too often the case. Play in this scenario is considered to be the opposite of work and to compete with it in children's lives. But distinction between work and play is not always easy to make empirically. Whereas adults speaking of children tend to draw a line between work and play, such as by telling children they cannot play until after their work is done, for children the difference is not always clear, and the two may in fact overlap (Thorne, 1987, 100; for a fuller discussion, see Liebel, 2004, chapter 7, 176–193). For example, Indonesian children who take a household buffalo to water may be performing a necessary household task, but they also enjoy riding on the animal's back and playing in the water. Children often turn work into a form of play. They also turn play into work: Antonella Invernizzi describes how children in Lima, Peru, may start to trade in the streets as a game, taking a few vegetables from their uncle's cart to sell, and subsequently turn this activity into work for income (2003, 331–332). Some work, like guarding crops, grazing livestock, caring for infants, or work on the streets, can easily be combined with play. We will here simply warn not to make hasty and definite distinctions between play and work, and return to the topic in chapter 5.

Some tasks are considered apt for children. Light work in the home, for instance, is widely considered appropriate for them. Some tasks may be considered specifically children's work; many southern African pastoral societies, for instance, consider herding and leading cattle to be children's work, and may thus be left to children, even if it means missing school. Some work is assigned to children because it is considered abhorrent to adults. For example, in urban Bangladesh, collecting firewood is considered children's work in part because scavenging is considered degrading for adults (Delap, 2001, 14). In some societies, there are constraints on certain adult work for which children traditionally compensate. For example, where Muslim women in Africa are sequestered in their homes, their children may be sent in their stead to collect water and firewood, go to the market, carry messages, and run other errands (Bass, 2004, 28–30; Katz, 1996, 4). In such societies, one of the characteristics of childhood is freedom to cross household and gender boundaries that will be lost in adulthood.

Children's relative freedom often takes the form of high mobility in the labor market. Children living in Brazil's cities apparently move in and out of the labor force much more frequently than adults, taking on short-term jobs or quitting more often (Levison, et al., 2007). Many children enter, leave, or change jobs readily for reasons of their own. They often start at the lowest level with dull and repetitive low-wage jobs, moving on to more interesting and responsible work as their experience develops. At the same time, children from poor communities often have little choice in the kind of work they can find, and their mobility between jobs does not necessarily open greater opportunity to them.

Children's work often supports or complements that of adults. When migrant families work together in commercial horticulture in Mexico, for instance, adults carry heavy crop buckets, while children pick, which is lighter work (Bey, 2003, 297). It can be reasonably surmised that most work of young children is in fact of this type. But children may also compete with adults, working at the same jobs for less pay and thereby lowering wages and adult employment opportunities: the employment of British children on milk rounds, for example, is explicitly aimed to cut costs (Lavalette, 2005, 158). Such undercutting of wages has been a fear of the trade union movement since the early days of industrialization.

Some crafts work is assigned to children on the alleged grounds that it can be performed better by their small hands, but this claim probably is not justified. An investigation of this "nimble fingers" argument with respect to children working in India's hand-knotted carpet industry found that children in fact have no special abilities that adults do not match or surpass (Levison, et al., 1998, 130). While there are a few jobs in which children do appear to have an inherent advantage over adults—such as begging, racing camels as jockeys, or creeping through small openings to mine ore or to rob homes—they are few. Children's main advantages to employers, many now think, are more likely to be ignorance or docility, thus making them easier to exploit.

On the other hand, children do not always work for less than do adults. In many cases, lower pay to children reflects their lower productivity in comparison to adults. Where their productivity is equal, it is not unusual to find their pay equal as well—such as in cases where workers are paid by piece rate. In some cases, they may even earn more than their parents or other adults of similar background. Chapter 6 will describe "earn-and-learn" schools in Zimbabwe in which child workers were paid at the same piece rate as were adults and received subsidized schooling besides. Sometimes children earn well because their greater flexibility and availability, such as for seasonal work, increases their value as workers. A study of child workers in Scotland suggests that most employers of school-going workers hired them for reasons other than cutting costs (Howieson, et al., 2006, 470). Sometimes, however, children consider the experience of work, or the chance to learn a skill, as more important than payment (see chapter 4), and apprenticeship practices in many parts of the world may require that children donate their work for at least an initial trial period.

As children become older, their work may increasingly resemble that of adults. Door-to-door hawking, a traditionally adult vocation, is now a common job for Scottish school pupils (McKechnie and Hobbs, 1999, 93). Although children serving customers in shops and catering are formally supervised by adults, in fact they are often left to deal with difficult customers on their own (Frederiksen, 1999). Any competition with adults for jobs is most likely to occur only after children have reached adolescence, which in most of the world is the stage at which they are eligible to become legal workers.

Like the Moroccan girls in Méknès, young persons can in most countries become legal full-time workers at some point in their early to mid-teens, at which point they may assume adult work roles, including full-time wage labor. The fact that young persons are considered in the UNCRC to be children until their eighteenth birthday leads to a slightly awkward situation in which perfectly legal teenage workers with a basic education are still sometimes considered "working children." However, their work is not considered problematic unless it is in some way harmful. On the one hand, the issue of legality is important because most countries have labor laws setting a minimum age for entrance to employment. On the other hand, its importance is diminished because these laws are widely ignored, with many or most children working illegally. This is true in rich countries as in poor ones.

The Range of Children's Work

In most societies, the range of children's work activities changes and expands as they grow. These vary with their gender, social and physical environment, and often with their social status. An adult level of function, knowing how to do many tasks, can in many cases be achieved by mid-adolescence. In Ghana, for example, children might start running errands and doing certain home chores at the age of four or five, taking on other tasks as soon as they are able. By the age of 14, they are expected to do all work that adults of their gender do, having gradually engaged in this work over the previous years (Hashim, 2004, 58). In highland Peru, children start herding domestic animals at the age of five (Bolin, 2006: 74). Tables 2.1 and 2.2 list child tasks in Vietnam to illustrate how the range of children's work there expands with age. Unfortunately, table 2.2, showing urban work, does not include domestic work in the child's home: it nevertheless shows a wide range of labor-force work as children grow.

These tables indicate that children grow up sharing household chores and economic activities from an early age. The following sections describe some of the most important kinds of work that children frequently do. A single child may at one time or another between young childhood and late adolescence engage in a number of them.

Reproductive Work

Studies from many places suggest that children are more involved in chores tending to the home and family—technically termed "reproductive work"—than in any other kind of work. Although both sexes are involved, this work falls predominantly on girls. Reproductive work is by definition unpaid (if it were done

TABLE 2.1

Starting age of work of children in different occupations in the Rural North Central Region of Vietnam

Age	Work undertaken
4	Look after young siblings Sweep house and yard. Watch house
5	Wash dishes Feed chickens, collect pig feed Dig up worms for ducks Catch crabs, shrimps, and snails
6	Wash clothes Cook food for humans Cook food for pigs, feed pigs
7	Fetch fuel wood
8	Boil water Dry paddy Process cassava
9	Tend cows and buffalos Collect grass, collect cattle manure Fetch water Harvest rice
10	Transplant rice
11	Weed and irrigate crops Plough and harrow fields Collect firewood from forest
12	Mill and husk paddy
13	Wage labor
15	Fish Migrate

Source: Adapted from Edmonds and Turk, 2004, 522; who cite as their source Save the Children UK, 1997, 676

for pay, it would be considered a form of "productive work," or economic activity). Someone has always to prepare food and maintain the home, whether it is men or women, adults or children, members of the homestead or hired help. Since such work is necessary and largely indistinguishable between households in a particular setting, it is often taken for granted and acquires little status

TABLE 2.2

Starting age of work of children in different occupations in Ho Chi Minh City, Vietnam (excluding household work)

Age	Work undertaken
6	Selling lottery tickets Peeling onions (at home) Making match boxes (at home) Weaving mats and baskets (at home) Scavenging at the dumpsite
7	Making shoes (local support workers)
8	Filling bobbins (at weaving enterprises) Catching grasshoppers
10	Making ball-point pens (boys)
11	Making lanterns Classifying waste plastic (home) Making operating parts of lamps
12	Recycling glass Making ball-point pens (girls) Making chains, making bag wheels Making silk screen prints Selling noodle soup
13	Making fermented pork Making furniture and wooden art products
14	Making scales, making chalk Recycling glue, recycling plastic (boys) Making shoes (migrant support workers)
15	Making plastic sandals Making bicycle tires Sorting/recycling plastic (at factories—girls)
16	Dyeing materials Catching locusts

Source: Adapted from Edmonds and Turk, 2004, 523; who cite as their source Save the Children UK, 1999, 677

compared with economic activities producing income. Household work is typically assigned to persons in subordinate positions, such as women (especially junior women) and children (especially children who have low status in the family such as step-children or adopted kin). In practice, reproductive work consumes a large proportion of their time. Researchers and advocates have long pointed out that maintaining one's own home has economic benefits for the family, so there is no reason why this work should be considered inferior to economically productive work. That argument also applies to children's household work, especially when it frees adults to participate in the labor market.

That said, children may receive benefits from working in the home, especially strengthened familial bonds that ensure their protection and long-term future security. Some children in high-income countries are in essence contracted by parents to undertake household chores and accept payment as just return for their work—usually in the form of "allowances." But many children regard their work as fair return for what they receive from their parents: accepting payment for their contribution could weaken their relations with their parents and their stake in the home (Zelizer, 2002, 380–383; Leonard, 2007, 155–156; Nieuwenhuys, 2005). It is recognized that children's feelings of competence and helpfulness in the home engender self-esteem (Call, 1996). On the other hand, various studies have found that young people may resent demands made on them when they do not feel their work is necessary or that it allows too little freedom (Call, 1996; also Hungerland, 2007, 170; Wihstutz, 2007; Larson and Richards, 1994, 99; Lee, et al., 2003, 115).

There is a huge variety in the level of the demands on children's contributions in the home. Girls usually do much more than boys. Working mothers may hand over reproductive chores to their daughters (Benería, 1992; Moser, 1996). Some homes demand little work of children because they are wealthy and use mechanized or hired help. On the other hand, poverty can increase workloads. In many homes throughout the world, waste must be disposed of and water and fuel must be fetched, which can be heavy work covering considerable distances (see, R. Ray, 2000b, regarding water storage and sewage disposal). A survey in South Africa showed that just over 20 percent of all children aged five to seventeen spent nine or more hours in the previous week fetching fuel and water (Clacherty, 2002, 33–34; Lehohla, 2001, 25, table 2.6; see also on Egypt, Assaad, et al., 2007). Besides, such work has little flexibility, since some chores, like food preparation and cooking, have to be performed at particular times of the day. Some studies of reproductive work have emphasized the time it absorbs and suggested that it can interfere with school performance, in developed and developing countries.[5]

Reproductive work can be especially confining when children are assigned heavy burdens of care for infants, invalids, and the elderly. In both rich and poor countries, children play a major role in care activities, and when those responsibilities are added to housekeeping chores, the total burden may become full-time work. With the epidemic of HIV/AIDS in southern Africa, increasing numbers of children there have inherited heavy household work and family care responsibilities. And as adults die, more and more households in southern Africa are headed by young people below the age of majority. Even in developed countries such as England, many thousands of young people are heavily involved in caring for invalids in their homes with little external support, sometimes interfering severely with schooling and socialization, and often damaging the health of the care-givers (Dearden and Becker, 2004; 1999).

The above discussion suggests that reproductive work can result in extreme lack of freedom, and because many children find it confining, they often go to some lengths to escape it. The relative liberty of outside work away from the stifling drudgery of reproductive work at home, it will be recalled, was one of the main reasons that the Méknès girls valued their factory jobs. In summary, reproductive work is not always benign for children, despite a widespread assumption that it is safer and more appropriate for children, especially girls, than are economic activities. The evidence does not support that assumption, for home chores can be even more disruptive to schooling and life satisfaction than is formal employment.

Unpaid Work outside the Family

Children may extend caring work relationships out into the community. Children in Germany voluntarily help elderly relatives and neighbors in such tasks as shopping. This gives them pride in their achievement and approval from adults, and sometimes disrupts the relations of dominance and dependency between adults and children (Hungerland, 2007, 174; Hungerland, et al., 2007, 265–266). Even when they are paid for such help, this may be a secondary consideration (Wihstutz, 2007, 82). In a study in Minnesota, U.S.A., up to a fifth of the adolescents were engaged in some unpaid voluntary work, spending an average of four to five hours a week on it (Mortimer, 2003, 96–97). In immigrant communities in California, twelve-year-olds took on some specially skilled work for their families and communities, such as interpreting between Spanish and English speakers (Orellana, 2001, 374, 378). As with helping kin, there may be a degree of compulsion from adults. The household head may provide the labor of children to a friend as a form of reciprocal help in times of need, such as repairing a house or bringing in a harvest or serving food at a feast or funeral (Bourdillon, 1987, 61).

Productive Work in the Family

Productive work in a family setting is often connected to reproductive work and the two are often hard to distinguish, especially in communities where part of the household's production is for its own consumption. In some such societies, gathering food is hard and requires walking some distance from home. Thus among the !Kung in the Kalahari desert of Botswana, families are kept small and children contribute little until they grow into adult roles. In other societies, food is more easily obtained, children are required to help, and families are larger (Andvig, 1998, 57–58).

Although foraging and subsistence production may have been common in some societies in the past, now it is extremely rare to find households totally outside markets and never producing a surplus for trade.[6] On the other hand, many families producing for the market grow crops and use animals for their own subsistence. So production for subsistence and production for markets are no longer clearly distinct. Where households choose or are obliged to produce large surpluses, more labor is needed and children may become more heavily involved (as we discuss further in chapter 4). Upwards of 70 percent of the world's working children appear to be engaged in family-based work (O'Donnell, et al., 2002, 8; Edmonds and Pavcnik, 2005a, 203, table 1). Like other work in the home, this productive work can become excessive and problematic, depending largely on demands made on children by circumstances or by controlling adults, and less on the nature of the work. We indicate areas in which children are frequently involved in family enterprises.

Much of children's work in developing countries lies in agriculture or animal husbandry on small-scale family farms (Bhalotra, 2003, 14). Children may start accompanying adults and imitating them in simple tasks such as harvesting, and move on to weeding and irrigating, with jobs similar to those of adults in their mid-teens (e.g., Punch, 2001, 811–812). In some societies, children take on responsible tasks in the care of animals from the age of five. They may be given their own animals to care for and to profit from. Agricultural work may present both rewards and risks. A big problem with agricultural work is that it can be so extensive as to interfere with schooling, in peak agricultural seasons, for example, or in herding, a task often assigned to boys. Development projects that encourage greater agricultural production for the market sometimes result in increased work and less schooling for children. Further problems can arise with hazardous tools and chemicals. Amanda Berlan points out that children on family cocoa farms in Ghana are taught to use machetes, a potentially dangerous tool, but are not provided protective clothing. Yet they work under supervision, learn to handle their tools competently, and show pride in their work and their skills (Berlan, 2009, 142–144).

Many urban children, in particular, work in family businesses. In Hanoi, Vietnam, even young children are assigned simple tasks in small family businesses (Burr, 2006, 85–87). Children of ethnic Chinese operating takeaway restaurants in Britain initially spend leisure time in the shop, perhaps to watch television when there is none in the living quarters upstairs, and later start to help. From casual help in their early teens, many became integral to the business in their late teens, able to provide particular skills, such as accounting and English translation. The work is combined with school, but may occasionally interfere with it. As in the case of reproductive work, some children are paid, but others disapprove of payment since they feel their work to be part of their reciprocal relationship with their parents (Song, 1999; see also Morrow, 1994, 133).

Where micro-credit support encourages households to develop business enterprises, children can be drawn into the work. This can be an opportunity for development for both the child, who can learn a variety of skills and acquire some responsibility, and the household. It can also be a problem, interfering with schooling and other aspects of a child's education (CIDA, 2007).

Many families take on home-based manufacturing under contract or for sale, and children may help their parents in such production. In Asia, this may include manufacturing incense sticks and garments, rolling cigarettes, stitching sacks, peeling shrimps, making home utensils and decorations, and producing and packaging vegetables (Malhotra, et al., 2003, 13–14); we will discuss stitching footballs in chapter 9. While such arrangements enable contractors to obtain cheap casual labor, the earnings are often more than the workers could otherwise obtain. The work of children in such family contracts ranges from light, willing, and free-time help, appreciated by caring parents (e.g., Burr, 2006, 104–105) on the one hand, to long hours that interfere with leisure activities and sometimes even schooling on the other.

Similar to such work in the home, children may accompany adults and contribute to work outside the home. In Mexico, children from poor agricultural areas travel with their families to earn seasonal money when their own agricultural season is over. Children remain with their families, learn about the wider world, including how to earn and to deal with employers, and work on light tasks to contribute significantly to their family economy. Although this movement may seriously disrupt their schooling—a huge problem for children in migrant labor—teachers also have commented that children are often sharper and brighter when they return from such trips, and show improved social skills. The wages for all are low and living conditions poor, but the work of children enables the family to earn the substantial amount that they need to meet their obligations at home (Bey, 2003; Taracena, 2003, 311).

Employment outside the Family

Concern about "child labor" usually focuses on the employment of children by persons outside the family, even though, as seen above, outside employment comprises but a very small portion of children's work. What is it that makes this sort of work of such prominent concern? One of the main factors is a popular assumption that work inside the circle of the family is safer, since the family has more interest in the child's well-being and development, while outside employers are assumed to be interested only in profit and to have little concern for the children. A powerful stereotypical image operates here, and it often appears in polemics for the "abolition of child labor." But a huge amount of documented evidence demonstrates that neither of these assumptions—the care of families or the callousness of employers—can be taken as generally valid. Reality is far more complex: this question needs to be investigated and answered specifically for each context.

Self-employed children often establish an enterprise of their own because they cannot find preferable wage employment, but some also are in search of an element of freedom in their work, and some want to develop entrepreneurial skills. For this reason, street workers often report a relatively high degree of satisfaction in their work. Not all self-employed street children, however, are outside the control of exploiting adults. For example, children selling small goods on the street often have to purchase their wares from adults at exploitative rates. Besides, self-employment sometimes involves substantial hazards, such as cuts, toxins, and infections among waste pickers, which could be effectively eliminated or controlled in supervised wage employment.

What Children Say about Why They Work

There is an extensive research, theoretical, and advocacy literature addressing the reasons why children work, and all the reasons given are currently under debate. The most common line of thought attributes child work in at least the developing countries to poverty, but how this relationship operates is a matter of intense research and discussion, the complex findings of which we will present in chapter 4. A second line of thinking associates children's work with the culture of child-rearing, treating children's work as a normal developmental factor in growing up. Chapter 5 will explore this perspective and its implications, based largely on social science research. Still another reason for child work is its educational value, as a vehicle for acquiring practical information and life skills. This will be discussed in chapter 6, as part of an analysis of the relationships between education and work.

However, such research-based discussions risk losing children's own voices and perspectives. If we authors have learned anything over our years of engagement in child work issues, it is the vital importance of hearing and considering seriously what children have to say about why they work and what they expect from it.

To ask why children work suggests that work is somehow unusual for children and so needs an explanation, even though most people in the world do some kind of work during childhood. It would be strange to ask why adults work, because it is accepted that work is one of the most fundamental ways people relate to each other (Spittler, 2001; Zimmermann, 2001). It is reasonable to ask of adults not why they work, but why they take up particular kinds of work, noticing that some take up professions for interest or enjoyment or status, even when remuneration is low. Similarly, we can ask young people why they are in the kinds of work they do. Maybe they were coerced by parents or others, or maybe they chose their work out of a special interest. It is worth knowing. It certainly would have been worth knowing why the girls at Méknès preferred to work in a factory rather than at home.

Some children, certainly, have no choice about whether or not to work nor about what kind of work they must undertake. Their work may bring them no material benefits or pleasure, indeed they may thoroughly dislike it. Chapter 6 points out that some children work under duress and would like to stop working altogether, although these appear to be a minority. In chapter 8, we comment on children's many complaints about their work situations, and express concern about children in various kinds of forced and harmful labor. The following sections of this chapter focus on children who exercise, or feel they exercise, some choice in decisions about work, and who see positive aspects in their experience of work.

Children Work for Income, and the Pleasures of Having and Sharing Income

The need for or desire of income is the most common primary motive that children report for seeking employment. They often say that their financial contributions, over and beyond the basic needs they help meet, generate for themselves greater respect and higher standing in their families. They often take great personal satisfaction in being considered a provider. Children also regularly report valuing the bit of independence they gain from having their own income. In an Indonesian tobacco-growing region, one child commented on work in the tobacco industry: "I like to save money for buying clothes and snacks. We want to earn money to help out our parents. When we need to spend money, we can spend our own money and not ask for it from our parents" (Amigó, 2005, 198–199).

Where work is an optional part-time activity, children value it for entertainment and luxury goods, such as fashionable clothing and electronic gadgets. While these items are not strictly necessary, young people clearly enjoy them, and may feel pressure from peers and advertisers to spend in this consumerist way, even occasionally to the detriment of schoolwork (Lavalette, 2005, 156; Mizen, et al., 2001, 45–49; B. White, 1996, 830–831; Zelizer, 2002).

Some children value paid employment, particularly if it is away from home, as a means for renegotiating their relationships with adults in their families, moving toward adult status while maintaining good relations through their contributions. The girls in Méknès reported motives of this type for working, which they saw as a way to enter modern society without causing a rupture in their far more traditional families. A study of children who had migrated from hill villages to work in carpet factories in Kathmandu, Nepal, showed the boys would prefer to be at home but that girls were happy to be there since factory work was easier than work at home (Johnson, et al., 1995, 57, 65). In Kenya, children, and particularly children who have been orphaned, have gained autonomy and influence in their families by earning money and remitting some of it home (Nyambedha and Aagaard-Hansen, 2003, 171). Child workers in Nicaragua, El Salvador, Guatemala, and Scotland claim to value their work and income for relieving them from dependence on others and giving them a degree of independence and control over their own lives (Liebel, 2001b, 61–62). In a survey of working children in Thailand, a little over half reported economic pressure as their main reason for working, and a little under half said their main reason was to achieve the autonomy of a separate income (Banpasirichote, 2000, 13).

Children Work for Social Access and Status

Some children work for reasons that are more social than economic. One reason young people give for taking up their jobs is to keep the company of their friends or expand social ties. Another is for social status and respect. In rural Nigeria, hawking is a way for girls approaching marriage age to be visible to prospective suitors, as these girls may legitimately be approached while selling by non-kin males in public (Robson, 2004, 206). Working children in South America argued that their work kept them from getting involved in criminal activities or begging, and allowed them to live a decent life in spite of their conditions of poverty (Liebel, 2001b, 60–61). In other ways, work may contribute to a young person finding a place in society: work enables them to be "someone in life" (Liebel, 2001b, 60). Children who are deprived of the opportunity to earn feel a loss in status. When asked what he thought was the biggest change brought about by a project to remove children from stitching footballs, an ex-worker replied dejectedly, "Football stitching helped stave off poverty for my family. . . . We used to use our hands in honest labour—now we will be left opening our hands, palms up, asking for help from donors" (Khan, 2007, 200).

Vinod Chandra's study of children of Indian descent in Coventry, England, and Lucknow, India, shows how children find meaning in their work, through which they assert their status in the family and their cultural identity (Chandra, 2008, 112–141). Related to status is a sense of responsibility: workers sometimes find that in their jobs they are trusted as responsible and competent in a way that they do not experience at school (Mizen, et al., 2001, 44–45; Morrow, 1994).

Future Prospects

Some children say they work in order to increase their long-term prospects. Many claim they work at least in part to pay for school expenses in the hope of a better future, and in fact it is very common to find children paying their own school expenses, and often those of younger siblings, out of their earnings. Bangladeshi girls reported seeking work that opened up prospects for desirable future employment, a positive factor that overshadowed possible hazards or working at night. Their experience was that contacts made in early employment may help a person to find appropriate work when older. Girls indicated that advantageous employment would help them gain control over decisions about their marriage, including through accumulation of a significant dowry, and perhaps lead to a more advantageous marriage than would otherwise be likely.[7] Despite some cultural tension around the idea of girls working, they saw work as producing a more successful pattern of transition to adulthood than do traditional early marriage and childbearing (Amin, et al., 1998). In various places, girls claim that contributing to their family's business may help to resist cultural pressures to confine them to home and to have their wishes treated sympathetically and with respect (Boyden, et al., 1998, 100; Chandra, 2007, 70).

Children Often Value and Enjoy Their Work

Children regularly report that they truly enjoy their work and value it for intrinsic qualities they feel are fun and constructive. Child workers meeting under auspices of the World Movement of Working Children declared in 2004, "We value our work and view it as an important human right for our personal development." They also announced in 2006, "We promote and defend the dignified work of children and youth."[8] Working children in Nicaragua surprised researchers with their positive attitude to their jobs: 55 percent expressly stated that they liked to work and half of these said it made them feel useful and important. Three quarters said that they would be worse off if they did not work and in discussions it emerged that the majority would still work even if their families had no need of their income (Liebel, 2004, 68; citing Pineda and Guerra, 1998). In a survey of full-time working children in Ahmedabad in Gujarat State, India, three quarters of the children gave reasons for liking their work and only a quarter gave reasons for disliking it: 72 percent would like to continue working (Sanon, 1998, 157–161). When child workers in Paraguay were asked what they liked most about their lives, the most popular response was their jobs, well ahead of school (Green, 1999, 24; see also Harwood and Mull, 2002, 17). In Nigeria, children who had no real need of income participated in street work as much for fun and excitement as for earning their own pocket money: many were not allowed to indulge in play at home and found recreation through work (Oloko, 1989, 17, 23). The appreciation of work for its intrinsic aspects can come from some surprising places and types of work. A study in Vietnam showed children working all night on rubbish dumps from 6 P.M. to 3 A.M. to be among the happiest, in spite of the dirt and dangers involved: they had good income, working among themselves (even as young as six) rather than under adult supervision, with flexible hours (Theis, 2001, 103). Children scavenging on rubbish heaps in the Philippines so valued and enjoyed their work for its excitement and companionship that it proved difficult to entice them to leave it (Gunn and Ostos, 1992).

Concluding Comment

An ILO study notes, "Decent and productive work is an unfulfilled aspiration of many young people" (Brewer, 2004, 3). It points out that unemployment and underemployment of youth (aged 15 to 24) are a serious problem, with high economic, social, and individual costs, and that early unemployment can permanently affect future employability. Could earlier workplace experience reduce youth unemployment and underemployment? Does it make sense to consider the employment of young persons of 14 to be a (child labor) problem, and then a few months later when they turn 15, suddenly to consider their lack of employment to be a (youth unemployment) problem (see, e.g., ILO, 2006, 6)? This unlikely shift can be understood only in the light of history behind current policies, and that is what we turn to next.

3

Children's Work in Historical and Comparative Perspective

In this chapter we compare the history of children's work, and ideas and interventions about it, in countries with different economic and social histories. We first take the case of Britain, where the notion and discourse of "child labor" as a social problem first appeared, and where the first attempts at its regulation were developed during the Industrial Revolution. We look at changing patterns of children's work, factors that influenced these changes, and changing ideas about childhood, through the nineteenth and early twentieth centuries. We then contrast brief histories of children's work in two low-income countries, Zimbabwe and Indonesia. As further contrast, we look at the substantially different experience of children's work in societies that attempted to follow "noncapitalist" roads to industrialization and modernization, using the examples of China and the former Soviet Union.

These cases throw doubt on a common view of the emergence and abolition of child labor that has influenced current thinking and international standards, namely that urbanization and industrialization are the main causes of the large-scale exploitation of child workers, and that laws prohibiting child employment, prompted by social concern for the welfare of children, have been the main instrument for its elimination.[1] In the last part of the chapter we explore the evolution of international standards in regard to children's involvement in work, and some contradictions embodied in currently adopted standards and policy approaches based on them.

Child Labor and the Industrial Revolution in Britain around the Nineteenth Century

The first legislation intended to protect working children appeared in Britain in the late eighteenth century and developed further in the nineteenth century.

These developments arose in the context of a number of radical changes in British economy and society during the period 1750–1900.

Although there has been more research on the history of children's employment in Britain than in any other part of the world, historians still debate a number of important issues. In what kinds of work were children mainly involved in pre-industrial times? What was the scale of their involvement in the rapidly growing industries of the late eighteenth and early nineteenth centuries? Did industrialization bring an increase in the numbers of working children, or merely a shift in the patterns of child employment? Did it cause children to enter employment at younger ages than in earlier periods? How harmful was industrial employment to the health and well-being of children, compared to other kinds of work? And what was the relative importance of the various factors contributing to the later decline of full-time child employment (Heywood, 2001, Ch. 8; Cunningham and Stromquist, 2005, 59)?

Children's Work on the Eve of the Industrial Revolution

In England (and to a lesser extent in Scotland, Ireland, and Wales) on the eve of the Industrial Revolution, quite radical agricultural changes were in motion. Through the enclosure of commons and other measures, small family plots were being replaced by large farms using waged labor. The displaced rural poor were becoming more dependent on wages, and rural crafts and trades became important sources of income alongside the inadequate incomes provided by farm labor or marginal smallholdings.

The children of poor families worked in agriculture, domestic service, commerce, and home industries. They might make themselves useful in farms or workshops as young as six or seven, but were unlikely to take on skills training or more exacting work before ten, and the majority were "unoccupied" well into their teens (Heywood, 2001, 122–123). While agriculture could involve long hours during times of harvesting, the work was seasonal, and children had much time relatively free of this work. The employment of children in home-based crafts and industries was widespread. Prior to the development of urban, factory-based industrialization, merchants put out contracts for home-based production of commodities and supplied raw materials (Medick, 1976). Scholars have pointed to the low and often declining returns to labor in this form of production, as a result of which the earnings of women and children became a central component of family income for a vast section of the population (D. Levine, 1987, 112–114).

Outside the home, the most common form of children's employment in crafts and trades, particularly for boys, was apprenticeship. Apprentices received training, board, and lodging, but no wages, and parents were sometimes required to pay premiums as in various metal-working trades (Nardinelli, 1990, 55). In England, besides children being placed in apprenticeship by their parents (usually as teenagers), the Poor Law authorities often placed "pauper apprentices" with farmers or craftsmen, often at the age of seven or eight. Charities and parishes sometimes obtained income by exploiting the cheap labor of such "apprentices" (Heywood, 2001, 127; Nardinelli, 1990, 88).

Urbanization, Industrialization, and Children's Work in the Nineteenth Century

Innovations in steam power and machinery made possible the large-scale factory industries, concentrated in rapidly growing urban centers, which dominate images of child labor in the Industrial Revolution. Long working hours and harsh working conditions had existed in small industries before the Industrial Revolution: even in 1801 only a third of the population were engaged in agriculture. Industrial growth created more employment opportunities in the cities: in the first half of the century, the proportion of the British population living in cities rose from around 30 percent to over 50 percent (Woods, 1992, 23). Over this period, life expectancy increased dramatically. Nevertheless, at the end of the nineteenth century, a survey in London suggested that a third of poor households were unable to survive on the wages of the male head (Heywood, 2001, 135); at the beginning of the twentieth century, many working-class families were struggling in poverty until their eldest children started working full-time (Childs, 1992, 1–3, 41–43).

The development of cottage industries and then large-scale industries changed children's experience of work. In cottage industries, children started productive work often as young as six years old. Before machinery took over, they engaged in a variety of tasks to help adult workers, such as blowing bellows, winding, and spinning, and often worked up to twelve hours or more a day. The impacts of machinery on children's work in the textile industry were varied and are debated. Some machines made work simpler and lighter and removed the need for skills and strength of adults: the earliest spinning machinery was designed to be operated by children to cut costs (Heywood, 2001, 131). Other machines meant that less labor was needed. In coal-mining, the more primitive technologies were associated with the employment of more children (Peter Kirby, 2003, 74–76). Work became harder in the larger factories, but children usually started working in them only after the age of ten (Heywood, 2001, 130–132). Waged labor outside the family made children's entry into full-time work more abrupt, rather than a gradual induction into work routines as the child grew. Industries made it possible for a child to be fully occupied in work all the year around, in contrast to the seasonality that had marked rural life (Cunningham, 1995, 81–89). The inadequate protection accorded to apprentices crumbled further, and children termed "apprentices" often became no more than underpaid workers, doing routine tasks and receiving little training that would allow them to compete with their masters for jobs (Childs, 1992, 52–56). In some cases, the long hours and poor conditions produced twisted limbs and curved spines of the poor "factory cripples" (as they were known in Lancashire, Heywood, 2001, 13), but available evidence does not show that the health of children was always worse in factories compared to conditions outside (Nardinelli, 1990, 76–81).

The precise role of children in the general labor force at different stages during the Industrial Revolution is disputed. In the early part of the nineteenth century, children comprised one- to two thirds of the workforce of many textile mills, and regularly comprised a quarter of the workers in mines (Humphries, 2003, 177). Child labor was already decreasing as a proportion of the labor force before legislation was introduced to control it (Nardinelli, 1990, chapter 5). Then, as now (see chapter 1), much reporting focused on horrifying and sensational cases, chosen to mobilize political and social action, and not reflecting the lives and conditions of the majority of children.

Even at the height of the Industrial Revolution, only a minority of working children and adolescents were employed in factories and mines (see Heywood, 2001, 133). Industrial employment was highly localized, concentrated in the areas in which textile manufacturing expanded. When child labor in textile mills peaked in the 1870s, less than 10 percent of children aged ten to fourteen appear to have been employed in factories and workshops in England and Wales, and these amounted to less than a third of all children in employment (Nardinelli, 1990, 5). Many girls and some boys worked in domestic service. Alternatives in the urban areas included working on the streets, helping in shops, begging, providing services such as cleaning, and stealing. Children also helped parents contracted to produce at home, as well as performing domestic chores (Davin, 1996, 157–197). Many boys and some girls were employed in agriculture, especially at harvest time. "Gangs" were formed for contract work in large-scale agriculture, including men and women, boys and girls. A report in the mid-nineteenth century showed half the gang members in the eastern counties to be aged between six and eighteen; they often worked a fourteen-hour day (Heywood, 2001, 124–125).

Work also depended on class, engaging primarily children of the poor. There remained many British children from all classes who did not work during the Industrial Revolution. At many times and in many places there was considerable unemployment among children, sufficient to place reducing their "idleness" high on the agenda of local authorities (Cunningham, 1990).

Education and Child Protection

The growing concern for both control over and protection of children during the nineteenth century showed itself in various ways. In the first half of the nineteenth century, there were attempts to rescue children from the streets, reinforced by worries over their disruptive lawlessness. Whether the concern was for children's welfare or for social order, many children were placed in institutions or schools, which often hired out their labor to cover expenses. In some cases, protection involved placing children in families where they could be employed in domestic service or in agriculture. Some were shipped to Australia, supposedly for their protection. Toward the end of the nineteenth century, the idea grew that children of the poor should be rescued rather than disciplined, even sometimes protected from abuse within their own families (Cunningham, 1991, 134–151).

By the early part of the twentieth century, the British state was taking more responsibility for the welfare and development of children, leaving less autonomy for families and parents, culminating in the Children's Act of 1908. This act strengthened the power of the state to act against child abuse and neglect, even to the extent of removing children from their homes. The professional classes thus gained in power over poor parents. The Act established the dependence of young people up to the age of 16, including them all in the category of "children." This legislation could not ensure that children had a joyous and carefree childhood, but it established this ideal as the norm to strive for (Davin, 1996, 208–216; Hendrick, 2003, 82–86).

Schooling was widespread even in the eighteenth century, but occupied only a few hours a day and a few years for the poor. The long summer holidays were supposed to allow children to take part in harvesting, but absences from school were common in agricultural areas at other times of year when children's work was required. Schools were run by churches, or sometimes by private individuals, although in eighteenth-century Europe, governments were increasingly taking a role in schooling and there were moves to make it compulsory at the turn of the nineteenth century (Cunningham, 1995, 117–24).

The growth in school attendance was not steady. There is evidence from industrial areas that schooling and literacy dropped as a result of factory employment around the beginning of the nineteenth century (Cunningham, 1995, 103–104). A part of the debate about getting the children of the poor into Sunday schools and other schools was more about keeping them under control and structuring the time of the idle than about teaching them anything useful or removing them from harmful employment. As historian Hugh Cunningham observes, "in the long run, it was the unemployment of children as much as their exploitation within labor which was a matter of concern to those in authority" (Cunningham, 1990, 121).

One factor that enabled poor children to receive some schooling was the policy allowing them to combine work and school. The Labor in Factories Act of 1844 restricted factory working hours for children to ensure that they were able to attend school in the face of competing demands: the families of the poor needed income from their children, but there was also a growing demand that children receive schooling. The policy of allowing children to work part of the day and to attend school received widespread support for the next thirty years, and some argue that this was a key factor in the relatively rapid spread of literacy in Britain. Toward the end of the century, however, the view that children should be in school and not working for wages began to dominate (Cunningham, 1995, 138–142; 1991, 170). With the introduction of policies to establish a school in every neighborhood in 1870, compulsory schooling from the ages of five to ten in 1880, and the abolition of school fees in 1891, the proportion of children aged five to fourteen in school in England and Wales rose from 24 percent in 1870 to 70 percent in 1900 (Cunningham, 1995, 158).

It is not clear that children and their parents always valued a school system that was severe, restrictive, and often of poor quality. Around 1890, about a quarter of those who should have been in school in England were regular truants. Around 1910, virtually all working-class boys had some experience of employment before they left school. Eighty percent left promptly at the school-leaving age of fourteen (or thirteen when they could get exemptions), often on the week or the day of the birthday that allowed them to do so, and immediately sought full-time employment (Childs, 1992, 39, 73–78). Prosecutions to enforce school attendance eventually resulted in effective universal primary education early in the twentieth century (Cunningham, 1995, 157–158).

Regulation of Child Labor

In the second half of the eighteenth century, the plight of poor working children began to receive sympathetic attention. The first working children to receive attention were the "climbing boys," normally apprenticed to a master chimney sweep. Their job was to climb up narrow chimneys and flues and brush them clean, an unhealthy task known to cause respiratory ailments as well as scrotal cancers. There were incidents of children being sold into this work, and strong rumors of kidnapping for it. The boys were sometimes pricked and prodded to force them up the chimneys, and there were accounts of fire being used for the same purpose. The climbing boys were visible, in that they visited private houses to clean the chimneys. The first labor law in Britain intended to protect children from poor working conditions was the Act for the Better Regulation of Chimney Sweepers and their Apprentices of 1788. This stated that apprentices must be at least eight years old and that a master may use no more than six apprentices. It was largely ignored at the time, but the work was increasingly seen as inhumane and in 1803 a society for the protection of sweeps changed its aim from protection to abolition. The minimum age of apprenticeship in this trade was raised to ten in 1834, and to sixteen in 1840, when entering a chimney or flue was prohibited for anyone under twenty-one.[2] The employment of climbing boys nevertheless continued into the second half of the nineteenth century (Cunningham, 1991, 58–59).

The conditions of children in the textile mills came to public attention partly through the efforts of medical professionals responding to epidemics in industrial towns, who drew attention to the health hazards created by conditions and hours of work in factories (Cunningham, 1991, 65). In 1802, the Factory Health and Morals Act regulated hours, conditions, and training for pauper apprentices in textile mills. In 1819, the Cotton Mill and Factories Act banned employment in this sector up to the age of nine, and it limited the working day to twelve hours for those under the age of sixteen. In 1833, the Factory Act reduced the working day to nine hours up to the age of thirteen. It also established paid inspectors to enforce the laws, although their power and effectiveness remained limited (Peter Kirby, 2003, 105–106; Cunningham, 1991, 170–172).

Toward the middle of the century, the cause of children outside the immediate view of urban industrial centers began to receive attention. The Mines and Collieries Act of 1842 prohibited underground work in mines and collieries for women and children under ten and provided for inspectors; we have already mentioned that in 1844, working hours were limited to allow children to attend school in the mornings or afternoons.

Restrictions were gradually extended to other sectors and branches of employment. The Factory Acts Extension Act of 1867 extended restrictions of working hours for women and children to any manufacturing establishment employing fifty or more people; in the same year, the Workshop Regulation Act prohibited the employment of children under the age of eight years in any handicraft, and the Agricultural Gangs Act prohibited the employment of children under the age of eight in public agricultural gangs (it also prohibited mixing sexes in gangs). In 1872, the Metalliferous Mines Regulation Act prohibited women, girls, and boys under the age of twelve years from employment in metal mines. The Agricultural Children's Act of 1873 stated that children between the ages of eight and ten years could be employed in agriculture only if a parent certified that the child had attended school 250 times in the previous twelve months, or 150 times for those over ten, but there was no enforcement of this law. The Shop Hours Regulation Act of 1886 stipulated that the hours of work of children and young persons in shops should not exceed seventy-four per week, including meal times. The minimum age at which a child may be put to work in manufactures was raised to nine in 1874, to eleven in 1891, and to twelve in 1901.[3] The Education Act of 1918 required that employment of young persons attending school be suspended during the hours of school, and it restricted the permissible hours of employment before and after school and on Sundays, thus confirming the official view that a child's place is in school.

These laws and regulations, passed over a period of more than a hundred years, initially attacked what were considered the most harmful sectors of child work and were gradually extended to improve conditions and to limit employment more broadly, establishing a pattern of intervention that was followed in several other countries and (as we shall see later in this chapter) in setting international standards. Although enforcement was often ineffective, these legal and administrative changes were responses to, and reinforced, changes in the way people thought about childhood, and particularly the way middle-class people thought about children of the poor. Yet right through to the early twentieth century, many children remained working in areas in which work was available (Cunningham and Stromquist, 2005, 63–65). Many children were still combining work and school, often in breach of legislation and with the support of their parents (sometimes to the embarrassment of labor unions). In 1912, evidence suggests that 7 to 10 percent of elementary school children over the age of seven were employed. Well into the twentieth century, prosecutions against parents for the failure of their children to attend school continued, and there were reports of children working long hours before and after school—but they were on the streets or in sweatshops, not in the more visible formal-sector factories where inspection was more feasible, and the story of success could be preserved (Cunningham, 1991, 13, 182).

In explaining the gradual shift in the dominant activity of (poor) childhoods from full-time productive work to school, there has been much debate on the relative importance of key influences, including: changing ideas about childhood; labor regulations and the development of institutionalized monitoring and enforcement; improved access to schooling; the changing economy and rising working-class incomes; lower mortality rates and smaller families; and changing technology and needs of manufacturers.[4] Changing interests of factory owners, particularly in suppressing competition, together with a concern of adult male workers to protect their jobs, were also relevant (Nardinelli, 1990, 133–136). It could be argued that the successive efforts in legislation were not so much in the cause of social change as the reflection of changing values in society and changes that were already underway in the economy. Probably all these factors were partly responsible, and influenced each other.

As the Industrial Revolution spread to North America and to other countries in Europe, similar patterns of child labor and protective legislation followed. As in Britain, this legislation always began with restrictions on the employment of children in factory industries, although it was only in parts of the United States and a few other countries (including Belgium and The Netherlands) that child employment in factories was found in anything like the numbers that had been seen in Britain. Thus, the typical evolution of European and North American child labor legislation has involved the gradual broadening of the category of prohibited employment to include previously excluded sectors such as retail trade, office work, hotels and restaurants, the caring professions and domestic service, and agriculture, as, simultaneously, who is a "child" has been gradually redefined by raising the minimum age of employment.[5] As in Britain, there were mixed motives for the suppression of child labor, one being the desire of adult male workers to protect their jobs.

The Work of Young People in Contemporary Britain and
Other Wealthy Countries

It is commonly assumed that in the developed world, employment of children is a minority experience; that children do only acceptable light work appropriate for children; and that legislation effectively controls and monitors such work (McKechnie and Hobbs, 1999, 90). It is further assumed that children work not out of economic necessity to provide for family sustenance, but only at their own choice to buy luxury goods and to pay for entertainment with peers. In the last twenty years, however, these assumptions have been challenged and more attention is now being paid to children's work in Britain and other wealthy countries.

Paid employment is not a minority experience for adolescents in the developed world. It is true that few very young children are involved in paid employment, although a survey in Denmark in 1992 showed that 7 percent of ten-year-olds already had work experience (Frederiksen, 1999). In most high-income countries, however, paid work is a majority experience for adolescents. A survey of pupils aged fourteen to fifteen in selected areas in Scotland and the north of England showed those who had paid work experience ranging from 50 to 79 percent.[6] A recent study of school pupils in Scotland showed that over half had some paid work experience by the end of the fourth year of secondary school (when they would be turning sixteen), increasing to over 80 percent by the time they left school two years later (Howieson, et al., 2006, 29). In The Netherlands, in recent years typically more than 10 percent of all twelve-year-olds have had paid jobs, rising to over 30 percent by age fourteen and over 50 percent by age fifteen.[7]

Most developed countries have complex legislation about children working below the age of compulsory schooling, controlling the minimum age for employment, the kinds of work that may be performed, the number of hours that children may work, starting and finishing times, and requiring permits. In Britain, the minimum age for employment is thirteen, while those under the minimum school-leaving age (currently sixteen) may not be employed during school hours, nor for more than two hours on a school day (and not more than one hour before school). Hours of work are limited to between 7 A.M. and 7 P.M. There are also restrictions on weekend work and work during school holidays, and on the kind of work that may be undertaken (no industrial work). The regulations also stipulate that anyone employed under sixteen must have a permit. However, the work that adolescents do is often in breach of these regulations: they work younger than the permitted age and outside the permitted hours (Lavalette, 2005, 157–9). Even when the work is in accordance with the regulations, only a small minority of those employed under the age of sixteen take the trouble to acquire permits (Howieson, et al., 2006, 83; McKechnie and Hobbs, 1999, 94). Adolescents in high-income countries sometimes claim a right to choose to work, and see no reason why they should require permission

(Leonard, 2004). In practice, the regulations are largely ineffective in controlling the work that children and adolescents undertake.

Children and adolescents undertake a variety of work in developed societies, nearly always in combination with school. While they often do light work that is considered appropriate for young people, such as baby-sitting or newspaper rounds, school-aged adolescents also undertake work usually associated with adult employment (Mizen, et al., 1999, 425, and see the discussion of children's work in chapter 2). Regulations are largely ineffective at controlling this work, and schools and teachers largely ignore it, in marked contrast to the much greater efficacy of compulsory education regulations. The study in Scotland showed that teachers were often only partially aware of the nature and extent of the part-time employment of their pupils, and recommended that school teachers both take account of their work experience and utilize it in the overall education process.[8] This would be a step toward overcoming the assumption that a "good" childhood is properly free of work. The assumption that a carefree and work-free childhood, without responsibilities, is ideal for all children arises from the romantic notion of childhood discussed earlier. What are the consequences of such notions for the development of children, for their families, and for the future of society? To what extent are they shared, and put into practice, in other kinds of society, and to what extent are they reflected in international standards?

Child Work, Education, and Interventions in Asia and Africa: Examples from Indonesia and Zimbabwe

We now consider briefly the very different histories of children's work in two low-income countries. Colonialism brought with it the incorporation of their populations into commodity economy and export production, and a distinctive, non-European pattern of economic growth without industrialization (indeed, sometimes destroying existing small-scale industry). How did colonial policies toward production, extraction, and labor affect childhood and child work? What, if any, policies attempted to shift the normative definition of childhood, in relation to such issues as work and education? And how did children themselves respond to these changing constructions of their lives and interventions in them?

Children, Work, and Education in Colonial and Independent Indonesia

Author Ben White has studied the history of children's work in Indonesia.[9] Local reports from the early nineteenth century suggest that children participated in productive work from five or six years old, in such tasks as agricultural work, guarding fields against birds and other pests, looking after livestock, and household chores: they were fully engaged in work by their early teens (Elson, 1994, 24). British Governor Thomas Stamford Raffles had this to say about children in Java's peasant economy, based on information collected by his team of field investigators in 1811–1815. "Children, which are for a very short period a burden to their parents, become early the means of assistance and a source of wealth. To the peasant who labours his field with his own hand, . . . they grow up into a species of valuable property. . . . As the labour of the women is almost equally productive with that of the men, female children become as much objects of solicitude of their parents as male: they are nursed with the same care and viewed with the same pride and tenderness." (Raffles, 1817, vol. 1, 69–71.)

In 1830, after the return of the Indies to Dutch rule, the colonial government introduced a system of forced cultivation that required peasants, as condition for access to land for their own crops, to cultivate also export crops to be delivered against fixed prices. Children became widely involved, not only in household work and subsistence production, but also in expanding export crops, such as indigo, cochineal, coffee, tea, cinnamon, tobacco, and sugarcane. They frequently replaced adults in fulfillment of labor-tax and labor-service obligations (Elson, 1994, 119). It was common for households with larger landholdings to take in the children of landless and marginal households as live-in, hired servants, receiving food and clothes for their labor (Boomgaard, 1989, 151–152; Elson, 1994, 294). Among the large landless population, children's wages were generally on a par with women's wages (at about 60–80 percent of the rate for adult men). We cannot tell how much work interfered (or possibly was combined) with children's needs for rest and play. Since very few children attended school, work was the main medium for learning life skills.

The rapid expansion of large-scale plantations in the late nineteenth century brought new patterns of wage employment. The labor force came largely from Java's landless workers and impoverished, near-landless peasants, recruited as indentured "coolie contract" workers to Sumatra and on shorter-term arrangements in Java. The labor inputs of children were common, but not always essential, in both native and European enterprises. In rural crafts and small industries, children commonly worked both as family helpers and for wages. Earnings in this sector were much less than prevailing agricultural wage rates, so all family members had to participate in production in order to attain a survival income for the household (as in Britain's "proto-industries" on the eve of the Industrial Revolution).

The employment of children was not considered a social issue in Indonesia before the First World War. At the beginning of the twentieth century, only about one in 200 native children attended any kind of formal school. It was only with the gradual establishment of village schools from 1907 onward that villagers in most regions had any access to education. Even by the 1930s, only about one-third of native children attended primary school, and then only for two and a half hours a day for three years. This did not interfere greatly with their other work, except for full-time work away from home.

Late-colonial interventions in child employment applied legislation establishing minimum ages for admission to employment, based on European concerns about child labor in factories. These interventions left untouched the majority of working children, who were working in agriculture, and did nothing to promote their access to education.

As signatory to the Treaty of Versailles, the government of The Netherlands was obliged to apply to its colonial possessions the ILO Conventions 5 and 6 (1919), which established fourteen as the minimum age for industrial employment, and forbade night-time employment in most industries. The colonial government adopted an ordinance in 1925 which set the minimum age for industrial employment at twelve (although in The Netherlands, a new Labor Law had raised it to fourteen), reduced the definition of night work from eleven hours to the specified 10 P.M. to 5 A.M., and made no attempt to engage the overwhelmingly agrarian employment of children. In the tobacco industry, many female children worked in drying and packing sheds, carrying bundles of tobacco leaf for women to sort, stack, weigh, and pack. The tobacco industry's objections to the new ordinance were overcome by redefining "industrial workplace" so that the drying sheds, which were open at ground level for ventilation, were not included.

When attempts were made to introduce a voluntary ban on children under the age of fourteen working in drying sheds, Labor Controller Raden Iskandar noted that there was no danger that the children would be hanging around idle, at the mercy of the "demoralizing influences of the village." "The young child can look after little brothers and sisters, whose working mother might otherwise have to hire help for this; the girls can cook rice and vegetables, clean the house and yard, bring meals to the parents [in the fields], gather firewood that otherwise would have to be bought, look for wild vegetables in the fields; the boys can graze the animals or ducks, cut fodder, help their fathers in all stages of rice and tobacco cultivation; many children earn money selling snacks, serving in food stalls, or running errands for neighbours" (de Kat Angelino, 1929, 140). Besides giving a fine example of stereotypical gender divisions, these remarks underline the point that the child labor ordinance and its enforcement were intended only to ban children from the world of "industry" and large-scale, formal sector agro-processing in enclosed buildings. The ordinance was not intended to exclude children from the world of work, from agricultural production, or even from earning money, and certainly not to push them into school, which is hardly mentioned in the entire report.

The 1925 ordinance remained in force without changes for more than 20 years. In the late 1940s, various developments in labor legislation in a newly independent Indonesia left the legal status of child workers in a state of some confusion. Most experts agree that the amended 1925 ordinance remained in force until a new Labor Law was introduced in 1987. During the half century after independence (in 1945) the lives of Indonesian children changed in many ways. Childhood was extended and modified through a combination of a higher age of marriage, the rapid spread of primary and junior secondary education, and correspondingly changed patterns of work for most children, both boys and girls. For the first three decades after independence, the child labor problem was given little if any attention by the government or the labor movement (although sporadic reports appeared in the media), and no employers were prosecuted for employing underage children.

Much greater efforts were directed at rapidly extending access to primary and secondary schools. By the time of the introduction of compulsory education in 1984, more than 90 percent of boys and girls aged seven to twelve, and around 70 percent between thirteen and fifteen (just under this figure for girls and just over for boys) were already attending school. By the end of the twentieth century, attendance had risen to 96 percent in the seven-to-twelve age group, and 79 percent among those aged thirteen to fifteen (Oey-Gardiner, 2000, 127).

In the first decade of the twenty-first century, very few children in factory employment or domestic service are still in school, but most of them have completed at least some years of primary school. In contrast, more than half of children in informal-sector employment, including "street children," are still attending school (B. White and Tjandraningsih, 1998, chapter 3; Irwanto, et al., 1995). The majority of Indonesia's working children are, thus, school-going children involved in part-time work. School attendance, although occupying only 4–5 hours per day in the first six years, places limits on the kinds of work available to children, and restricts employment to a part-time activity. A good example is given by East Java's tobacco industry. Today's tobacco companies still make widespread use of child labor, but all the children attend school for at least some years. Many, particularly girls, begin working in the drying or sorting sheds before they are twelve years old, but the majority combines this with school attendance, working four hours or less on school days. Also in contrast to earlier times, child workers generally keep their own wages, although some give part or all to their parents (Tjandraningsih and Anarita, 2002).

Indonesia ratified the UN's 1989 Convention on the Rights of the Child in 1990 and was one of the first four countries to join the ILO's International Programme for the Elimination of Child Labour (IPEC) in 1992. Under IPEC, a set of time-bound programs was established for Indonesia, to eliminate the employment of children in selected "worst forms" including off-shore fishing platforms, commercial sex work, and footwear factories. Indonesia ratified the ILO Minimum Age Convention in 1999 and the Convention on the Worst Forms of Child Labor in 2000.

Children, Work, and Education in Colonial and Independent Zimbabwe

Author Michael Bourdillon has studied working children in Zimbabwe, where again the history of children's involvement in work is very different from that of Europe. Before colonial settlement at the end of the nineteenth century, children were involved in herding, agriculture, and domestic work. Colonization brought new markets for agricultural produce and created a demand for labor on the part of wealthy African land-owners, resulting in increased workloads for women and children. At the same time, many men took up paid employment on farms, mines, and in towns, leaving domestic agriculture in the hands of women and children who remained behind.

On the other hand, adolescent boys, from as young as ten years old, were quick to take up opportunities of work away from home. Some were encouraged by their fathers to earn for the family, while others welcomed the chance to resist patriarchal control and unpaid toil at home. They worked in a variety of occupations, from mining to domestic help. Movement into the migrant labor force enabled them to purchase clothes and other consumer goods, and to acquire some control over the fruits of their work. Girls and young women were more restricted in opportunities for employment, but they could find work in domestic service and seasonal agricultural work. Many girls fled to towns, farms, and mission stations to escape marriage and other arrangements whereby fathers or guardians effectively sold their labor to other men (Grier, 2005, 69–109).

Labor migration also created problems of control and discipline in the urban areas. The young migrants, having challenged parental authority, were ready to challenge colonial controls. They also defied employers, regularly and unilaterally breaking off contracts when they so desired. Early regulation was concerned more with controlling labor than with keeping children out of the labor force. The Native Juveniles Employment Act in 1926 actually facilitated the recruitment of boys and girls under the age of fourteen. It allowed children to register and obtain passes to seek employment away from home, without necessarily having parental permission. It also allowed involuntary apprenticeships for unemployed boys in the towns (Grier, 2005, 111–159).

One major concern leading to this act was unruly behavior of young boys in the towns and mine settlements. Registration was intended to control young people by making it easier to identify them when they escaped either from patriarchal control at home, or from disagreements with employers at work. The regulations did not state a minimum age for employment, although officials were eventually instructed not to issue registration documents to children under ten years of age. When it became clear that young people were not so easily molded by legislation and employers, the Chief Native Commissioner noted, "These young people are the coming generation, and if we countenance the facility with which they can denounce their parents and their schools and wander off wherever they like, coming back hardened little vagabonds and rogues, it is not in the interests of the native community that that state of affairs should be tolerated any longer . . ." (Grier, 2005, 157, citing a 1931 Conference).

Early schools were started by missionaries toward the end of the nineteenth century and were much in demand for the benefits they could bring in the newly colonized country, particularly to boys. Attendance, however, was irregular, with children staying away at peak agricultural seasons or when livestock needed attention. Some schools had boarding facilities, allowing pupils to stay away from home. The labor of school pupils was often utilized by mission schools, and particularly boarding schools, to grow food for pupils and staff and to sustain the schools: some missionaries even used the labor of pupils to enrich themselves personally (Grier, 2005, 161–195).

Primary schooling expanded throughout the colonial period, but schools were racially segregated, and government expenditure on Black education was low. Secondary schools, usually with boarding facilities, also expanded, but much more slowly than primary schools. Although by 1974, almost all children received some primary schooling, less than half of those starting would reach the sixth grade, and less than 4 percent would find places in secondary schools (O'Callaghan, 1977, 54, 61).

Some schools were more explicitly associated with the employment of children. From 1930, certain tea estates advertised free schooling and boarding in exchange for work on the estates. These schools provided reliable and cheap labor for the estates, and made schooling possible for some who would not otherwise receive it.[10]

The work of children changed little immediately after independence in 1980.[11] However, there was a massive expansion in secondary education. Primary education was free, and within a decade nearly half of all children entered junior secondary school, the highest figure in Africa. The quality of the new schools, however, was often poor, and there remained a demand for the more expensive private, but government aided, schools. In the 1990s, school levies were introduced at the primary level and, together with secondary school costs, increased relative to earnings as the economy of the country deteriorated.

According to a survey covering the period 2000–2006, just over 80 percent of children of primary school age were enrolled in schools, as were 33 percent of girls and 35 percent of boys of secondary school age.[12] These figures are likely to be dropping with the economic collapse in the country in the first decade of the twenty-first century, as school expenses become unaffordable and teachers look for work elsewhere in order to survive.

In 1997, the Zimbabwe government amended its Labour Relations Act to forbid the employment of children under twelve, while those aged twelve to fourteen were permitted to work a maximum of six hours a day in light work during school holidays. Zimbabwe ratified ILO Convention 138 on Minimum Age for Entry to Employment in 1999, raising the minimum age to fifteen, and ILO Convention 182 on the Worst Forms of Child Labor in 2000. The minimum age legislation is occasionally enforced, but it is widely considered inappropriate to the difficult circumstances of the country and is thus frequently breached. Economic collapse and the HIV/AIDS epidemic have left large numbers of children with little or no adult support. Young people have increasingly to fend for themselves, sometimes crossing national borders, and protective legislation is of little help.

Children, Work, and Education in Communist Revolutions and Post-Communist Transitions

The important socialist revolutions of the twentieth century (in Russia, China, and various other Asian, African, and Latin American countries) led to fundamental changes in structures of ownership, production, and distribution. They also had major implications for childhood: "wherever communism seized control, changes in concepts of childhood and in government initiatives toward children followed quickly" (Stearns, 2006, 91).

Pre-revolutionary Russia (prior to the First World War) and China (prior to the Second World War) showed features similar to those of other poor countries of Europe and Asia, respectively. The majority of their populations was rural and engaged in small-scale peasant agriculture or agricultural labor, crafts, and petty trade. Illiteracy rates and child mortality were high, only a minority of children went to school, and the state was largely indifferent to children's survival and upbringing.

In Russia, new attention to children surfaced almost immediately after the 1917 uprising, with laws forbidding employment below age fourteen (1917) and promoting the eradication of illiteracy (1919). The new regime began quickly to establish new schools, including nursery schools and kindergartens, and to introduce programs to improve children's health, as well as to abolish corporal punishment in schools. Communist ideology included beliefs that problems with childhood resulted from imperfect social arrangements, poverty, and class inequalities, and that the state should play an active role in childrearing.

Education policy in early Soviet Russia included work for youth in school gardens or workshops, or in factories, as a means of becoming acquainted with technology. "Schools organized productive activities, [...] and the youth groups certainly called on children's service in harvesting grain, helping take care of veterans, making toys and a wide variety of other activities. The goals were to aid the state—not the family economy—while not interfering with the primary educational mission, and to teach the children both relevant skills and the nobility of work itself" (Stearns, 2006, 87). Child work thus took on a communal character, rather than an individual one based in the family or in capitalist wage relations.

In China after 1949, the new communist regime was also determined to construct a society different from modern Western models and from the Confucian tradition: the culture of instilling conformity in children and extensive patriarchal controls were seen as responsible for many social problems. There was thus a strong emphasis on curtailing family influence, expanding access to school, and modernizing education with more emphasis on intellectual creativity (following Russian research on the subject). It could also be argued that one form of indoctrination (Confucian) was replaced by another (Maoist), as rote learning and recitation of slogans continued to play an important role. During the 1950s primary school enrolment tripled from thirty to ninety million, and expansion has continued to the present, with a new state commitment in 2003 to provide university education to 15 percent of the relevant age group. As in the Soviet Union, a huge effort went into the provision of nursery schools and kindergartens, and into the mobilization of youth groups, which played important roles both in providing labor in collective enterprises, and in political work (Stearns, 2006, 89–90).

During the Cultural Revolution of the late 1960s, secondary and tertiary education were severely disrupted and millions of secondary school students found themselves waiting to graduate and to be assigned jobs. Partly as a way of addressing this problem, Mao Zedong's "send-down" policies resulted in seventeen million urban youth being sent to live and work in rural areas between 1967 and 1978. All urban families with children who had graduated from secondary school were expected to send their children to designated rural areas, where these transplanted youth worked long hours. They generally stayed in rural areas for several years, visiting their families for only a few weeks every three years. Opportunities to stay in urban areas, or to return after being sent down, became scarce and valuable. Most college students were children of those with political connections, and on graduating most were able to remain in urban areas. After Mao's death in 1979, the send-down policy was abandoned and the government was forced to legitimize self-employment (previously forbidden) in order to generate a greater variety of job trajectories for urban youth leaving schools (Zhou and Hou, 1999, 12–16). The population policy of one child per family introduced in the early 1980s also encouraged new levels of emotional investment and material indulgence of children, as well as a return to a preference for sons and the corresponding female infanticide or abandonment.

In Communist ideologies, introduction to productive work is seen as integral to education, not as antagonistic to it as implied in the ILO's Minimum Age Convention. Nevertheless, work was detached from income, and it has been argued that the policy suffered from lack of resources in schools and lack of incentive on the part of factories (Holmes, 1991, 9, 41–42).

The transition from socialist to market economy has seen qualitative changes both in education and in child employment. In Russia, serious constraints on education budgets have weakened the influence of schools: "For many . . . school has ceased to be credible as the cultural and educational centre of childhood. . . . Children themselves cannot protect their right to education; many see it as having no relevance to their lives." At the same time, "social and economic transformations . . . have brought about a number of long-forgotten social phenomena, such as child vagrancy, begging, and homelessness" (Mansurov, 2001, 165, 151). As Alyesha, a fourteen-year-old newspaper distributor, commented: "Now, everything depends on money. It depends how much you can spend" (cited in Mansurov, 2001, 155). The provision of job placements for children within the educational system has declined, as many labor and recreation camps have closed down (Mansurov, 2001, 151). At the same time there has been a sharp increase in children's work in the informal sector (particularly in urban areas), sometimes from very early ages and with a semi-legal (and thus unprotected) character. Working street children, both boys and girls, have become a cause for official concern, as shown in studies carried out in Moscow and St Petersburg in 2001. About half of these children were under thirteen years of age, and in both cities more than 60 percent of the working street children reported that they were still attending school every day or "nearly every day" (International Labour Office, 2002a, 22, 24; 2002b, 24–25). In rural areas the collapse of infrastructure and production has reduced the number and kinds of jobs available to children, and the absence of a market infrastructure seriously limits the opportunities for self-employment. Rural girls find it particularly hard to get work. The researchers were told of instances in which thirteen- or fourteen-year-old girls were living with well-off older men in return for economic support (Mansurov, 2001, 157–158).

In China, after the adoption of market-oriented policies and rapid economic growth since 1978, childhoods (particularly urban childhoods) have begun to resemble those of other Asian societies. Little research is available and there is no comprehensive information on patterns of child work, but there is general public recognition that child work, including its harmful forms, has increased along with economic development during the reform period. As in Russia, large numbers of "long-forgotten phenomena" such as abduction, forced child labor, and trafficking have been reported (International Labour Office, 2005, 55).

In summary, Communism did not abolish children's work but changed its character in three important ways: first, the worst kinds of abuse of working children were largely eliminated; second, children's work was combined with (rather than getting in the way of) schooling; and third, it took on a collective rather than individual character. The subsequent collapse of Communism led to a resurgence of the forms and conditions, and some of the abuses, of child work that have characterized the non-Socialist world. These rapid changes in children's lives, education, and work involvement in Socialist revolutions, and their partial reversal during post-Socialist transitions, underline the importance of broad state policies (such as development policies and social policies, especially education) and of larger political and economic forces in shaping the life course of children and young people—as already seen in the cases of Britain, Zimbabwe, and Indonesia. Children's involvement in work and their experience of it are only to a minor extent (and in some cases probably not at all) affected by "child labor" legislation.

International Standards and Trends in Interventions

The evolution of international standards and national legislation on children's work since the late nineteenth century has been dominated by the "British model" of progressively more restrictive prohibition through minimum-age regulations or conventions. A recent book by ILO expert Alec Fyfe, *The Worldwide Movement Against Child Labor* (2007), provides a useful overview of the key global actors in international campaigns, including the ILO and other UN agencies, international NGOs, donor governments, consumer movements, the media, the research community, and movements of working children and youth. Among international agencies, it is the ILO that positions itself as playing a "convening role" in the current worldwide movement against "child labor" and providing policy leadership through its standard-setting role (2007, 3). It is useful to reflect in greater detail on the background to the ILO's two key "child labor" Conventions 138 (1973) and 182 (1999).

Minimum-Age Conventions

At its inauguration in 1919, the International Labour Organisation (ILO) was mandated to work for "the abolition of child labor and the imposition of such limitations on the labor of young persons as shall permit the continuation of their education and assure their proper physical development" (Treaty of Versailles, 1919, article 427). It adopted a series of minimum-age conventions, first focusing on industrial employment (1919) and later extending to prohibitions on child employment at sea (1920), in large-scale agricultural work (1921), and various forms of nonindustrial labor (1931).[13] In all these conventions, the employment of children within their own families was exempted from the prohibition. Finally in 1973, the ILO established a general Minimum Age Convention (no. 138) aiming to achieve the "total abolition of child labor" and prohibiting the admission of children under the age of fifteen (or the age of completion of compulsory schooling, if this is higher) in "employment or work in any occupation."[14] This Convention has been adopted (in 1998) as one of ILO's "core conventions" in the Declaration on Fundamental Principles and Rights at Work and its Follow-up (along with freedom of association, the right to collective bargaining, elimination of all forms of forced or compulsory labor, and the elimination of discrimination in respect of employment and occupation). This means that all member states must "respect, promote and realize" the Minimum Age Convention, regardless of whether they have ratified it or not. The ILO has claimed consistently—even after the adoption of the highly successful "worst forms" Convention 182—that Convention 138 is still the central pillar of its work on child labor.

Marianne Dahlén's *The Negotiable Child: The ILO Child Labor Campaigns 1919–1973* (2007) provides a thorough and revealing exploration of the evolution of the ILO's Minimum Age Convention. Her study shows a genealogy running in a direct line from the British Factory Acts (and similar French and German legislation on minimum age for admission to industrial employment). The preparations for Convention 138 were linked by the ILO's Director-General to the broader preoccupations of the ILO, in particular the growing concern about unemployment, economic crisis, the effects of the technological revolution on employment, and the shift in the global division of labor as labor-intensive manufacturing shifted away from the high-income nations to the emerging economies of Latin America and Asia. Meanwhile the gap between rich and poor was increasing and the Director-General's report contained a plea for far-reaching social policies to address these problems. These policies, incorporated in the Minimum Age Recommendation No. 146 (1973) adopted together with Convention 138, include family allowances, social security, insurance, a commitment to full [adult] employment, full-time school and vocational training, and other facilities for the protection and welfare of young people (articles 1–4). As nonbinding recommendations, however, they have been ignored in subsequent discussions and implementation efforts.

Among the thousands of delegates at the ILO conferences leading up to the adoption of Convention 138 there was almost no representation of organizations supporting the interests of children (beyond UNICEF and UNESCO, which each sent one representative); furthermore, no expertise on childhood was consulted in establishing the proposed age boundaries for prohibition of employment. However, in preparation for the drafting of Convention 138, the ILO itself had gathered a large amount of information on the state of education and children's employment worldwide. The results of the ILO's survey were summarized in the "Grey Report" of 1972,[15] which provided "many relevant facts about the situation of working children . . . which might have given rise to new, alternative approaches in the new Convention and recommendations" (Dahlén, 2007, 281). The Grey Report found that child labor "in the classic sense" (which the report defined as mass exploitation of children in large-scale factories and mines during industrialization) was largely "an evil of the past," and more generally that "child labor [was] least apparent in large-scale, reasonably modern industry" (that is, in conditions relatively amenable to conventional labor inspection); it was "more so in small, marginal factories; very common in small-scale and cottage industries, handicraft workshops, industrial home work, small retail shops, hotels, restaurants, services, street trades and domestic service; and more prevalent by far in agriculture" (Grey Report 1, 23).

The ILO, therefore, was aware that "most child labor was performed under conditions that were difficult to control by laws and labor inspection" (Dahlén, 2007, 283). The report also noted that "child labor is a very broad term and that the employment of children does not have the same characteristics everywhere. Such considerations as the formal status of the working child . . . the nature, intensity and regularity of the work, the hours of work and the conditions of employment and the effect of work upon schooling are at least as important as numbers in judging the seriousness of the problem in a given situation and determining how to tackle it" (Grey Report I, 23).

The ILO's own survey of its member states also revealed the very high proportions of children who were not in school, particularly children aged eleven to fourteen years, children in rural areas, and girls. While there was much regional variation, the survey concluded that only about one-third of children in developing regions went to school on a regular basis, which led many delegates to the Convention to point out the huge numbers of children that would be left in a vacuum of "no school and no work" if the standard minimum age were set too high, and enforced. The Grey Report also showed an awareness of the difficulties of enforcement of minimum-age regulation in agriculture, domestic service, and many informal-sector activities in which the majority of working children were employed. Delegates to the conference pointed out the impossibility of enforcing the obligation on employers to keep a register of the names and dates of birth of all children and young persons employed (Dahlén, 2007, 303).

All these findings and concerns, however, were ignored and the ILO's new knowledge base on working children does not appear to have influenced the formulation of Convention 138 in any way. The debate leading up to the adoption of the Convention was almost entirely about whether the standard minimum age should be fourteen or fifteen years (Dahlén, 2007, 317). The ILO has never abandoned or questioned the minimum-age model first adopted in the 1919 Convention, based on the Western industrial experience of the nineteenth and early twentieth centuries; because of this, it can be argued that the ILO's campaign suffered—and continues to suffer—from a "permanent hang-over from history" (Dahlén, 2007, 333). The strategy of eliminating abusive child labor by eliminating "*all* forms of [child] work or employment," besides being largely unenforceable, tends to discourage protective legislation or other efforts to improve conditions of child work. It also makes the work of labor inspectors more difficult, because when most forms of child work are considered illegal, then most child work goes underground.

The "Worst Forms" Convention of 1999

Only a minority of governments ratified ILO Convention 138 during the ensuing twenty-five years, and the ILO itself paid relatively little attention to child labor issues during this period. However, the late 1980s ushered in a period crowded with new developments, new international actors, and new initiatives in relation to child work and education. Among these are the 1989 UNCRC; the 1990 Jomtien Declaration on Education for All (and renewed EFA commitments in

Cairo 1994 and Dakar 2001); the ILO's "Worst Forms" Convention 182 (1999), and the reflection of all of these in the UN Millennium Development Goals of 2001. It is also in this period that international donor funding for child labor interventions became available on a large scale; that the ILO became a major actor in programming interventions alongside its traditional role in standard-setting; that child labor became debated as an international trade issue; and that UNICEF, the World Bank, and many international nongovernmental organizations declared themselves important actors in the struggle against "child labor."

Starting in the late 1980s several organizations and experts, and some ILO members, began to argue for a change of main strategic focus, and in the mid 1990s the ILO for the first time began emphasizing harmful forms of work, adopting in 1999 Convention 182 on the "Worst Forms of Child Labor."

The UNCRC, as we have noted earlier, marked an important milestone in international discourse and consensus on problems that work may cause for children. Besides its important role as the formal basis for all international discourse on children's issues to be cast in a rights perspective, it also marked a turning-point in UN discourse on children's work. As labor expert Bjorne Grimsrud notes, previous conventions up to and including ILO Convention 138 had defined the child labor problem simply in relation to the labor market. In the UNCRC, however, for the first time "child labor was defined not according to the activity [of work] but according to the effect of the activity on the child. This laid the ground for a new understanding of child labor . . . [and] was influential in the adoption by the ILO of Convention 182 in 1999" (Grimsrud, 2002, 9). As we pointed out in chapter 1, the UNCRC established the right of the child to be protected, not from all work or employment, but from exploitation and from work that is likely to harm the child. In defining the "child labor" problem as one of *harmful* work rather than of work itself, the UNCRC follows the line taken by previous League of Nations and UN declarations on the rights of the child, rather than that taken by the ILO conventions, thus marking a shift away from rigid labor-market approaches in international discourse.

The UNCRC has also provided support for a new, emerging discourse that picks up on earlier minority voices of the 1980s. The proponents of this discourse (mainly academics and NGOs) argue that child work and education should be looked at from a child-centered and child rights perspective, and that the voices of working children should be listened to. They tend to argue also for a differentiated approach, distinguishing more and less harmful forms and conditions of work and questioning blanket prohibitions; they are interested in exploring the potentials, and the potential problems, of combinations of school and work.

The ILO itself made an important advance in this direction when, in the mid-1990s, it decided to develop a new Convention on the "Worst Forms" of child labor, which for the first time would promote a differentiated approach to child work and attempt to establish priorities.[16] As Fyfe notes, the ILO's decision was based not only on the poor ratification record of Convention 138 during the past quarter-century,[17] but also on the realization that "a prevailing intellectual climate favored prioritization within the world-wide movement" (Fyfe, 2007, 26).

The new Convention—the most swiftly and widely ratified Convention in the ILO's history—requires its members to "take immediate and effective measures to secure the prohibition and elimination of the worst forms of child labor as a matter of urgency," and defines these "worst forms" in two ways. First are the so-called unconditional worst forms including slavery and similar practices, forced recruitment of children in armed conflict, and the use of children in prostitution, pornography, or illicit activities (see chapter 8). Second are the so-called hazardous forms. Work is considered "hazardous" for children when the work, "by its nature or the circumstances in which it is carried out, is likely to harm the health, safety or morals of children." The ratifying members are required to define this last category of "hazardous forms" themselves and to report them to the ILO. The Convention's accompanying Recommendation 190 (1999) provides guidelines on the "hazardous forms," which we discuss in chapter 8.

Abolitionist and Regulatory Approaches to Distinguishing between More Harmful and Less Harmful Work

The Convention thus follows more or less the definition of harmful child work in the UNCRC. In our view, Convention 182 is a very important step, not so much for the details of its definition of harmful work in the Convention and Recommendation (about which many questions could be raised, and further debate is still needed),[18] but simply for the international recognition it provides for the principle that it is both necessary and possible to distinguish between more and less intolerable and harmful forms and relations of children's work, and therefore to focus intervention on the most serious forms of abuse. Convention 182 furthermore offers the possibility for opening dialogue between diverse global and national actors, particularly between NGOs and the international agencies, in what had previously been a polarized field of debate and intervention (Fyfe 2007: 75).[19] Compared to Convention 138, the "Worst Forms" Convention can more easily accommodate views of children as holders of rights and as agents, as well as a broader view incorporating the macro-political economy of development, which sometimes gets lost in "child-centered" perspectives. This broader view reminds us of the two fundamental historic tasks of policies and interventions in the area of children's work (B. White, 2005, 321): first, the urgent, universally accepted and so far largely unachieved goal of eliminating harmful forms and conditions of children's work (as now firmly established in UNCRC article 32, and ILO Convention 182), and second, promoting the historic shift from work to school as the main (but not necessarily the only) activity of all children. The achievement of this second task is not realized by regulation or prohibition of children's work, but by provision of universal compulsory education and the commitments of governments to the large investments necessary to make quality education available to all.

Although the principle of differentiating between intolerable and benign forms of children's work may now seem self-evident to many readers, it is one that is still opposed by many national and international agencies and, until recently, would have been opposed by the ILO itself. Many organizations remain entrenched in a rather rigid abolitionist stance inspired by ILO Convention 138. This is articulated as a general principle, for example, in the mission statement of the EU-based "Stop Child Labor" campaign:

ALL CHILD LABOR IS UNACCEPTABLE

The Convention on the Rights of the Child along with a host of other international agreements unequivocally affirm the right of all children to live in freedom from exploitation. Approaches to the issue have tended to prioritize and segregate solutions to different types of child labor depending on certain categories.... The Stop Child Labor campaign believes that such distinctions, while helping to cast a spotlight on the worst abuses, tend to be too narrow in their focus and offer only partial solutions. Efforts to eliminate child labor should focus on all its forms, preferably aiming at all children in a certain community.[20]

This imposition of homogeneity on all child work situations is quite different from the position adopted by the Save the Children Foundation, which in our view, provides a more balanced, reasonable, and practical approach on children and work, derived explicitly from a child rights perspective.

Our goal, our understanding of children's work and our beliefs about appropriate responses are shaped by the UN Convention on the Rights of the Child (UNCRC) and a rights-based approach to programming. Implicit in our goal is a belief that children's work is not a uniform activity and we must recognize that, while some forms of work violate children's rights, other forms of work do not. Most forms of work have both good and bad elements, and for this reason, can be both harmful and beneficial to children's development and well-being. Therefore, we accept neither blanket bans of all child work, nor an approach which unequivocally promotes children's work. We believe that different responses are appropriate for different forms of work and for different working children. (Save the Children Alliance, 2007, 1)

The same kind of divide may be seen in the position statements of NGOs operating at regional level and/or in specific sectors. Contrast for example the "non-negotiable" principle of India's MV Foundation that

All labor is hazardous: it harms the overall growth and development of the child. There must be total abolition of child labor.[21]

with the Declaration adopted by the International Conference of Working Children in Karnataka (and in many similar forums of organized working children in subsequent years):

> We are against exploitation at work, but we are in favour of work with dignity and appropriate hours, so that we have time for education and leisure. (International Working Group on Child Labour, 1997)

or with the position taken on "street children" by the successful Canada-based NGO Street Kids International (see chapter 7):

> When we use the term street kids, we use it with pride, respect and recognition for the unique individuals who get on with life every day on the streets despite the barriers and challenges they face . . . Street Kids International believes that street involved youth have the potential for transforming their own lives when given non-judgmental support in developing skills, making choices, and accessing opportunities.[22]

Trade unions, as the civil society bodies that have the mission to protect and promote the interests of labor in society, have largely stuck to ILO Convention 138.[23] The ILO continues to espouse universal ratification and application of Convention 138 as an "overarching goal" (International Labour Office, 2006, 6, 23). Attacking child labor's "worst forms" as defined in Convention 182, and at the same time insisting on a universal minimum-age policy as defined in Convention 138, is in our view an awkward pairing of "abolitionist" and "regulatory" approaches that are not easily compatible (Bourdillon, et al., 2009, 108). There are clear fault lines between approaches that aim to clear all labor markets of children and assume that work itself is the problem, and approaches that allow a differentiation of children's work into more and less harmful forms as a basis for setting priorities in intervention.

In this chapter we have seen that child employment historically has been primarily nonindustrial and outside factories, in all parts of the world including most of Europe. Child labor legislation itself has played a relatively modest role in shaping patterns of children's involvement in work, compared to other state policies (including development models and specific sectoral policies, in particular education) and the larger political and economic forces that shape the life course of young people.

In chapter 1, we saw how opportunities and aspirations of teenage girls in Morocco were damaged by outsiders' assumptions of what is appropriate activity for young people. Given the huge variety of contemporary child work situations and conditions that we have sketched in chapter 2, and the contrasting longer-term trajectories of childhood and child work that we have explored in this chapter, there remains the question how generally applicable are strategies and policies developed in and for a particular time and place. Are current "modern" notions of carefree childhood applicable to all situations, and which if any situations do they accurately reflect? As a next step toward exploring these questions, in the following chapters we focus in turn on current assumptions about the relations between child work and poverty, between child work and child development, and between child work and education.

4

Child Work and Poverty

A Tangled Relationship

In this chapter, we untangle the complex and varied connections between poverty and children's work. Although poverty may affect household work as well as paid and unpaid work in the labor market, this chapter will focus on labor-market work, both paid and unpaid. Since a general assumption is that poverty is the main reason that children work, and the implication is that families are seeking resources beyond those they have, here we are examining the child as labor-force worker.

Many adults in low-income countries are reluctant to condemn children's work, because, as they frequently point out, many children take on productive work out of dire necessity. If they do not work, they cannot eat:

> I had no choice [about sending my son to work], it was not possible for me to run my family on my income. My job is very unreliable. I have to feed all of my children. (Lipi, forty-year-old domestic servant and female household head—Delap, 2001, 9)

> It is a poor family so everybody should work. What point is there in thinking about the future? If you can't eat now, you will not see tomorrow. (Kabir, fifty-year-old scrap metal dealer and father of a fifteen-year-old working child—Delap, 2000, 667)

It seems wrong to forbid or limit child work under such circumstances. Not all child workers, however, are in this situation: some children work when it is not necessary for basic survival. Some children from very poor families have heavy workloads, while children from other very poor families do not. In chapter 2, we pointed out that there are many reasons why children seek employment. In this chapter we will question the belief that poverty is the primary and most important reason why children work in the labor force. Does existing evidence support this belief strongly, partially, or very little?

To the extent that children engage in harmful work because of poverty, policy solutions are not easy or obvious. There is a limit to how much can be done to fix poverty at the local level if it is mainly being caused by global macroeconomic trends. Worldwide markets determine prices for many agricultural products and natural resources, and worldwide production of goods and services demanded by high-income countries means that recessions in Europe and North America have severe ramifications for low-income countries. Inequalities between the poor and the well-off around the world persist both between and within societies (Pieterse, 2002; Chotikapanich, et al., 2007).

Children widely list economic factors as the main reason, or at least one reason, for undertaking productive labor. Often, the motive is to contribute to a stretched family economy. Adolescents in particular are often aware of their families' economic problems and wish to help. In many cases, however, the motive for working is to be recognized as a contributing member of the community, to acquire a degree of independence from parents, or to enjoy modern consumer goods and lifestyles. Youth's perceptions of what they need, in terms of possessions and lifestyles, may be part of the "economic factors" that affect their desire to work. It is not always true that poverty has forced them to work.

What Is Poverty?

The word "poverty" can mean many different things.[1] One important distinction is between absolute and relative concepts of poverty. Relative measures contrast better-off and worse-off members of one community or one geographical area. For example, percentile measures of poverty rank all the households in one country with respect to total income or wealth, from poorest to richest. Average characteristics of the richest 20 percent of households (the "top quintile") are compared to those for the poorest 20 percent of households (the "bottom quintile"). In contrast, absolute measures of poverty aim to determine who is "poor" or "very poor" based on whether they lack adequate income (for example) to obtain a minimal amount of food, water, shelter, and other things that are considered essential for life. A further discussion in this area is about whether these "essentials" should include only material needs or a much broader set of needs.

While these concepts continue to be debated, there are also fundamental problems with putting them into practice, which requires reliable measurement. Even if people report their incomes honestly, they may not remember them accurately. Moreover, there is substantial agreement that income (even if measured accurately) is not a good measure of well-being. One problem is that income is a static measure, but poverty is dynamic—someone who has adequate income today may still be vulnerable to health problems, labor market fluctuations, or any of a number of crises that could lead to poverty. Moreover, income does not capture social disadvantage, humiliation, lack of opportunities, disabilities, and a number of other dimensions of poverty that poor people care about.

In this chapter we refer to studies that use a range of definitions of poverty. We will use the term loosely rather than attempt to adopt any particular definition, while recognizing the conceptual and measurement problems involved.

Defining and Measuring Labor-Force Work

There are also many problems with the definition and measurement of children's participation in the labor force. There is, for example, a lack of agreement about labor-force work rates for children aged ten to fourteen years in higher-income countries (discussed below) that has to do with the many difficulties of measuring labor-force employment. Standard problems arise from things like not remembering how many hours one worked the previous week. In addition, many survey questionnaires use the same questions, often including technical jargon, for children and adults, even when that is developmentally inappropriate for the younger children. Even for adults, the questions may be problematic. Anker, Khan, and Gupta (1988, 142) studied how to capture more accurately Indian women's work in surveys. They found that typical questions used in censuses and surveys around the world were "grossly inadequate," with acceptable responses only for wage or salaried employment. Since the majority of child workers are unpaid, the same questions undercount their work as well.

An additional issue for children is that often adults give proxy reports on the children's behalf; even if the child is present, an adult may be allowed or required to give answers about the child's work, whether or not the adult is particularly well-informed about it. Sometimes, too, questionnaires force respondents to make a choice between labor-force work and school as primary activities, even if children are doing both; this can lead to substantial under-reporting of part-time work.

In-depth small qualitative studies have found children moving in and out of labor-force work much more quickly than is usual for adults. One study looked at this issue on a larger scale (Levison, et al., 2007). The researchers tracked the movements in and out of labor-force work of thousands of ten- to sixteen-year olds in Brazil's biggest cities using data from a monthly labor-force survey, following each child from one month to the next for four months. They concluded that, because children start and stop employment more frequently than adults, the usual way that labor force and household surveys identify adult employment—by asking about work in the past week—is not effective for children. A child may work one week, not work the next week, and have another job the following week. The authors argue that such a child should be counted as someone who usually works even if not working at the time the survey is taken. Further, they claim that by ignoring intermittent employment, the numbers of child workers are substantially undercounted.

Many Poor Children Do Not Work for Pay

Before trying to understand the connection between poverty and children's labor-force work, it is important to consider some statistics mentioned in chapter 2. Edmonds and Pavcnik analyzed household surveys conducted by UNICEF in thirty-six low-income countries (Edmonds and Pavcnik, 2005a, 203, table 1). While there is reason to believe that these surveys missed many child workers for the reasons explained in the previous section, they still found that less than 3 percent of children aged five to fourteen worked for pay outside of their households, and that 25 percent participated in labor market work. This figure rose to 35.2 percent when considering only those aged ten to fourteen years: 4.0 percent in paid work, 7.3 percent in unpaid, non-family labor-force work, and 29.7 percent in work in family businesses or on family farms. Clearly, then, children whose work was reported in the surveys mainly worked for their own families. Edmonds and Pavcnik argue that their findings are typical for sample surveys.

Labor Supply and Labor Demand

When adults speak of the necessity of work for children in poor families, they are considering only one side of the labor market: the supply of labor. The total supply of (child) labor is determined by the total number of hours of work that would be undertaken if all these children could find as much work as they (or their families) want them to have.

However, this does not necessarily determine how much work such children actually do. If employers, including families who "hire" their own children, do not want or need as many work hours as children are ready to supply, then the employers' demand for labor will limit the work of children. It is likely that in many places child labor-force work would be much greater than it is if there were more work available for children. Because the desire to work does not in itself determine children's labor-force work, poverty cannot be the sole driving force behind children's work for money.

In Andra Pradesh in India, the risk of drought in some areas explains why households seek work outside agriculture. It is, however, the traditions of craft work in particular districts that create opportunities for children to work. These enterprises are usually run by families, and the profit margins are low, so they draw on children in the family rather than more expensive hired adult labor to meet commitments (B. S. Reddy, 2000; cited in Kabeer, 2003, 360).

In Karnataka, India, more children are involved in agriculture in areas where rainfall is low: there is more scope for employing children for harvesting crops like cotton, chilies, and groundnuts than for paddy, which is grown in high rainfall areas and requires skilled adult labor (Kanbargi and Kulkarni, 1991, 146).

There is debate about the extent to which the demand for labor has a substantial effect on how many children work and how much they work. Some evidence indicates that children living in areas where economies are thriving are more likely to work than children in areas with fewer economic opportunities.[2] When this effect is due to an up-turn in an economic cycle, it is called a pro-cyclical effect: at times when there is more work for adults, children also work more. Other evidence, however, suggests that children's work is counter-cyclical: when there is *less* work for adults, children work more. Grootaert (1999) documents the effects of a severe economic recession in Côte d'Ivoire on children's labor-force participation: rates rose from 31 to 44 percent for children and adolescents in very poor households, but fell for those in somewhat better-off (although still poor) households. The implication is that effects of labor demand may be different for children with different levels of household resources. This is supported by a study from Brazil, whose authors found that ten- to fifteen-year olds tended on average to work more in better times. However, not all children behaved this way. Rural children and children from poorer households worked more in better times (pro-cyclical labor), but younger children (ages ten to twelve) and children from better-off families worked less (counter-cyclical labor—Manacorda and Rosati, 2007).

Do limits to child work due to a lack of demand apply to self-employment? Children in poor cities often work on their own account in such occupations as selling candy, snacks or newspapers, polishing shoes, watching parked cars, and washing windshields. This kind of self-employment may not be much affected by the demand for candy or clean windshields. Such jobs, sometimes akin to begging, may bring in very little money. If adults set these kinds of tasks, they may be assigned mainly for the work experience, or to provide children a well-defined task to keep them out of trouble when they are not in school. As we saw in chapter 2, children may have a variety of reasons for undertaking such work, including the lure of adventure on the streets as compared to the confines of a small living space at home.

Possibilities for more productive self-employment vary enormously, because they depend so much on the context. In Honduras, rural boys cut trees on steep hillsides belonging to others, then carry heavy bundles of branches and logs, sometimes for kilometers, to sell to people in towns. This kind of self-employment is responsive to people's need for fuel, but it does not pay well because there is too much competition from other boys and men doing the same thing.[3]

On the demand side of the story, as economists tell it, employers also consider wage and piece-rate levels against their expected production in determining how many children they want to hire, or how many hours they want children to work. In practice, employers are also affected by social expectations and customs about hiring children. They may refuse to employ children for fear of losing business. Or they may try to help children by hiring them, even if the employers do not strictly need the children's contributions. For example, in Madagascar, when fourteen-year-old Theo's grandmother could no longer support him, she asked another couple to let him become their domestic servant—and "the couple took pity and agreed, despite having enough troubles of their own," barely getting by with too few customers for their seamstress and carpentry work (Ravololomanga and Schlemmer, 2000, 301).

It is clear from considering the basics of labor supply and demand that the amount of work done by children from poor families cannot be decided only by the poverty of the family, although poverty is certainly one factor that matters. What are the other factors, and how are they related to poverty?

General Patterns

Some patterns with respect to children's work occur so frequently that econo-mists call them "stylized facts." Such patterns are not always true for every fam-ily or child, or even for every country. But they are general patterns that have been documented in many studies.

Some are unrelated to poverty. For example, work generally follows gen-dered patterns, with boys doing more labor-force work and girls doing more domestic work. Another pattern relates to age: older children are more likely to work, and they tend to work longer hours than do younger children. Children rarely work at all before about five years old, and they rarely do labor-force work before they are ten. Other general patterns are closely related to the economic well-being of children and their families.

Comparisons between Countries Show That Young Children Are Much Less Likely to Undertake Full-Time Labor-Force Work in Richer Countries

Perhaps the most widely accepted general pattern is that as a country's percent-age of people in poverty falls, fewer school-aged children participate in full-time labor-force work. Younger children (under age twelve or so) are also less likely to participate in any labor-force work as a country's prosperity increases. The data, however, are not completely consistent on this pattern of an inverse rela-tionship between poverty and labor-market employment. Child labor statistics produced by the ILO usually show very low participation in labor-force work by younger adolescents (ten- to fourteen-year olds) in higher-income countries (see, e.g., Edmonds and Pavcnik, 2005a, figure 1), yet these results are inconsistent with other studies showing the majority of adolescents in high-income countries are engaged in part-time employment by the age of sixteen. For example, in the

Netherlands in 2009 more than 10 percent of ten-year olds, 30 percent of twelve-year olds, and half of fourteen- to sixteen-year olds were breaking the law by working at jobs that were technically prohibited (chapter 3, above. See also B. White, 1994, 860; Huijsmans, 2004, 4).

The pattern can also apply to regions within a country. Studies in India and Bangladesh showed that in their more developed regions, measured by more advanced technology and developed infrastructure, children are likely to work less and more children are likely to go to school (Kabeer, 2003, 359). This pattern is likely to be related to the degree to which the population is engaged in agricultural production, in which there is a greater role for young children.

On the other hand, Andvig's study of twenty African countries for which 1995 figures were available shows that low GDP per capita generally means high percentages of working children, but one of them (Zambia) has the lowest percentage of working children, and other low-income countries (Nigeria and Benin) have a smaller percentage of working children than some of the wealthiest nations (Andvig, 2001, 5–6). While there is considerable doubt about the reliability and comparability of the figures, they alert us to the danger of assuming a simplistic relationship between children's work and poverty.

One problem with this general pattern is that much evidence comes from single points in time, when a survey was conducted or a study performed; the data come from a single cross-section of society. It would be more useful for our purposes to have information about the same people at several different times in their lives. We would like to know whether, when families become less poor, their children are less likely to do labor-force work, or do fewer hours of labor-force work.

In at least one case, this kind of information exists. As the economy of Vietnam improved during the 1990s and living standards rose, there was a dramatic decline in children's work. This is true for all kinds of work, both boys and girls, all age groups (except those in ethnic minorities aged ten and above), for both urban and rural areas, and all regions (except the Central Highlands). The evidence strongly suggests that rising living standards have been important in driving this reduction in labor, and that the children who are still working are doing so largely because their families cannot support their basic needs without an economic contribution from their children (Edmonds and Turk, 2004).

Living standards rose in Vietnam in part because of a rise in the world price for rice, a major export crop from Vietnam. Increases in the price of rice meant that farming families could afford to stop relying on their children as field workers—even though it was increasingly lucrative to do so. Households selling the most rice had the largest declines in children's work. Edmonds and Pavcnik (2005b) found that 45 percent of the 1993–1998 decline in child labor was explained by the higher price for rice.

In South Africa, when democracy was established and privileges for Whites abolished, the state set up a system of substantial pensions for elderly Blacks.

When this happened, there was a significant increase in attendance at school and completion of schooling together with a noticeable decrease in hours of labor-force work and chores by boys and girls (Edmonds, 2006, 412).

Correlations between the economic state of countries and the amount of work that their children undertake do not indicate relations of cause and effect. Successful intervention requires determining what the causal relationships are in specific contexts, as in the Vietnam and South Africa examples. Sometimes policy experiments can help to clarify the relationships, as discussed below.

In Low-Income Countries, Children in Poorer Families Are More Likely to be Working in the Labor Market

The pattern associating children's work with poverty often, but not always, applies at the household level. For example, a study in urban Bangladesh showed that both boys and girls were more likely to be working for pay if they are part of households with low income (Delap, 2001, 8–9).[4] This is a very typical finding; we could list dozens of studies with similar results.

Several factors may make income or goods produced from children's economic work essential. The child may be orphaned or for other reasons have no adult support, a situation we discuss in chapter 7. The adult support may be inadequate to keep the child, either because the adults are incapacitated or because gainful work or adequate wages are not available. Income from children may be especially important if the incomes of poor families are unstable, when, for example, they depend on seasonal work, or during family crises (Kabeer, 2003, 366; Chakraborty and Lieten, 2004, 156; Grootaert and Patrinos, 1999, 6: crises are discussed below). In these situations, unless support is available from elsewhere, income from the child's labor is necessary for survival and must take priority over other needs and wishes, including schoolwork (we shall discuss the relationship between child work and schoolwork in chapter six).

It is not, however, necessarily children from the poorest households that have heavy workloads. As discussed below, better-off families often require more work from children than the very poorest families do. Some theories about how families and societies get richer argue that the unpaid economic labor of women and children allows families to accumulate surplus up to a certain point, after which they begin to hire labor and reduce the inputs of family members. Using all the labor available to a family allows it to produce more than it needs to survive, and this extra can be put into funding a small family business or buying machinery, for example. Economic anthropologists refer to this process as "endo-familial accumulation" (e.g., Cook, 1986, 79; Cook and Binford, 1990).

This is thought to hold in industrialized countries as well as low-income countries. Studies of immigrants in industrialized countries show, for example, that immigrant children work hard to help the family get ahead. Children's work is viewed as a way for poor families to move up in the economic and social hierarchy of their country, not only a means of achieving a minimum level of survival (e.g., Song, 1999, 74–75).

In the short term, it is incontestable that some families need economic help from their children for family stability or even family survival. It is widely alleged that this need for children's labor may also perpetuate a cycle of poverty, hindering schooling and trapping children—and the adults they grow into—into low-productivity work that is often physically arduous, repetitive, and unpleasant. More learning and/or more training is often necessary to allow a person to move into a more productive, better-paying position. In some labor markets, however, those who start work young may get the experience they need later, and may strategically position themselves in the labor market. Whether and to what extent children's work actually perpetuates their poverty seems to be very context-specific.

Adults' Spending on Alcohol Affects Poverty Status and in Turn Children's Work

Another context-specific factor is adult consumption patterns. In some cases, children would not need to work if their parents were not drinking up the food money.[5] The values of parents and the way they spend household income can also affect the work of children. Research shows that different types of adults consider different uses of money to be "essential." Studies on the intra-household allocation of resources show that men (on average) spend substantial portions of income under their control on alcohol and tobacco. Women spend much higher proportions of income under their control on the health and education of their children (Alderman, et al., 1995, describe a number of studies that reach this conclusion).

Families in Crisis Depend More on Children's Labor

Recent studies have shown that children's work frequently increases when their family experiences an unanticipated crisis or "shock." Shocks may be collective or family-specific. Among collective shocks, which affect whole communities, are natural disasters, armed conflict, crop failures due to weather or pests, and high unemployment due to macroeconomic recessions. If the rains do not come after the dry season, and there are no crops to sell or eat, how will the family cope? Family-specific shocks include a variety of events that reduce the family's income unexpectedly. If one of the primary income earners in the family falls ill and is unable to work, how will the family cope? A common response is to depend more heavily on children's work.

There are a number of good studies on how unexpected crises affect poor families, and these show the extent to which poverty can cause children to work, or to work more. Studies of this sort do not need to track the same households for many years. Instead, researchers can learn from information from two time periods, as long as some families experience an unexpected crisis in-between the dates when data were collected.

A study of how floods affected poor families in Bangladesh showed that in some cases income from children provided an important coping strategy for the household, especially when the work of adults was prevented by the floods. For example, the father of fourteen-year-old Liton could not work at his tea stall, which had been submerged by flood waters, and his mother earned little in domestic service. So Liton's work in collecting rubbish for recycling during the floods was important to the family. Children appreciated the fact that they were able to provide help in this time of family crisis (Delap, 2000, 668, 671).

As usual, there are limitations to such studies. Orphanhood or abandonment of children is a phenomenon that especially affects populations in areas with a high level of HIV/AIDS. It is especially hard to enumerate children living without adult assistance, because surveys are best at documenting the lives of people who live in fixed locations. Also relatively hard to document are effects of the loss of an important income-earning family member—often the child's father—and thus the loss of those earnings.

These losses happen because of death, illness, divorce, or abandonment. In the urban Bangladesh study mentioned above, boys and girls were especially likely to be working for money in female-headed households where marital breakdown had recently taken place (Delap, 2001, 9). Illnesses and deaths of family members can also lead to illness-related expenses and funeral expenses. Income losses because of the unexpected unemployment of an important earner can cause crises. For example, in Brazil, a sixteen-year-old girl with uneducated parents was 50 percent more likely to become employed if her father lost his job (Duryea, et al., 2007).

Shocks affecting entire communities include natural disasters (mudslides, earthquakes, floods, hurricanes, typhoons, tsunamis, plague); the unexpected loss of crops and/or livestock due to drought or disease; loss of income due to a drop in the world price of an internationally traded crop or mineral, such as coffee, sugar, or cocoa; and loss or abandonment of a farm/dwelling due to war or civil unrest. Since most poor people do not have access to relatively safe ways of saving, such as insured bank accounts, their savings for potential crises are particularly vulnerable to crime and, in some cases, to the crisis itself. Sometimes having savings would not have helped, if, for example, the savings had taken the form of jewelry that got buried in a mudslide, or materials for future home-building that were swept away in a flood, or livestock which starved. Given these limitations, it may not make sense for the very poor to try to prepare for unknown catastrophes, when just maintaining calories is a daily struggle. Instead, in a crisis they make the most of their primary resource: the labor potential of family members.

A number of studies provide details on some of the kinds of crises, or shocks, that have been found to increase children's work—either number of hours worked, or the likelihood that a child works in the labor force at all.[6] While a number of these studies have found that recessionary environments increased the likelihood that children work in the labor force, or work longer hours, in at least one case there is evidence to the contrary. Shady (2002), for example, found that macroeconomic crisis in Peru *reduced* children's participation in market work, presumably because of reduced demand for workers of all ages. Because the types and intensities of shocks vary so much, a few researchers have attempted to distinguish among them in terms of their effects on children. Guarcello, Kovrova, and Rossi (2007) point out that shocks may have varying or no effects on children's labor-force work. They found that in Cambodia, children were much more likely to work after a crop failure, while floods had no effect.

Long-lasting crises may change social norms about children's work. In Madagascar, a twenty-year-long economic crisis has meant that many children work or beg to support themselves and other family members. Ravololomanga and Schlemmer (2000, 311) argue that economic needs have transformed the way that city dwellers, at least, think about children: "the idea of making children pay for the right to sleep at home already exists in the milieux worst hit by the recession, which is proof enough that no ideological barrier can remain standing forever when faced with the ordeal of a reality with which it has become far too incompatible."

Boys Do More Labor-Force Work, and Girls Do More Non-Labor-Force Work

A pattern found in most, but not all, communities in low-income countries is related to gender roles. Boys are often found in labor-force work in substantially higher percentages than girls, whose work is more likely to fall in the realm of "reproductive work," such as cleaning, cooking, collecting fuel and water, and caring for others in a variety of ways. Exceptions to this pattern may occur when girls are employed as domestic servants, but there are few opportunities for boys in this field.

Children in Rural Areas Work More Than Children in Urban Areas

One of the most common patterns, worldwide, is that rural children are much more likely than are urban children to be engaged in the labor force (Andvig, 2001). This is not surprising, since being "rural" is also related to a number of other factors that themselves are likely to affect children's propensity to engage in economic work. Their parents are more likely to own or work on farms, with crops and livestock needing tending. Children learn farm skills by working on farms. Bachman (2000: 35) argues that the structure of production in a country is the best predictor of the proportion of children who work in the labor force; in particular, "child work is more likely to occur in economies with a greater share of agriculture" in their gross domestic product (Bachman, 2000, 30–41).

People in rural areas also have less access to infrastructure. In many parts of the world, rural villages do not have piped water or a connection to an electricity grid. Fuel and water have to be fetched, usually by children, and often at some distance from home. While the same applies to many poor urban areas, water sources in those cases are often closer. In urban areas, fuel is often purchased rather than scavenged. Illegal and unsafe supplies of electricity are tapped by urban poor. Access to infrastructure has implications for children's economic work, as described below.

Better Infrastructure Reduces Children's Work

Not debated, but often overlooked, is the general pattern that better infrastructure reduces child work. Aspects of infrastructure that seem particularly to affect children's work, as we pointed out in chapter 2, include whether or not piped water is available in the home or in the neighborhood; whether or not there is piped sewage disposal; whether or not the household's solid waste (trash) is collected; and, sometimes, the availability and reliability of electrical power.[7] Other kinds of infrastructure include hospitals, clinics and health services, and paved roads and highways.

If There Are More Possible Tasks for Children, Children Are More Likely to Work

The preceding patterns suggest that children from poorer families in poorer countries will work more than other children do. Some factors, however, work in an opposite direction.

Poor families have few resources with which to work. If a household is landless, has no animals to care for, no tools with which children can work, and a very basic dwelling, there is limited work for children to do within the family. Children can help support the family by earning in the labor market, but this may not be possible if there are no jobs available or if available jobs interfere with schooling. If, however, a household has a garden to tend, poultry to care for, sheep to herd, or a family business, there may be obvious roles for children to play. More household productive assets often imply more work for children.

While younger children from wealthy families in any society rarely have to undertake productive work, as they get older they may be requested to participate in family businesses. Yoram Ben-Porath discussed a complex, interconnected set of reasons why it makes sense to rely more on family members when running a business (Ben-Porath, 1980).

A study of Ghana and Pakistan showed that children in households with larger landholdings tended to have more productive work to do than do children of presumably poorer households with less land (Bhalotra and Heady, 2003). When landholdings decrease in size because of population pressure, it appears that children have less work to do (Andvig, 1998, 345). In Karnataka in India, when families owned more cattle, more children were in productive work rather than school (Kanbargi and Kulkarni, 1991, 146). In Botswana, on farms where adult males were involved in commercial crop cultivation, boys had more work to do in cattle husbandry (Mueller, 1984, 359). Similarly, there is a variety of evidence that children in families with business enterprises are more likely to be involved in economic work (see, e.g., Edmonds and Turk, 2004).

Further Investigation May Find More Patterns

Other patterns are not so widely documented but have appeared in a number of studies. For example, a study in Brazil showed that adolescents belonging to families whose incomes exceed the minimum wage were more likely to be in productive work than those in poorer families: the education of the better-off children helped them to find jobs (Alvim, 2000, 167). Similarly in Britain, middle-class children were more likely to have connections that provided part-time employment than were poorer children (Lavalette, 2000, 220).

Children's Earnings: How Much, and Who Gets Them?

When children earn money (a minority of working children), how much do they receive for their effort? Economists believe that earnings, when determined by the market rather than labor regulations, reflect not only one's time spent working but also one's productivity. For example, if a child produces a paper flower in 6 minutes, but his mother can produce a similar flower in 3 minutes, then the child is half as productive as his mother. If the two of them are paid the same amount for producing the flower, they have earned the same piece rate. Piece rates are often paid when production is clearly defined by number of units produced or by the provision of a particular service, like a haircut.

Payments to Children versus Adults

An ILO study run by Peter Dorman (International Labour Office, 2007) focused on the demand for children's labor and their productivity in eight sectors of employment in four countries: Ghana (small restaurants and coastal fishing), Philippines (fireworks and jewelry making), India (vehicle repair and zardosi textile production), and Uganda (fishing and construction). Among these eight sectors, the researchers documented a variety of payment practices for children relative to adults. In two sectors, children and adults received the same piece rates. This was especially evident in what Dorman calls "distressed labor markets": when labor-market conditions are bad for everyone, as in the Ugandan construction industry, then all workers are paid very little. In Ghana's fishing industry, men and boys also seemed to be on relatively equal footing: like adults, boys "are selected for their ability to do the work and paid accordingly" (7).

In the other six sectors, the evidence showed that children's piece rates and wages were lower than those of adults. It was possible to compare adult and child productivity in some cases. They found "strong profitability motives" for hiring children in Ghana's small restaurant business, in the Philippines' pyrotechnics industry, and in India in the vehicle repair sector (in Delhi) and in zardosi production. In other words, if children were less productive than adults, this difference was not great enough to explain the divergence between child and adult piece rates or wages. Other researchers found a similar result for India's hand-knotted carpet industry, where "even children who are fully trained may receive lower piece rates" (Levison, et al., 1998, 100).

Contributions to Family Income

Being a good child in a particular cultural context may involve contributing to one's own and family expenses (Whitehead, et al., 2007, 20). Moreover, the work of children often provides income that is significant for their families and buffers them from the worst effects of poverty (Aitken, et al., 2006). In Brazil in 1995, only 29 percent of workers aged five to fourteen received monetary payment, but children from very poor families were much more likely to have paying jobs compared to other child workers. In 32 percent of urban households, children earned over 20 percent of total household income; this was also the case in 41 percent of rural households. In almost 10 percent of households, children contributed over 40 percent of household income (Kassouf, 1999). Similar patterns have been found in more recent years (Ilahi, et al., 2005). A series of studies of children working in prohibited, hazardous industries in India found that each working child contributed on average 20 to 25 percent of family income (Anker and Melkas, 1995, 9).

In some situations, children's income may not be essential for survival but may still be important for improved livelihood and to pay for such things as clothing and schooling, or perhaps capital items such as livestock or a sewing machine (Bissell, 2004, 277–281; Whitehead, et al., 2007, 35). Carla Madsian describes child street vendors, mainly selling peanuts in a middle-sized Brazilian town. She notes that "luxury goods and household durables are within the expectations of all the people, even if not within reach of most of the people" (2004, 132), leading even households in poor neighborhoods to save and borrow in order to buy the symbols of middle-class success, gain respect, and overcome the stigma of poverty. Many of the children in her study worked at the request of their parents, and their earnings helped pay not only for food but also for "those gadgets that are common to mainstream social life" (133). Even among young school pupils in high-income countries, earnings from part-time employment might be used to relieve stress of family budgets, buy groceries, and relieve the need to ask parents for expensive items (Mizen, et al., 2001, 45–52; Ingenhorst, 2001, 142; Hungerland, et al., 2007, 271–272).

When children contribute significantly to the incomes of impoverished households, banning them from work may deepen their own poverty as well as that of their families. Working children in poor communities are commonly better nourished than their nonworking peers of similar background: a study in India showed working boys up to the age of seven and girls up to the age of ten to have better weight for height ratios than their school-going counterparts (Cigno and Rosati, 2005, 86). Income from work can also provide access to health facilities (Liebel, 2001b, 59). Although some studies suggest that productive children may receive a disproportionate amount of food to the detriment of nonworking siblings (O'Donnell, et al., 2004, 25), it is common for older working children to play an important role in the support of younger siblings who do not work. A study in a semi-arid agricultural region of India showed that higher child wages related to more time spent at school by nonworking children in the household (Skoufias, 1994, 348).

Who receives the money that children earn? Do their families have prior claims on all of it, or do child workers keep part or all of it? If so, what do they do with it—is it used for food and other essentials, or is it essentially "pocket money?" Relatively little information exists with which to answer these questions, and the answers we do have vary depending on the context. While some children work to provide basic provisions, the earnings of others allow the workers and/or their siblings to attend school by paying for fees, uniforms, supplies, transportation, and other expenses. Some children have relatively little control over income, although they may use portions of their own earnings on snacks. Others use substantial portions of their earnings on luxury items (as we pointed out in chapter 2).

As we pointed out in chapter 2, the domestic work of children, and especially of girls, often frees adults in the household for productive work. Thus, many children contribute indirectly to family income.

Are Children Working Instead of Adults, or Undermining Adult Wages?

One motive for promoting the abolition of "child labor" has been a worry that children's participation in the labor force undermines adult employment and wages (Myrstad, 1999, 75; Hanson and Vandaele, 2003, 126). Trade unions have historically been against the use of child labor because of this concern (among others).

The argument is applied at both global and local levels. Some fear that child workers in developing countries steal adult jobs in developed countries by driving down product prices to the point that rich countries can no longer compete. It is also claimed that removing children from the workplace will allow unemployed adults to work and will result in higher adult wages at the local level, thus making the work of children less necessary as a family survival mechanism. If child workers take jobs away from adults, or undermine adult wages, then a local economy that depends heavily on child labor could be one that keeps entire families poor, by lowering the earning capability of adults.[8]

There is little evidence that this is generally the case, although such substitution can take place at the level of particular firms or industries. For one thing, jobs that children do are often jobs that adults do not want—as discussed in chapter 2. For another, children's work often makes adult incomes possible in enterprises depending on family labor for economic viability (such as small farms and services). A study in Mexico suggested that removing children from the labor market increased adult wages, but not enough to make up for the lost earnings of children (Edmonds, 2008, 3694, citing an unpublished work by K. Doran). On the other hand, a study of data from Egypt found the work of children to compete modestly with the work of women and to complement the employment of men. For the society as a whole, the work of children did not appear to affect adult employment (Diamond and Fayed, 1998). A study using data from Venezuela and Mexico also argues that children's work usually complements rather than competes with adult work (Freije and Lopez-Calva, 2000). Other studies address the substitutability of labor-force roles within the household. For example, Ray (2000a) finds evidence suggesting that when a Peruvian parent's wage increases, his or her children will be less likely to work, but in Pakistan, an increase in a woman's wage makes her daughters more likely do labor-force work. Such findings do not allow us to draw conclusions about the aggregate effect of changes in child work on adult employment or wages.

Is Child Labor Necessary for Enterprise Survival?

In some cases, the use of child labor is common in particular economic niches, and their employers argue that, rather than taking jobs from adults, children allow the business to be competitive enough to survive in the global economy. In chapter 2, we pointed to a claim sometimes made that children are better able to perform certain tasks on account of their small hands (the "nimble fingers" argument), and that such claims were not justified in a study of India's hand-knotted carpet industry. The same study explored the possible costs of replacing child workers with adults and found that the cost increases would have different impacts, depending on who bore them—the small enterprises, the Indian exporters, importers in the USA, or the final purchasers. The cost increases could be devastating to the small businesses, but foreign retailers and consumers would face extremely small price increases (3 percent and 1–2 percent, respectively). On the other hand, even that small increase might have made Indian carpets lose market share to Chinese carpets. In this particular case, low-paid child workers seemed to be necessary for enterprise survival because such a small share of the profits from the final product went to the family businesses. A redistribution of profits from importers and exporters to the small enterprises would have been necessary to simultaneously replace child workers with adult workers and maintain market share. The small businesses exist in a context where they have no control over global economic forces—in this case competition to sell hand-knotted carpets to high-income countries.

Conditional Cash Transfers as Compensation for School Enrollment

One of the ways of removing or minimizing conflicts between children's work and their education is by addressing family poverty directly. Since there seem to be many poor families who depend for their day-to-day survival on their children's work, replacing their earnings might allow children to participate in the formal education system. Conditional cash transfer (CCT) programs provide poor mothers with a small payment for each child who attends school regularly. A number of CCT programs have been conducted as experiments. For example, in Mexico, residents in some rural villages had the opportunity to participate in the PROGRESA[9] program, while similar rural villages elsewhere did not: 320 poor localities were randomly chosen to be participation sites, while 186 comparable localities were assigned to be in the control group. Data about people in both sets of villages was collected before the program began in 1997, and again at regular intervals after that. Women in participating households—and only households in extreme poverty were eligible to participate—received cash transfers when their children attended school regularly, among other things. An evaluation one year after the program began showed that PROGRESA had a substantial positive impact on school enrollment of eight- to seventeen-year olds. There was also a decrease in the likelihood that girls aged fourteen to fifteen and boys aged twelve to thirteen undertook market work; however, the absolute differences between pre-program levels and post-program levels were small (Skoufias and Parker, 2009, 176–177). Because the data comes from a careful experimental study, its results are convincing, and the program has greatly expanded and been emulated widely.

A review of CCT programs for which evidence exists concluded that all the reviewed programs were effective at reducing poverty and increasing school enrollments. PROGRESA, for example, reduced poverty in participating communities by about 17 percent, compared to nonparticipating communities; it raised the income of rural poor households by 10 to 15 percent, which, as the authors note, is a large effect for one program (Morley and Coady, 2003, 97). In general, children who benefit from CCT programs rarely stop working altogether, but they work less, and they attend school much more, and make more progress from grade to grade. Still, if poverty were the main reason why children work, we would have expected to see more substantial declines in child work from these poverty-reducing programs. It remains questionable whether they are sustainable in poorer countries (Bissell, 2004, 285).[10]

Is Child Work a Cultural Phenomenon Rather Than an Economic Necessity?

We have shown that children's work is statistically related to poverty, and is particularly likely in response to crisis, but that not all poor children work. With respect to India, Myron Weiner argued that "child labor" is primarily due to a "culture" in which status differences are established in a caste system, and according to which it is considered appropriate for children in lower castes or classes to work while other children go to school. Upper classes fear that "excessive education" of lower classes might disrupt the social order. Such attitudes are dominant in upper and middle classes, extend to teachers and other educationalists, and are sometimes accepted by the poor themselves (Weiner, 1991; see also Burra, 2003, 75; and the discussion in Kabeer, 2003, 355–373). Such attitudes affect the way children of the poor are treated at school (see chapter 6). A further problem is the attitude in some poor communities where parents believe "children were born to serve and support them and saw nothing wrong in their not being in school or not being able to play" (Burra, 1995, 170). Against these arguments, Sumi Krishna points out that ranking states with highest incidence of "child labor" bears no correlation with their ranking in terms of school attendance (Krishna, 1996, 98–99), so it is not simply a question of cultural assumptions that some children should work rather than attend school. Moreover, much evidence shows that "an overwhelming majority of Indian parents today, even among deprived sections of the population, attach great importance to the education of their children" (Dréze and Sen, 2002, 154).

Nevertheless, a program in Calcutta, India, illustrates the importance of attending to knowledge and values, while at the same time attending to accessible effective schooling. Initially parents did not consider school important and sent their children to work in order to keep them out of trouble on the streets. The program did two things: first, it sensitized parents to how education could help their children and how school was possible for their children; and second, it provided initial informal education and subsequent support for children entering formal schools. The result was that children reduced their hours of productive work, and sometimes stopped entirely. Once families became aware that school was a possibility for their children, adults were prepared to live on less income and to take on more housework to allow their children to attend school (CINI-ASHA, 2003).

Social sciences have brought attention to problems of treating "culture" as an autonomous influence, pointing out that patterns of thinking and behavior are intimately related to material factors. Culture cannot therefore be considered independently as an explanation for harmful work. Other studies have argued that the dominant factor when children work instead of attending school is lack of resources (e.g., Bissell, 2004; Lieten, 2000, 2177). Nevertheless, social expectations and values do influence decisions on children's schooling and work, and intervention should take this into consideration. The dominance of girls in reproductive work and of boys in labor-market work reflect cultural values. In the next chapter we will discuss how different ideas about childhood are reflected in different work patterns of children.

The Effects of Child Work on Poverty Dynamics:
How Learning Matters

Part of the difficulty in determining whether poverty causes child work is due to the fact that child work can also affect well-being of children and their family members, in the present but also in the future. That is, there can also be a causal effect from child work to poverty. In the present, for example, the earnings or in-kind payments for child work may improve her own and her family's nutritional levels. In the future, however, the effects may be more substantial. These longer-term effects may be positive or negative, or combine elements of both. It is generally assumed that longer-term effects are predominantly negative, to the extent that work reduces children's educational attainment and thus keeps them from acquiring skills that would allow them to get better jobs in the future.[11]

Economists have long been exploring the relationships between certain aspects of human development, with special attention to children and youth, and national social and economic development, in what is known as the human capital literature. The driving idea is that healthier and more skilled populations contribute more to society and the economy. For this purpose, child development is defined very narrowly in terms of measurable education and health variables that can be analyzed to gauge their contributions to national economic development. Such analyses have generally found that investments in children's education, especially universal primary education, provide extraordinary economic and social returns that are difficult to match from any other kind of investment (e.g., Psacharopoulos, 1997). Investments in children's healthy physical development through immunization, nutrition, disease prevention, and similar programs also turn out to be highly productive in national economic terms. The United Nations tracks certain national statistics pertinent to this human capital perspective, and reports them annually through two publications: the UNDP's *Human Development Report* and UNICEF's *The State of the World's Children*.

There is reason to believe that estimates using human capital approaches may substantially overstate the effects of education on future earnings. Most estimates fail to take account of school quality, but children are likely to stay in school longer if they are learning something. Glewwe (1996) argues that it is more useful to estimate rates of return to investments in school quality. Neither do most estimates control for individual ability, although children with greater academic abilities are likely to stay in school longer. A further problem has to do with the assumption that very high rates of return to an additional year of schooling will continue, even if entire cohorts of children enter school instead of the most advantaged children. Once everyone has completed primary school, having a primary certificate will not confer particular advantage on anyone, and the measured return to primary education is likely to fall substantially.

From a rigorously economic perspective on child development, the primary concern about children's work has been that it may detract from their schooling, and the corresponding high national social and economic returns such schooling provides, or result in poor health and nutrition that drive up national medical expenses and reduce worker productivity in adulthood. Emerson points out that most economists assume that such negative relationships exists. Yet, as he points out, "Though almost every theoretical study of child labor posits a fairly rigid relationship between child work and diminished human capital, there is very little empirical evidence to support or refute this assumption" (Emerson, 2009, 8). A few studies using Colombian and Brazilian data suggest that early school-leaving and/or starting work at a young age have long-term negative effects on earnings due to reduced education; while positive effects of experience exist as well, these are overwhelmed by the education effect (Knaul, 1998; Emerson and Souza, 2007; Ilahi, et al., 2005). Even when carefully conducted, such studies have methodological limitations that reduce their credibility. Most importantly, the causality may not be in the assumed direction. In Egypt, for example, Richard Carothers has observed that poor school quality and children's poor performance in school (both correlated with poverty) leads to children dropping out. Sometimes these children then take on unpaid or low-paid work that provides opportunities for skill acquisition (e.g., apprenticeships, discussed in chapter 6)—and, in the long run, a way out of poverty.[12] This suggests that adults in retrospective studies may have been worse off had they not started work at a young age. A study that considered the effects of early commencement of child work for adults working in different sectors suggests that this is sometimes the case: in Brazil, early work in the manufacturing and service sectors had long-term positive effects, while early work in agriculture had long-term negative effects on adult earnings (Emerson and Souza, 2007). A study in Vietnam indicated that work experience resulted in increased incomes, which more than compensated for lower school attainment in the medium term (five to ten years) (Beegle, et al., 2005, 31–32); the Bangladesh case study in chapter 9 suggests why this may be so in a particular context. In the U.S.A., part-time employment in adolescence has been correlated with subsequent employment up to ten years after graduating from high school and appears to reduce the amount of time youths spend unemployed

(D.M. Hansen, et al., 2001, 131). The precise effects of work on future earnings appear to depend on the situation of the children and on the context.

There is evidence that children look for work that has long-term prospects, defined broadly. Contacts made in early employment may help a person to find appropriate work when older, or, in the case of a girl, lead to an advantageous marriage (Camacho, 1999, 70; UNICEF, 1998a, 14). In Bangladesh, children considered work good if it opened up prospects for future employment, a factor more important to them than possible hazards or working at night (which worry adults—Save the Children U.K., 2005; also Groves, 2003a, 3). Increased later income may be partly due to learning to use time in a disciplined way, and learning how to deal with employers and people one meets in the work situation (see also Pole, 2007, 158). These "soft skills" are hard to measure or quantify.

Many economically essential skills are conveyed from one generation to another through work rather than through formal education. Farming is a good example. All but an infinitesimally small percentage of farmers learn to produce food and fiber through experience of working in family or other agricultural enterprises, usually beginning in childhood. To the extent that work in farming is shown to result in skill-building that will contribute to the economy, should it not be credited with this contribution, perhaps similarly to schooling? It is well known that, in many countries, most mechanics, small builders, and other tradespeople learn their craft by working in it, starting as children. This function of cognitive and skills development has immense economic importance yet, again, it has not been subject to substantial analysis, and thus is too frequently overlooked. Economic logic suggests that national economic accounting should, at least in theory, credit the contributions to child development of this kind of learning in a manner similar to schooling.

Does Poverty Cause Child Work?

There is no one answer to the question, "Does poverty cause child work?" However, because children usually cannot work in the labor market unless some adult (often a family member) is willing to employ them as paid or unpaid labor, poverty can never be the entire explanation for children's labor-force work. It is true that some children are self-employed—for example, as garbage recyclers—but these are relatively few of the millions of children who work. The large percentage of children doing labor-force work who are unpaid also suggests that the common supposition that children mainly work in order to earn money is not supported by evidence. Children who are unpaid may well be productive, and their products may eventually be sold, but these children's work is not necessarily causing daily or weekly family income to rise.

Many of the general patterns imply that poverty and child labor-force work are highly correlated, but most of them cannot go further than that without more evidence. What causes what? In some cases—as documented for Vietnam—it is clear that poverty-reducing economic growth led to less child work (Edmonds, 2005). In other cases, child work seems to lead to skill acquisition that, eventually, reduces poverty. The studies about the effects of shocks show that families under economic stress increase their use of child work—that is, as poverty increases, so does child work. On the other hand, the conditional transfer experiments show a decline in poverty with little accompanying decline in child work.

When Barros and coauthors asked, "Is Poverty the Main Cause of Child Work in Urban Brazil?" in the 1990s, they cited 36 studies that reached the conclusion that poverty was the main cause, and yet they concluded that there was no hard evidence supporting that hypothesis. They considered the hypothesis on three different levels: (1) compared to other Latin American countries; (2) by region and across time—they expected to find higher child work in areas and time periods with higher poverty, but did not; and (3) between rich and poor households living in the same city, where they found an effect of income that was much too small for poverty to be the main explanation for child work (Barros, et al., 1994). It seems that distinguished and careful researchers may reach quite different conclusions, depending on the evidence they consider and the methodologies they employ, even within the same context. Across different contexts, an even wider range of answers can be expected. This suggests that designers of programs to reduce child work—or improve children's conditions of work—should keep an open mind about the underlying reasons for children's work. The same programs are unlikely to succeed with, on the one hand, youth working to obtain fundamental necessities of life and, on the other hand, youth determined to buy a cell phone or an iPod.

5

Work in Children's Development

The questions we raise in this chapter regard whether the legitimate concern about harm deserves to be the only major policy interest when considering working children. If the objective of policy is to promote children's development, should not the contributions that work makes to development merit as much interest as the risks that undermine it? We argue that children are not well-served by one-sided policies and interventions that consider only threats that work may pose to child development and ignore its perhaps equally important benefits. Why should it be assumed that work risks are more important and deserving of attention than work benefits? Might there be good reason to consider positive effects of work in child development as seriously as negative ones? That needs to be explored, for a balanced approach that considers the impact of work on child development from multiple perspectives promises a more logical and better-informed foundation for policy than does a focus on one aspect alone.

The last chapter explored relationships between child work and poverty, recognizing that most economically active children work at least partially out of necessity. In chapter 2, we showed that economic rewards are not the only benefits of working. Field studies widely report that children value work as an important developmental activity, viewing it as a means through which they acquire responsibility and useful skills, establish a positive community reputation, and form relationships essential to their integration into society. One finds this positive attitude toward child work to be widespread among children, their parents, and others in both industrialized and low-income countries. It is so ubiquitous that perhaps most of the world's parents believe that childhood work is natural and conducive to growing up, and many children are on record with the same opinion. The ILO recognizes that some work is developmentally valuable to children. "Not all work is harmful to children. . . . Light work, carefully monitored, can be an essential part of children's socialization and development process, where they learn to take responsibility, and gain pride in their own accomplishments. Work of this kind is not without risk, but it is not what is generally meant by child labour" (IPEC, 2002, 3).

However, popular culture does not create law, and child work is a topic in which culture and law are out of step with each other where it most counts—in national and international policies governing child work. While current policies reflect a legitimate public concern that some kinds of work and working conditions may put children's physical and mental development at risk, they neglect to take into account equally important developmental advantages that work may be seen to provide. This imbalance implies that risk should be the unique consideration in assessing child work, and it encourages the spurious presumption that the very act of working places children's development at risk. This subtext is apparent in two of the most important international convention clauses:

Each member for which this Convention is in force undertakes to pursue a national policy designed to ensure the effective abolition of child labor and to raise progressively the minimum age for admission to employment or work to *a level consistent with the fullest physical and mental development of young persons.*

ILO Convention (No. 138) Concerning Minimum Age for the
Admission to Employment, 1973, Article 1. (Emphasis added)

States Parties recognize the right of the child to be protected from economic exploitation and from performing any work that is likely to be hazardous or to interfere with the child's education, *or to be harmful to the child's health or physical, mental, spiritual, moral or social development.*

UNCRC, Article 32 (1) (Emphasis added)

As these provisions from ILO Convention 138 and the UNCRC suggest, policymakers, program staff, and advocates seeking the well-being of working children must squarely face the issue of how work figures in child development if they are to be responsive to international standards governing child work. Beyond mere compliance with the law, however, any responsible intervention to protect or assist working children must take into account the fact that a child is physically and mentally in the process of growing up, with all the special conditions and dynamics this process entails. This involves viewing children more broadly than just through their work status and relationships: it requires examining the role of work in child development in wider perspective. But assessing the role of work in a child's growing capacity is not easy, in part because national and international laws governing the work of children have framed the issue too narrowly, in part because "work" as experienced by children does not lend itself to universal generalization, and in part because there are contradictions between policy assumptions and empirical observations. This chapter will present a brief overview of these problems, suggesting conceptual approaches helpful for circumventing or resolving them.

Framing the Issue

How an issue is framed shapes the content of policies to address it. Official response to the work of children has been determined by the fact that national and international law frame child work primarily as a threat to children's immediate welfare or long-term development; that is, as a social problem that merits legal intervention. Policies to discourage child work flow naturally from that perspective. Accordingly, the two convention clauses cited above seek to protect children from developmental risk assumed to be posed by working. The first, from the ILO Minimum Age Convention (No.138), is concerned about age, assuming that the younger the child is, the greater are the threats from working. It calls for progressively raising the minimum age of legal admission to work. The second clause, from the UNCRC, is concerned about many kinds of harm that might occur. It wants "development" to be interpreted comprehensively to encompass the whole child, and it lists some aspects to be considered.

Together, these two clauses portray work exclusively as a present or potential threat to children's development. Certainly a concern about risks is justifiable, because many children do in fact work in hazardous, exploitative, or otherwise harmful circumstances that many have long observed to undermine their development in various ways. Child trafficking and slavery, for instance, are real and present, and demand concerted action. We urge prompt and serious attention to such abuse of children.

However, a broader view of child work that encompasses developmental benefits as well as risks rests on information and ideas uncommon in conventional "child labor" discourse. In order to present the less familiar conceptual foundations that must underlie a more balanced policy framework, this chapter is devoted primarily to consideration of the constructive role of work in child development. The more harmful aspects will be taken up in chapter 8.

What Is Child "Development"?

Since international policies on child work seek to safeguard children's development within a legal framework, one might reasonably expect an accompanying international definition of child "development" and criteria—according to which the impact of work on development can be evaluated—to determine whether or not the legal mandate is being met. Manuals for guiding the implementation of human rights and other international standards are common and are expected to address definitional and interpretive issues key to their application. However, UNICEF's official manual for applying the UNCRC does not define or indicate how to define or assess child development, even though protecting child development is the stated objective of Article 32 on child work, and promoting it is a main goal of Article 29 on the aims of education (UNICEF, 1998b, 427–444, 391–406). Nor does the ILO provide guidance in its implementing suggestions for Convention 138.

If the international institutions do not provide guiding criteria according to which interested persons can assess progress toward the development, protection, and promotion they mandate, what other source might provide an acceptable standard for international use? We have not found sufficient consensus to create a workable international definition with respect to which characteristics and actions of children should be considered signs of "development" and which not. The challenge is not trivial. With UNCRC article 32 in mind, how would one come up with universal criteria for measuring a child's moral or spiritual development, for instance, and determining whether work has impinged on it? In the absence of standardized criteria, judgments about the ways and degree in which children are thought to be developing probably must be situational, culturally relative, and to some extent subjective. This means that it is not possible to measure progress internationally, and it raises questions about mandating international objectives against which there can be no measurement.

Having no ready-made definitions of "development" at hand, policymakers and others seeking to abide by the above ILO and UNCRC standards have no choice but to wrestle with the issue on their own. In this chapter, we discuss some of the currently prominent approaches to conceptualizing "development," and their implications for thinking about the role and effects of work in child development.

Ideological Influences

Ideology—a system of normatively charged, related ideas expressing the views, values, and aspirations of a particular group—is a major source of thinking about childhood and children that drives much current policy regarding children's work. Several such ideological frameworks, sometimes referred to in the literature as "discourses," are especially significant (Ennew, et al., 2005; Myers, 2001), of which we will highlight two. If there is a leading candidate for an official international ideology around child work, it would be the historically crucial Romantic view of childhood introduced in chapter 1 and which chapter 3 presents as the line of thought leading to ILO Convention 138. As powerful as this view has been historically, it has never been entirely consistent with empirical evidence, even in the time and place of its origin. Today it is rarely encountered in serious studies. Analytical approaches to children's work tend to be more nuanced and to draw distinctions between benign work and harmful work, sometimes labeling the latter "child labor" and reserving that term for work injurious to children's well-being and development (Lieten, 2009). However, international standards and national policies lag behind new insights from research and experience. Although most specialists have long since moved away from the Romantic view of childhood and child work, it continues to drive national and international policy.

Other ideologies also are important to current political and social thinking about child work (Myers, 2001). One of the newest, and increasingly influential, can be termed "children-centered," and this is the second ideological discourse we highlight. It is driven largely by human rights, especially child rights, and is advocated by UNICEF and various international child defense NGOs. Although historical roots of this perspective can, like the Romantic ideal, be traced to a Rousseau publication in 1762 (in this case *The Social Contract*, developing a concept of a society of free citizens with rights), it is mostly a product of the twentieth century. Its concept of childhood virtually opposes the Romantic view of children as weak, inept, and dependent. Instead, this "children-centered discourse proposes that children are resilient, capable, and knowledgeable. . . . Children are conceptualized as participants in their own defense when given the chance" (Ennew, et al., 2005, 30). Central to this ideology is the image of children as citizens rather than subjects, and as citizens children are considered to have full human rights—including the right to work, if they wish—that are granted to adults, as well as a voice in the affairs of society. By this mode of thinking, children must have a voice in actions taken on their behalf, which would apply to protective interventions in their work. This view of childhood, and of work in it, both underlies the UNCRC and is supported by it. It does not oppose child work as such, but is concerned that work should not be harmful to children, keep them from school, or otherwise impinge on their rights and well-being.

Notions about child development derived from normative ideological discourses have the advantage of being internally coherent, but because they are driven more by values and rhetorical reasoning than by facts, they are a poor guide to reality. That makes them a precarious basis for policy, especially if those policies are to be judged by their consequences. They might help get intentions sorted out in a logical way, but they offer very little information about the world in which those intentions must be applied, and the best of intentions are undone by ignoring the facts or getting them wrong. That is what happened in Méknès (see chapter 1). A problem with ideologically driven ideas of childhood is a tendency toward moralism that overlooks the complexity of life. This can be seen, for example, in the claim that rights should trump all other considerations. While we are firm supporters of children's rights, we are not convinced they should take priority over consequences to children. When applied as policy, even UNCRC provisions should be subject to accountability for their results in the lives of children.

Beyond honorable motives and intentions, one needs facts by which to understand situations and assess the results of actions. Neither the Romantic nor children-centered ideologies provide that, but social science can. What can we learn from concepts of children's development based in social science theory and research, in order to discover and act on the realities of children's lives? These days most social scientists understand that their own subjective views influence their studies, implying that there does not exist one objective reality that can be discovered. Nevertheless, the procedures and protocols of social science force a healthy attention to empirical detail that is essential for understanding at least aspects of children's development and the role of work in it.

The Idea of Human "Development" in Social Science

Unfortunately, social science does not provide an agreed operational definition of human "development" adequate to serve as an international standard. Most social scientists studying the human life cycle accept and use the term "development," but at the same time they realize it is problematic. It is an abstract, socially constructed metaphor that may not describe very accurately whatever processes actually occur in nature. The very notion of an individual's "development" is surprisingly elusive. In most general terms, it might be thought of as "the growth of children with age in bodily size, neural connections and the differentiation and organization of their mental life" (R. A. Levine and New, 2008, 3). This concept takes account of physical and neurological growth, including size, various motor skills, strength, and sexual maturity, all of which may be relevant to the work that children undertake. But others stress that development is holistic, with many interrelated physical, psychological, and social aspects that cannot be understood outside specific cultural and historical contexts (e.g., Smidt, 2006, 2–3). Some authors prefer an even broader concept: "patterns of change over time which begin at conception and continue throughout the life span" (Keenean and Evans, 2009, 4). It is far from clear that "development" provides the best account of a human life cycle that includes processes not only of increasing strength and competence but also of deterioration and decrepitude, often mixed together. For example, as people age they may grow intellectually wiser and socially more adept as they become physically weaker. Nor is it clear what about "development" pertains to individuals and what to society, given that one becomes a functioning individual through processes that are social. Some scholars even question whether the very concept of "development" is either scientifically valid or socially useful (e.g., Burman, 2008a; b).

Does this mean that social science cannot contribute to giving substance to the mandate of the UNCRC to serve children's development? Not necessarily. The different professions and sciences deal with the ambiguities of the concept of "development" largely by ignoring the big conceptual issues and simply defining "development" operationally according to their respective disciplinary viewpoints. "Development" need not mean the same thing to psychologists, anthropologists, and economists, which is of course confusing to outsiders. Therefore, when policymakers, child advocates, and others apply the notion of children's "development" to child work, they need to be conscious of how the term is being used, realizing that any one viewpoint provides but a partial and imperfect approximation of what actually occurs in children's lives.

If applied to articles of the Minimum Age Convention and the UNCRC, this approach would imply that the mandate to protect children's "development" is open to various interpretations, none of which can be legitimately considered to be universally definitive, but which can nevertheless provide helpful structure and guidance for particular situations. Those responsible for applying the standards have to decide how to define "development" for purposes of the situation and context in question. For making contextualized decisions, social science can be especially useful because its solidly empirical foundations allow it to address real people in real contexts and situations. This kind of thinking from social science has in recent years proved useful for addressing issues of work in child development (see especially chapters 1 and 2 of Boyden, et al., 1998).

Three social science perspectives on children's development, and hence on the mandates of international law, are today especially important for the consideration of child work issues. They are the views from developmental psychology, anthropology and sociology, and, to a lesser extent, economics. We will discuss each in terms of how it addresses child work, and then will conclude with a few comments.

The View from Developmental Psychology

Developmental psychology focuses on the individual person, investigating the processes through which individuals grow cognitively, emotionally, and socially. Some of the most insightful studies are longitudinal, following a sample population from childhood into adulthood in order to determine how the experience of early years plays out over time. A famous longitudinal study by psychiatrist George Vaillant has followed the mental health and life success of a sample of nearly 400 Boston men in a poor and largely immigrant "inner city," starting from 1939, when they were about fourteen years old, up to the present, when the survivors are in their 80s. One of the items on which the youths were originally scored was their work. In this case, "work" was defined broadly to be an indicator of industriousness, including not only whether the boys held jobs, but also noting the extent to which they did home chores, performed exceptionally well in school, and took on other responsibilities. Vaillant found that "the willingness and capacity to work in childhood is the most important forerunner—more important than native intelligence, social class, or family situation—of mental health" in adulthood (cited in Lane, 1991, 247; and recently re-expressed in an interview, Wolf, 2009).

While most research in the field focuses on infancy and early childhood, before children start engaging in most kinds of work, certain findings from this period do have important implications for thinking about child work. One especially useful insight comes out of a branch of child development psychology originating in the ideas of Russian psychologist Lev Vygotsky early in the twentieth century, and built on since then by various modern researchers. This line of thinking begins from the observation that human beings become developed individuals by the act of being social—through transactions with each other—since they have evolved to survive and thrive not so much by individual capacity and independence as through culture, cooperation, and interdependence. For thinking about child work, one of the most valuable insights from this line of research is that children best learn in community with others in order to join and become a part of a community. In fact, they seem "hard-wired" to learn most life skills best when focused with others on a common task in which people are working together. At the core of this process is learning-by-doing through imitation and team involvement.

This process is so pervasive in human experience that developmental psychologist Barbara Rogoff suggests it is the most fundamental social mechanism of human cognitive development. She terms the process "apprenticeship in thinking"—the allusion to on-the-job training is intentional—and she describes in some detail how the "apprentice" (child) learns through "guided participation" with the help of one or more mentors (Rogoff, 1990). Much of children's work, even for routine home tasks, is normally organized this way, its very structure facilitating child development. That is what one sees, for example, when a small girl grabs a branch or broom and, imitating her mother in a commonly gendered task, joins in sweeping the floor. That is only a beginning, for by joining her mother or other women in this way as she grows, she is likely to acquire more sophisticated knowledge of home maintenance and child care, as well as attitudes, customs, and skills. And she will learn how to engage successfully in the complex human relationships involved in doing all these tasks. This is how most of the world's women learn to manage homes and care for children. Likewise, the agriculture that feeds most of the world's population depends on farming knowledge and skills—plus supporting attitudes—that almost everywhere are learned from childhood, beginning with the work of children in fields and pastures. Because there is no realistic way to teach these skills in classes, children's cognitive, emotional, and social development through work continues to be an essential pillar of human survival.

The implications of this approach for evaluating how specific jobs or tasks play out in the development of individual children are enticing, but only now are psychologists starting to explore them. Leading the way, so far, is psychologist Martin Woodhead, who has been uniquely interested in the impact of work on children's psychosocial development. In an essay, "Is there a place for work in child development?" he explores what scientific research can tell us about how work affects child development. Citing the above-mentioned work of Barbara Rogoff, he notes that "sociocultural approaches to child development offer the most promising way of constructing a more inclusive framework for child development" (1999, 18). "Acceptance of this view—that children's behaviour, thinking, social relationships and adaptation are culturally as much as biologically constituted—has profound implications for prescriptions about the place of work in child development. Children's 'needs,' the 'developmental appropriateness' of their experiences, and the 'harmfulness' or 'benefits' of their work cannot be separated from the cultural context in which they are developing, the values and goals that inform their lives and their prior experiences of learning skills and ways of thinking" (Ibid., 19). Woodhead, as many others, notes that most of the research and thinking about "child development" comes from rich countries, and hence the danger of ethnocentrism exists in any attempt to draw universal conclusions from such culturally specific data. Cultural contexts are innumerable and so varied that universal generalizations about specific effects of work on child development are probably impossible. So, how can one make sense of anything?

Woodhead suggests utilizing the notion of a "developmental niche" (Super and Harkness, 1986). All children grow up in a specific environment with particular physical and social settings, cultural customs and child-rearing practices, and values and beliefs. Taken together, these tightly woven, interconnected characteristics constitute the particular "developmental niche" in which a child lives and matures. Children relate to and transact with the characteristics of niches they inhabit, often themselves impacting on the niches. The nature, organization, and impact of children's work are shaped by the features of that niche, and the way work affects children is also determined by how they, the children, interact with their environment. For example, do the people around them reward and praise their work, or castigate them for it? Although Western ideas about work—such as the notion that children should not engage in it—seem appropriate in developmental niches of certain rich countries, they may be irrelevant or inappropriate where the characteristics of children's developmental niches are radically different. On the other hand, "globalized" ideas, tastes, and customs increasingly form a part of developmental niches in many societies, and notions about children's work may be among them. The point is that a developmental niche is specific to the particulars of context, and that context may include elements shared across national and cultural boundaries as well as those that are purely local. The effects of work on children are strongly influenced by the specifics of how that work is physically, socially, and psychologically contextualized in children's lives. Child protective interventions in work, where they are needed, have to be equally sensitive and adapted to the specifics of children's developmental niches. Woodhead implies that there is little justification for mass generalization about how a particular type of work affects children everywhere or for universalized prescriptions for action.

Woodhead led a comparative field study (1998) in which 300 working boys and girls, mostly aged from ten to fourteen years, participated in forty-nine discussion groups in six countries (Bangladesh, Ethiopia, Philippines, Guatemala, El Salvador, and Nicaragua). The researchers used a variety of projective tools to enable the children to indicate how they saw the role of work in their wider lives, and the researchers found that situational factors—especially how others valued children's work and the children doing it—were central determinants of whether and how children perceived their work as having positive or negative effects on them. Whether work could be considered harmful to children's development appeared to be more closely tied to the social context of that work than to the nature of the work itself (chapter 8 will present more on this topic). What came through Woodhead's study with great clarity was that most children valued their work, saw their own value as attached to their work, and thought they gained from it in ways one might consider developmental. It had a lot to do with building their sense of efficacy.

This is in line with our informal observation of many years, and now supported by recent research, that working may help build children's sense of efficacy—an extremely important developmental factor reflecting the combination of self-esteem and competence. Findings from a rigorously controlled longitudinal study (beginning in 1988) of adolescents in a U.S. city strongly suggest that regular employment helps build a sense of efficacy not only in regards to economic skills, but also generally in personality development. Starting regular work younger and continuing with it through adolescence seems to yield greater self-efficacy than does starting later or working only intermittently (Cunnien, et al., 2009).[1] Such findings from a single place, especially in an atypically rich society, should not be interpreted to convey a universal truth, but they certainly pose a serious challenge to the opposite generalization that starting work older and engaging in it only intermittently is better for children than starting young and holding a regular job—a generalization that has long been the untested assumption behind much child labor legislation and the conventional wisdom preached by the ILO and others of similar thinking.

Feelings of self-efficacy are known to be related to children's "resilience," the term used to describe their ability to cope successfully with stress and adversity.[2] Some believe that children's work can build resilience. For example, a famous longitudinal study of resilience in Hawaiian children found that regular nurturing responsibility, such as care for younger siblings, seemed to act as a protective factor promoting it (Werner and Smith, 1992). An ongoing longitudinal study of Ethiopian children similarly suggests that even somewhat risky work that is family-supported and fosters important competencies in children acts as a protective ("steeling") factor that reduces their vulnerability to hardship. From this study, it is not clear that adversity and resilience are two separate things, or that the results of risk are necessarily negative (Boyden, forthcoming).

The weight of field research to date clearly indicates that, as Woodhead and his colleagues found, children have a substantial psychological stake in their work, and the sensitivity with which society respects that personal investment has a lot to do with the way and extent to which work affects their development. It has been widely observed, including by working children themselves, that the pain of social disrespect for their work, such as denigrating or criminalizing it or arbitrarily removing them from it, can be more damaging to their self-respect and socialization than are stresses within the work itself (Woodhead, 1998; Boyden, et al., 1998, 27–111; Boyden, 1997).

A very clear implication for policy is that the traditionally recommended solutions to child labor (criminalizing it, banning or removing children from work, etc.) may, from a point of view of child development, end up being a "cure" worse than the perceived social ill they address. Chapter 9 will provide some programmatic examples in which this seems to have been the case. This not uncommon situation poses a dilemma, and raises the question whether it might not be possible to eliminate the dangers of work while retaining its positive developmental contributions. Clearly, this is not always possible, and we recognize that some work situations are so inappropriate that children have to be removed from them. However, beyond the literature, our own direct observation and field experience with working children and programs that affect them suggests that children should be removed from work they want to do only as a last resort, and then with great sensitivity, because self-esteem and other factors linked to their psychosocial development are likely to be involved. Care needs to be taken to ensure that interventions in children's work to provide the protection required by the UNCRC Article 32 and other national and international norms do not themselves become threats to children's development and well-being. Policies and activities intended as child protection can turn out in practice to be threats to child development. There is significant anecdotal evidence that this is a widespread problem, and that it is especially tied to minimum-age policies banning "underage" children from all work (Bourdillon, et al., 2009).

Honoring children's sensitivities, however, does not address the hard fact that some work children do really is so hazardous, exploitative, demeaning, or otherwise inappropriate that it deserves to be discouraged, prevented, or eliminated. There is little argument about the need to intervene in the kinds of observably harmful work targeted by ILO Convention 182, but some child labor activists have long claimed that even work that does not seem on the surface to be dangerous—especially paid work outside the home—may undermine children's development in subtle but effective ways. For example, they worry that a child's enhanced sense of independence can adversely affect family solidarity and unity. A study of working and nonworking adolescents (aged sixteen to eighteen) in the U.S.A. showed that those who worked were a little more likely to disagree with their parents over such things as dress, friends, going and staying out, helping in the house, sex, smoking, money, school, and family (Manning, 1990, 192). Some literature suggests that employment of children leads to behavioral problems (see Greenberger and Steinberg, 1985). It is not clear, however, whether work is the cause of these problems, since children with prior problematic behavior at school or at home are more likely to look for paid employment (Werner, 1989, 182; Apel, et al., 2006, 358–360). Neither is it clear whether the problems are temporary or more enduring. Mortimer's long-term study in the U.S.A. (see chapter 6) showed working children entering earlier into smoking and drinking than their nonworking peers, but multivariate analysis linked this trend more closely to particular peer groups than to work. When the adolescents reached early adulthood, behavioral patterns evened out, and children who had worked during high school moved into adult family roles in a normative manner (Mortimer, 2003, 165). Working children in South America argued that, far from making them delinquent, their work kept them from getting involved in criminal activities or begging, and allowed them to live a decent life in spite of their conditions of poverty (Liebel, 2001b, 60–61).

The question of when and to what extent work provokes behavioral problems that could be considered developmentally disabling remains open, and it probably hinges on situational factors. At this point, we think a generalized claim that working puts children at risk for behavior and family problems would be difficult to sustain on the basis of existing evidence. But it is a possibility deserving to be kept in mind.

By explicitly recognizing that work can have both positive and negative influences on child development, it becomes possible to frame psychosocial factors in a way conducive to analyzing the situations of particular children and to establishing balanced policies and activities helpful to them. Table 5.1 (page 100) presents an example of a balanced framework.

Children's Work in Anthropological and Sociological Perspective

Anthropologists and sociologists—who have overlapping interests and methodologies these days—are concerned to discover and describe the variety and breadth as well as the inner dynamics of human culture and social experience. They aim to provide a carefully disciplined perspective, free from ethnocentrism, to understand more completely what it means to be human in society. Their focus is generally on social groups, such as villages, ethnic groups, or socioeconomic classes, and the complex processes and relationships between people within and between groups, rather than on individuals. They not only travel to distant places to identify the world's cultures and document them in

TABLE 5.1
Psychosocial factors in child work

Factors	Major positive influences	Major potential hazards
Secure relationships and consistent settings	Stable environment, predictable routines Changes occur in context of supportive relationships	Breakdown of social networks, emotional bonds Disruptions to familiar surroundings without supportive relationships
Activities and guidance	Progressive participation in socially valued activities, skills, and responsibilities under sensitive, consistent guidance	Unstimulating, monotonous activities Induction into inappropriate behavior, e.g. crime, drug abuse, peer exploitation
Responsible adults	Positive, consistent, and considerate treatment, respectful of children's integrity	Negligent, inconsistent, harsh treatment Emotional abuse, humiliation, and discrimination. Physical and sexual abuse
Peer support and solidarity	Opportunities for positive and wider peer relations and mutual support	Isolation from or rejection by peers Bullying, violence, stigmatization.
Physical environment and daily schedules	Safe, healthy environment with appropriate balance of work, learning, play, and rest	Adverse working conditions. Accidents, ill-health Exposure to toxins Excessive workload
Relationships with employers and supervisors	Positive modeling with adequate protection, expansion of relations with adult world	Financial and job insecurity, harsh supervisors, lack of protection Powerlessness in face of exploitation

(continued)

TABLE 5.1

Psychosocial factors in child work (continued)

Factors	Major positive influences	Major potential hazards
Work and family lives	Expected contributions respectful of children's interests and well-being Positive modeling and teaching	Unreasonable parental expectations, coercive treatment, collusion with exploitative employers
Behavior	Learning responsibility toward others	Conflicts with family, adopting problematic behavior patterns
Other factors affecting the impact of work	Positive opportunities for participation in school and other community settings Basic economic and social security, political stability, and social justice.	Incompatibility of work versus school demands Social exclusion, stigmatization, e.g. by teachers, police, or others in authority Acute poverty, political/ social upheaval, social injustice, and exclusion.

Source: Based on Woodhead, 2004, 338

great detail, but also turn their professionally distanced perspective on their own societies. They draw comparisons between societies, finding commonalities that join them as well as differences that divide them. A practical effect is to expand the range of human behavior that can be considered "normal."

In recent years, anthropologists and sociologists have increasingly studied childhoods, focusing on children's diverse "lifeworlds" and the different social structures and processes that affect them, studying in great detail how children learn about the world and engage in it. In general, they have confirmed that children thrive in a wide variety of different environments and child-rearing systems. They also have discovered that many Euro-American ideas about what is universal in human development and what is universally essential for children to flourish are neither borne out by fact nor shared by most of the world's societies. They find no reason to conclude that Euro-American child-rearing theories and practices are better or more universally applicable than those of most other societies. Nor do they find any objective justification for imposing

on other societies Euro-American notions of what constitutes a proper childhood, or the place of work in it.

A recent overview of findings from the field of anthropology of childhood
notes, "Nowhere are Euroamerican views on childhood and those of the larger
world more at odds than on the issue of work." Writing from a Euro-American
perspective, the author adds, "While we hamstring our children to keep them
from the labor force, fearing their loss of innocence and studiousness, the norm
elsewhere is to open the pathway to adulthood" (Lancy, 2008, 234). He goes on
to note that, in most of the world, part of a child's essential education for life has
long occurred through a home "chore curriculum" of tasks graded to suit a
child's age and abilities, and that through their work children enjoy a sense
of achievement and increased respect from others. By working, children are
expected to learn more than just how to perform the tasks competently; they also
pick up connected social norms and practices and learn how to work with others.
A description of child-rearing practice from Kenya probably represents a viewpoint of parents throughout most of the world today: "[They] attach importance
to providing children with duties that teach responsibility and mutuality. In
their view, a mother who does not expect her children to help is remiss, even
neglectful. A child so treated would inevitably emerge as an adult with few
prospects and without the respect of the community" (Wenger, 2008, 290).

Some societies, recognizing the role of work in helping root children in
family and community, consider children to have a moral right to assume
responsibilities as they are able. They believe that work is an intrinsic part of
the broad social processes and institutions through which children gain knowledge, experience, status, and self-expression in their community and society.
Life is not simply divided into separate components of work, play, and education, parceled out piecemeal as happens in modern industrial societies. Where
there are no such divisions, the arbitrary removal of children's work risks
undermining the web of social mechanisms through which children are social-
ized, included, and empowered, thereby leaving them isolated and vulnerable.
Anthropologists have long recognized links between children's work and their
socialization, including the development of their moral sensibilities and standards. This has been especially noted in rural settings, still the prevailing environment for most inhabitants of many low-income countries.

> In agrarian models of life, child labor at home is a virtuous activity, one
> part of a long term reciprocal exchange between parent and child that
> constitutes the moral order of kin relationships. This exchange is by no
> means limited to economic goods and services but includes many sym-
> bolically significant forms of obligatory social and ritual actions. Child
> labor is seen as an expression of the work domain of this broader rela-
> tional concept. Reducing it to its economic component is taking the child

labor out of the indigenous context in which it is experienced by a large number, probably the majority, of Third World families. (R.A. Levine and White, 1986, 175)

We illustrate this point with a study by anthropologist Inge Bolin (2006), which describes the role of children's work in their development and socialization into a pastoralist society in the highlands of Peru. She draws a picture of rich cultural and social lives in the midst of crushing economic poverty. In that context, child work is both an economic necessity and a vehicle of cultural transmission, inclusion, and expression. It is also tightly woven into the full fabric of life. She demonstrates how play, learning, and work are integrated and sometimes indistinguishable from each other, whereas in rich industrialized countries they would be separated from each other and compartmentalized in different processes and institutions. In their play, young children imitate the tasks they see family and community perform, and as they become able they voluntarily join in the work, from which they learn not only competence in carrying out tasks, but also the cosmic beliefs, the patterns of social cooperation, the binding rituals, the arts of self-expression, the intricacies of moral discernment, and the expected standards of behavior in which the tasks are embedded. Chores entrusted to children, such as herding animals, are consistent with child capacities and provide opportunity for play while working, as well as for learning essential skills. Children generally take pleasure and pride in their work, which is rewarded with praise and, at certain points, with more substantive recognition, such as a rise in community status or the gift of an animal of one's own. The sexes are valued and treated equally. A climate of mutual respect between the generations is established in which children enjoy considerable freedom. They participate fully in the social, cultural, and religious rituals that define their culture. When properly nourished and provided with decent schools within reasonable walking distance, they are reputed to be among the better students, with a special facility and fondness for mathematics.

This longitudinal study conducted over more than a decade reveals that, despite the burden of severe poverty, children grow up happily, they suffer little conflict and violence, they acquire a rich store of life skills, and they apparently adapt well to their own society while remaining flexible enough to fit into formal education and modern town life where that is an option. Bolin attributes much of this developmental success to the empowering and mutually respectful social environment in which the children are reared. Participation in work is a central vehicle of that empowerment and mutual respect. Similar findings regarding the socializing value of children's work come from a study by Antonella Invernizzi of street workers in urban Peru. She concludes, "It seems important to revise the notion perceiving children's work solely in terms of economic necessity. That approach makes it difficult to deal with facets of socialization" (2003, 338).

The point is not to romanticize either work or traditional societies—there are hazards aplenty for children in both—but to point out that ideas and assumptions common in industrial society about work, and about the role of work in children's development, have been shown by anthropological research to have very limited applicability elsewhere. Even some work that is so dangerous or otherwise inappropriate for children that it merits outside intervention may at the same time help them develop skills, attitudes, and relationships they must acquire in order to succeed in their society. That does not obviate the case for protective intervention, which may in any event be necessary, but it does suggest that a good remedy will retain the developmentally positive effects of working while reducing the negative ones. In many instances this will mean making work more appropriate for children rather than taking them away from it, and we note that such a strategy is consistent with the UNCRC. Unnecessarily draconian measures barring or removing children from even safe work may pose unanticipated developmental risks to children when that work is linked to other social mechanisms that protect and empower them.

Some anthropologists have looked into the effect of interventions on children at risk based on the discourse of child rights, and have found cases in which biases of industrial countries against child work have led to actions inimical to children's cognitive, social, psychological, or moral development. How this occurs can be glimpsed in a rather emblematic little incident related in a study by anthropologist Rachel Burr (2006) of Vietnamese children at risk.

She cites a case in which a remand school for boys was trying to move from a punitive to a rehabilitative approach in dealing with the young people assigned to its care. Realizing that the students were trapped by poverty and lack of livelihood skills into likely recidivism when put back on the street, the staff started a vocational program to teach them bicycle repair. The school understood that these boys needed skills to make an honest living if they were to escape the cycle of crime and arrest. Not having money for a typical vocational school class, the school set up a small business which would take in bicycles that the boys could repair under the teaching and direction of a skilled workman. The boys learned their trade on the job. Apprenticeship arrangements of this type are usual for acquiring such skills in Vietnam and perhaps most of the rest of the world. However, this bicycle repair workshop, although established for a social and educational purpose, was surprisingly condemned as a case of child labor by a visitor representing UNICEF, who insisted that the program should be closed down. This visitor, a European, saw the program only in terms of its commercial aspect, ignoring its educational and developmental purposes.

What caused this unanticipated reaction that seemed so alien to the high purposes and unexceptional approach of the school staff? Was it because the learning and work components were joined together—actually, an educational advantage—rather than separated from each other, as they might have been in Europe or North America? It appears likely that an ethnocentric view of the role of work in children's development might have led the visiting official not only to misinterpret the facts of the case, but also to misconstrue international child rights and labor standards, which in fact could easily, logically, and legitimately have been applied in support of the bicycle shop as an educational program.

The View from Economics

Chapter 4 introduced the economic view of human development and discussed research into the relationships between poverty and children's work, presenting the economic finding that healthier and more skilled populations—those with more "human capital"—contribute more to society and the economy. For the purpose of this kind of economic analysis, child development is defined very narrowly in terms of measurable education, health, and similar variables that can be analyzed as contributors toward national economic development. The costs and benefits of schools, health programs, and other social infrastructure are assessed within that conceptual framework. Defining human development in terms of adult contributions to economic output is an extremely constricted notion that pays little attention to what people really expect and pursue to provide meaning in their lives. A purely economic construction of human development might be useful for helping plan economic development programs and relating to peoples' hopes for growing prosperity, but it neglects other domains and objectives of human development that are at least equally important, such as the broadening of individual personality, experience of social solidarity, and pleasure in the company of others. By regarding children's work only in economic terms such analyses miss entirely the wide range of personal and social competencies that other social sciences—especially psychology and anthropology—place at the very center of human development. Most national and international policy analyses of child work take this economic framework as given (e.g., Grootaert and Patrinos, 1999). We believe economists' perspectives on human development are far too narrow and incomplete to serve as the central intellectual basis for national and international policies governing child work. While the future economic prosperity of children as adults should of course be an important concern, context-appropriate psychological and anthropological indicators of children's broader personal and social development serve human development purposes better.

Concluding Observations

While a universal definition of child "development" is not available as an international standard for assessing progress toward mandated protection of children's development in regards to their work, the social sciences provide insightful concepts and tools that can be applied to particular contexts and situations. It appears to us that, at least among social science researchers studying child work issues in the field, there is an expanding consensus that

> [c]hild labour policy may have been "getting it wrong" for some time by focusing on the complete eradication of child labour and perpetuating western versions of childhood which dictate that work itself is harmful to child development. Research increasingly shows that children in fact see work as a legitimate right and opportunity to play a more active and important role in society and a right of passage to adulthood.... This perspective emphasizes the role of personal agency in children's labour market participation and recognizes that in addition to fulfilling a family need, there are benefits to children as they acquire skills, form social relationships, build friendships and identities. (Gamlin and Pastor, 2009, 119)

This view is not confined to academics. We have met practitioners who work closely with working children, and who are generally inclined to view many kinds of work as developmentally appropriate for children as long as safeguards are in place to prevent abuse. Many claim that work of the right kind and in the right circumstances is a developmental advantage. The social science perspectives presented above strongly suggest that children's participation in safe, non-exploitative work can be a fundamental mechanism of personal and social development. That raises the interesting question whether children who do not have access to some form of work are in fact being deprived of an important developmental opportunity. If work is a fundamental human process for developing important life skills, attitudes, and relationships, maybe society has a vested interest in making properly supervised developmental work available to children, just as it has an interest in making sure that all work is safe and appropriate for them. Perhaps the problem of "youth unemployment" begins in middle childhood rather than in adolescence. Understood this way, maybe children should indeed have a recognized right to work, as some of them now insist, perhaps as part of their right to education.

This suggests that the best policies to govern child work would be balanced, facilitating appropriate work as developmental for children while guarding against dangers and abuses in work. A parallel might be drawn with sports. Children's participation in sports is generally considered physically, socially, and psychologically developmental for them, especially when properly organized and overseen by adults. Adults coach children in skills, enforce rules of safety and fairness, encourage effort and good sportsmanship, and counsel children as needed in order to make sport as developmental as possible. But sports also come with risks, and almost all children who play them suffer minor wounds such as scrapes, bruises, and sprains, and sometimes more serious injuries as well. Some sports are so violent, exhausting, or otherwise inappropriate that responsible adults do not let children engage in them. But nobody deals with risk by banning children from all sports. Instead, schools, communities, and even governments organize child and youth sports to be as safe and as developmental as possible. Children are encouraged to participate as an experience conducive to their development. Might not children's work be handled in a similar way?

6

Education, School, and Work

"Stop child labor! School is the best place to work."[1]

This popular slogan inspiring a major international campaign against "child labor" sounds compelling because it supports children's education and opposes work that keeps them from it. Its subtext is a widely shared belief that children's work and schooling are incompatible, and that stopping children from productive work is necessary to ensure that they attend and succeed in school. This view is promoted by certain well-regarded experts and institutions, based on their reading of studies and official statistics that report negative correlations between child work and school attendance and achievement—the more work, the less schooling.

The ILO, for example, finds general incompatibility between work and school based on a cross-national comparison of working vs. nonworking children according to household survey data in 34 countries. It concludes that "[c]hild labour has to be taken seriously as an important obstacle to reaching the Education for All goals" (Allais and Hagemann, 2008, 17). In a major reference book article proposing to "bring together the international evidence on the interaction between education and child labor," economist Ranjan Ray asserts that "the literature is near unanimous on the harmful effects of a child's employment on her or his learning outcomes" (R. Ray, 2009, 118). We could not disagree more, either about what the literature reveals or about the actual relationships between children's work and their education.

This chapter will test the assumption of incompatibility between work and education by drawing on literature more extensive than that consulted by Ray and by citing research more sophisticated than the simple cross-country comparisons presented by the ILO. We will demonstrate that things are not at all as Ray and the ILO (and many others) would have us believe, and that the truth—or at least as close as we can get to it—is not only more complex, but also much more interesting and promising.

The assumption that work and school are mutually exclusive alternatives is challenged by much empirical evidence and by working children's views. In chapter 1, we questioned the assumption that stopping children from working will drive them to school and the last chapter (5) suggested that work be included in consideration of education. Because we think the illusion of work-education incompatibility is fed in large part by abstracted survey data providing only a simplistic and overly generalized fly-over view from the proverbial 30,000 feet, we will start our discussion at the opposite pole—on the ground, with an ethnographic case study presenting the complicated specifics of real life. We start with a case in which work makes school possible, and we go on to present children's views on work and school in different situations. Education is a right of children, bestows important benefits, and is reasonably considered a principle activity for them. Nevertheless, the previous chapter showed how child development and education cannot be relegated solely to formal schooling: this chapter further considers the severe limitations of some of the schools that are available to children in low-income communities. We then consider evidence for and against the belief that work necessarily hinders schooling. There are serious problems with many common statistical analyses, which fail to show whether work in fact hinders schooling or whether in certain situations failure of the school system encourages children to work. More careful research comes to more varied and nuanced conclusions. We look at a landmark study that resolved such questions in a particular setting by following a panel of children over time. Finally, we consider ways of combining schoolwork with other kinds of work, and of learning through productive work.

"Earn-and-Learn": Tea Estates in Zimbabwe

In the late 1990s, author Michael Bourdillon studied an "earn-and-learn" boarding school on a tea estate in the Eastern Highlands of Zimbabwe (2000a), meeting with teachers, pupils and their families, and employers on the estate. The school was one of several run by the tea company, at which pupils contracted to work for the estate as a condition of enrollment. Although these schools have been accused of exploiting cheap labor (as is suggested historically in chapter 3), it was the request of workers on the surrounding estates to have more such schools that prompted the investigation.

In the peak harvesting season, the pupils went to the fields at first light and worked for eight hours, plucking tea leaves and tossing them into large baskets carried on their backs. They attended school in the afternoon; teachers and pupils often complained of tiredness and dozing during class. In the evening they did their school assignments, and after less than seven hours of rest they were up again for work. They had Sundays off and some free time on Saturdays. They were required to work through some of the school vacations. In the off-season,

the regime was more relaxed: school came in the morning and work assignments on the estate were often completed in a few hours.

Many of the pupils had spent years out of school and some were over twenty
years old by the time they finished secondary school, but in the late 1990s, some
were being admitted to the scheme as young as thirteen—or even twelve if they
looked physically strong enough. At one stage, under international pressure, the
company stopped accepting pupils under the age of fifteen into the scheme: this
meant that a boy of twelve, son of a very poor single mother, who had just finished primary school with good grades, would have to wait a couple of years
before starting secondary school. Or perhaps he could earn enough from herding cattle and working on small tea farms out of the international eye to go to
the less satisfactory local day school.

All the pupils claimed to be in the scheme by choice. Indeed, some told of
difficulty in persuading parents to allow them to travel from distant parts of the
country. Local people appreciated that life was hard for the pupils. Nevertheless
past pupils generally said they had been happy at school because they had a purpose that they could fulfill. Several people in the district, including some working in the Ministry of Education, pointed out that the "earn-and-learn" schooling
had been their route out of poverty and into their current professional status.
One, now a white-collar worker on the estate, was earning enough to send his
youngest sister to a good school elsewhere, to ensure she did not suffer as he
had done. He pointed out gratefully that he was only able to do this because the
"earn-and-learn" school had given him the opportunity.

When asked how they came to be at the school, many of the pupils
described how they had dropped out of previous schools, often because they
could not afford the expenses. Some chose to come to this school because they
were dissatisfied with teaching and facilities in other local schools. The labora-
tories, libraries, and other facilities at the estate schools were better equipped
than those in government schools. One of the pupils had previously attended a
more relaxed day school, but often missed school at the beginning of term for
want of school fees, and he noticed that the estate schools had much better
examination results. Some pupils commented that although they had to work
hard in the "earn-and-learn" schools, even at home they had work to do, and at
the estate school they were saved several hours each day of walking to and from
school.

In one case, a thirteen-year-old girl and her three younger siblings, whose
parents had recently died, were taken in by her grandmother. The grandmother
had no income and could not grow enough food for the whole family. The girl
entered an "earn-and-learn" school (under the legal age for employment) where
she earned money to continue her own schooling and enough besides to pay for
provisions and schooling for her younger brother and sisters.

The children had many complaints about their treatment at the "earn-and-learn" schools. In particular, they wanted less time given to work on the estate, and they did not want to work in the plantations before school. These and other complaints together led, from time to time, to strikes and disturbances. Many children could not cope: the drop-out rate was around 15 percent in a normal year. But the pupils did not want the scheme to close.

The pupils were paid at the same rate as were adults for the tea they picked and other work they undertook (although in the past they had been paid less). Although some of their earnings were deducted for school and boarding fees, the school and meals were heavily subsidized by the tea company. The labor of the pupils was therefore more expensive, but also more reliable, than casual adult labor. In return the company guaranteed the children some employment, even when there was little demand for work. In management there was discussion about whether to mechanize for efficiency or to continue with the "earn-and-learn" scheme as a service to the community.

In this case, far from keeping children out of school, paid work made school possible. The situation was certainly unsatisfactory: the pupils should have had more time for rest and leisure, and the government should have provided better schooling at less cost to the children. They should have had more time with their families. In the peak picking season, work certainly interfered with school performance. Shortly after Bourdillon completed his research, there were some improvements to the conditions of work for the pupils. The work was reduced from eight to seven hours a day and subsequently shifted to the afternoon—after school. Refreshments and some protective clothing were introduced. While Bourdillon was disappointed that so little changed, teachers and pupils were delighted: a small improvement can be a very positive experience for disadvantaged children. In an ideal world, such schools would not exist. In the world we have, they provide the best available opportunity for many children to receive an education that could allow them and their families to break out of poverty.

In the earn-and-learn schools, work and school are interdependent. The pupils' work makes the school viable for the company. Employment makes school possible for pupils. The pupils are very clear on why they are at the school and are aware of both the advantages and disadvantages it held out for them.

Children's Perceptions

Elsewhere, researchers have consulted children's opinions on work and school, and this has revealed a variety of views. Many children go to school and do not want any other work; others would like to engage in some sort of productive work as well, while some even prefer such work to study. Some children who work without attending school have no desire for schooling, but many others

TABLE 6.1

Preferences by children aged 10–14 for school and work in four regions (percentages)

	Bangladesh	Ethiopia	Philippines	Central America
Paid work only	24	29	4	1
School and work	76	69	79	78
School only	–	2	17	21
	100	100	100	100
N	72	42	81	106

Source: Woodhead, 2001, 106

would like to attend school as well as work, or to give up their work in order only to study.

A number of studies illustrate this variety of views. One is Woodhead's study (2001, mentioned in the previous chapter) of working children in six countries, most of whom were living with their families and felt responsible to contribute to them. As shown in table 6.1, most did not see school and work as exclusive alternatives, and overwhelmingly wished to combine them. Whether the remainder wanted to drop school or drop paid work depended on where they lived and how they experienced the two. In the Philippines and Central America, the young workers more readily aspired after a different future, and regarded their paid work as a temporary necessity. Probably they experienced a higher quality of schooling than did those in the other two countries. In Bangladesh and Ethiopia, the children were more fatalistic about their future, and saw little chance of something different; nevertheless, another study showed Bangladeshi children equating "learning" with a classroom (Bissell, 2005, 388). Bangladeshi working children expressed a wish for school hours to be adjusted to allow them to undertake productive work if necessary, and for employers to allow them time off to attend school (Save the Children U.K., 2005, 9). A third of a sample of working children in Lima, Peru, did not prioritize between school and work: they considered both important, and about half said they would not like to stop working (Glasinovich, 1995).

The preference for a combination of school and work accords with what movements of working children have often asked for (we will be discussing these further in chapter 7). The African Movement of Working Children and Youth claim "the right to learn to read and write" and "the right to be taught a trade," together with "the right to light and limited work." The First International

Meeting of Working Children in Kundapur, India, in 1997 declared themselves in favor of "work with dignity with hours adapted so that we have time for education and leisure."

In most high-income countries and some low-income ones, children are not given the option of whether or not to attend school. When children do not wish to attend classes, it is assumed that they are putting short-term pleasure over their long-term best interests, and their wishes are overruled. We have pointed out that a majority of adolescents in high-income countries voluntarily take up part-time employment besides their school work; they value this kind of experience and some claim it as a right. The question remains whether or not children's preferences to combine work and school should be overruled in a similar way, since education must remain a high priority in the interests of children. In any case, the varied opinions of the children should alert us to positive and negative factors in both school and work that should be considered if good decisions are to be made about policy.

The decisional role of children's aspirations and agency typically is not picked up in the economics-oriented literature on work-school relationships because domestic decision processes have been modeled, and questions asked, on assumptions that exclude children as actors. For example, the World Bank has used a conceptual framework in which children are sent to work (instead of school) by parents or other family members owing to one or more of the following posited causes: (e.g. Bhalotra, and Tzannatos, 2003; Betcherman, et al., 2004)

- Incentives that favor work over schooling;
- Constraints that compel children to work rather than study;
- Family lack of altruism or ignorance of the value of education.

These categories reflect economics theory rather than what is already known about intrafamilial decision making in regards to family work from anthropology, sociology, and other social sciences. They miss how influential children can be in such decisions, and by excluding the culturally and situationally complex reasons often given by children for working or not studying, they miss the actual reasons for decisions. School incompetence or mistreatment that drives students away does not fit easily into this framework, nor does the frequently cited desire of children to help their parents out of feelings of respect, solidarity, and compassion.

The Right to Education

Children everywhere, including many who also put great value on work outside school, want to learn. We pointed out in chapter 4 that investment in education brings long-term returns for children (even if these are sometimes exaggerated). Studies throughout the world show that children and their parents generally appreciate the value of schooling, although, as we shall point out later in this chapter, they may be skeptical of the value of the particular schools available to them. Besides its economic value, schooling can empower children with a range of knowledge and skills necessary for development and for participation in modern society. So free basic education is widely accepted as a fundamental right of all children.[2] School is not the only, or necessarily the best, way of learning, but effective schools provide an efficient way of teaching large numbers of children. For most of the world's children, school is the only way to acquire certain skills and knowledge necessary for participation in the modern world, and consequently all children have a right to effective schooling.

Does the right to education impose an obligation on the part of children to attend available formal schools?[3] Or does it rather impose an obligation on society to provide schooling appropriate to the needs of all children? In high-income countries, appropriate and modified education is often provided for children with special needs, such as those arising from various kinds of disability. The right to education places an obligation on society to provide schooling that is appropriate to the children concerned and accommodates their needs. The right to education does not necessarily have overriding priority when it comes into conflict with other rights, such as the right to food and livelihood of children with inadequate adult support. If such children are compelled by their circumstances to engage in productive work, they still have a right to appropriate education and the obligation falls on society to provide it.

Motives behind compulsory schooling are not always related to children's rights and interests, and thus the conduct of schooling does not always keep the best interests of children as the primary consideration. When school is seen as a means of keeping children out of the labor force (as in Winrock International, 2008, 5), or indeed off the streets, this can have a negative effect on its role of developing the knowledge and skills of children. An example is when bright students are held back to the curriculum of their age cohort, rather than being allowed to progress rapidly and complete early.

The UNCRC requires that education be directed to the "development of the child's personality, talents and mental and physical abilities to their fullest potential" and "preparation of the child for responsible life in a free society" (article 29). During the 1970s and 1980s, the value of combining work and education—"education with production"—in the development of children and youth was commonly accepted by experts, by international agencies, and by NGOs promoting educational reform. In keeping with ideals that education should train children to become productive members of their society, a number of UNESCO and ILO publications explored models fusing education and work in ways that emphasized the dignity of work, both manual and intellectual, the role of labor in the social and economic formation of both children and adults, and the potential of earning while learning as an approach to protecting working children. This attitude, and the UNCRC, corresponded with an understanding of "basic education" as encompassing both "essential learning tools (such as literacy, oral expression, numeracy, and problem solving) and the basic learning content (such as knowledge, skills, values, and attitudes) required by human beings to be able to survive, to develop their full capacities, to live and work in dignity, to participate fully in development, to improve the quality of their lives, to make informed decisions, and to continue learning."[4]

These ideas were largely lost in a heavy emphasis on literacy and numeracy skills in the 1990s, and in the determination of some global actors to remove children from labor-force work (Myers, 2001b, 311–313). The term "basic education" is now largely used to cover formal primary schooling (sometimes extended to preschool and junior secondary school). Formal schooling, however, does not always fulfill children's right to education when it is not adequately directed at the overall development of children.

School as Work

In chapter 4, we mentioned the PROGRESA program in Mexico, designed to increase school enrolment and performance by paying cash grants to mothers provided that their children attended school regularly. Effectively, school became the income-earning work of children. Evaluation studies reported significant increases in enrolment, particularly for girls past primary school, and increased average length of time in school for the poor (Glewwe and Kremer, 2006, 979; citing Schultz, 2004). The idea that it makes economic sense to provide incentives to families that increase a population's overall literacy and numeracy has gained support in part because of the dominance of the human capital perspective in development economics (discussed in chapters 4 and 5). Jens Qvortrup pointed out that in this view, the primary and obligatory work of children is no longer to contribute to the livelihood of the household, but to acquire knowledge and skills for the future of the nation. This view considers schooling as investment in children for what society will need from them later. It is implicit in the policies of many countries, which see the value of formal schooling for the countries' economic development. Applications coming from this perspective are not limited to low-income populations. In 1995, the German Federal Government declared that because the educational system should produce qualified labor power, it is as economically important as, for example, traffic infrastructure (cited in Qvortrup, 2001, 91).

In practice, in both high- and low-income countries, the majority of young people do not wish to spend all their working time on school work. Moreover, schools available to children of low-income families do not always provide effective education. When this is the case, children must do the bulk of their learning outside the formal education system.

Problems with Schools

A significant growth in formal education in the last fifty years has resulted in the vast majority of the world's children receiving at least some schooling. Even in very deprived areas, primary schools can be found in which children learn with enthusiasm from teachers who manage with few resources. Many children, however, still miss out on schooling. In 2006, it was estimated that seventy-five million (13.6 percent, and over half of these in sub-Saharan Africa) of the world's children of primary school age, and 43 percent of secondary school age (over 75 percent in sub-Saharan Africa), were not enrolled.[5] Girls are significantly underrepresented in enrolment figures (Glewwe and Kremer, 2006, 955, table 6). Since 1980, the United Nations has repeatedly stated a commitment to achieving universal education, and has so far failed to deliver it.

To what extent should this failure be blamed on children's work, as the slogan at the beginning of this chapter suggests? Campaigns against "child labor" often contrast the worst kinds of work with an ideal picture of schooling. In practice, schools available to low-income communities are often far from ideal. Although parents are generally interested in education for their children, as Dréze and Sen point out, many take a dim view of the available schooling system (2002, 158).

Although the UNCRC states unambiguously that basic education must be provided "free of charge," and that secondary education must be "available and accessible to every child" (Article 28), for many children schooling remains expensive or unaffordable. Fees and levies are charged even for primary schooling. There are often costs in books, writing supplies, and school uniforms. When schools are not near the children's homes, transport may be an expense, whether in money or in hours of walking. A major cost for many families is the loss of children's contributions through their unpaid and paid work.

Apart from these economic considerations, children and their families make choices about schooling based on what is available to them in a particular situation. Far from being welcoming places for children that provide appropriate learning environments, schools—especially those serving the poor—are sometimes grim, demeaning places where little valuable learning occurs. Ali Khan illustrated the problem in Sailkot, Pakistan, with this comment from a girl who dropped out of school, "Half the time we were in school the teacher would not be present. On other occasions she would make us do her housework for her, like sweeping the floor of her house. Also she would hit her students with a cane so that most of the students were too scared to learn anything" (Khan, 2007, 183). Khan pointed out that, in these contexts, conditions in productive work appeared less severe against the yardstick of actual conditions at school and at home, and that many children who stitched footballs "showed confidence, self-esteem, and a sense of responsibility and purpose that was absent from their non-working, school-going counterparts" (2007, 188).

National budgets for education are often grossly inadequate. Many schools lack the most basic resources—textbooks, blackboards, desks, benches, and sometimes even classrooms (in which case classes meet outside and are cancelled when it rains). Teachers often have over fifty children in a class and sometimes over seventy. Qualified teachers may be reluctant to live and work in remote areas, which in turn results in teachers who have inadequate training being hired (Glewwe and Kremer, 2006, 947, 961). Teachers sometimes receive low salaries and have little incentive to teach well or even show up for class (e.g., Chaudhury, et al., 2006, 91; Hallack and Poisson, 2007, 164, 260–267).

Even when the children of the poor are able to attend relatively good schools, they are often disadvantaged by such factors as language differences, a curriculum designed for middle-class children, and humiliating discrimination from teachers and peers. Mohammad Talib and Myron Weiner, in separate studies in India, report teachers' attitudes that lower-caste children are unable to learn (Talib, 2003; Weiner, 1991, 199), reflecting a cultural belief that lower-caste children should work rather than go to school, and making poor children uncomfortable in the school environment. Working children may be disadvantaged in school because work and evaluation in school depends on classroom skills and a curriculum that takes no account of their experiences and achievements outside school.

Problems in school systems can result in low levels of achievement by children. In Tanzania, for example, between 1997 and 2001, only 22 percent of students passed the primary education final examination, and only 28 percent passed the certificate of secondary education exam (Glewwe and Kremer, 2006, 963). In Bihar in India, money and effort went into hiring teachers, getting children to school, providing free lunches, and making schools accountable. Yet a survey in 2007 showed that in the fifth grade, four children out of ten could not read and seven out of ten could not subtract (New York Times, 17 January 2008). Although many problems are system-wide, it is individual children who are given failing marks; such children may become humiliated by failures at school and come to believe that they have no aptitude for studies.

The knowledge provided by formal schooling is sometimes divorced from the practical lives of children. Much of what is learned at school may have little relevance for the kinds of jobs that are available. By giving much of their time to school knowledge, they may not acquire practical skills and environmental knowledge that they would otherwise learn through the performance of tasks in their home environment (e.g., Katz, 2004, 113–117, 174; Weiner, 1991, 76; Khan, 2007, 181).

How safe are schools? A study of schools in Ghana, Malawi, and Zimbabwe revealed sexual abuse of girls by teachers, other pupils, and sugar daddies to be part of a wider problem of school-based violence that included excessive corporal punishment and bullying (Leach, et al., 2003, ix). Throughout the world, large numbers of children report being bullied at school—over 30 percent in many European countries (Pinheiro, 2006, 122–125). Several people interviewed from Nairobi slums cited fear of assault at school or on the way to or from school as a reason for dropping out (Mudege, et al., 2008). Perhaps parents who try to protect their daughters by removing them from school at puberty are sometimes justified.

School work can be harmful in other ways. A system of constant testing can create stress and damage the learning process (Harber, 2004, 111–123, chapter 8). Excessive expectations can also be damaging. A study of Japanese school pupils showed that the pressure to do well separated them from families and allowed no leisure. As a result children were found to have a growing incidence of the kinds of illnesses that in other societies are associated with stress among adults (Field, 1995; see also Che, 1995 on South Korea). In India, extreme stress and anxiety concerning examination performance is common and sometimes leads to suicide (Oudenhoven and Wazir, 2006, 47). Such treatment is more disruptive of children's development than are many economic activities that young people undertake.

The problems outlined here refer to situations that are not envisioned or taken into account when experts speak of the advantages of education. The problems indicate that children and their families are not necessarily irrational when they see available schooling as of little value to them (Dréze and Sen, 2002, 158), and work in their particular contexts as more valuable than schooling. These problems underline the importance, and the enormous challenge, of improving schooling and making adequate schooling available rather than simply relying on legislation and compulsion. Researchers rarely pay attention to quality of schooling; when they do, the results show that quality, like costs, affect attendance (e.g., Hanushek, et al., 2006, 24–27; Hazarika and Bedi, 2003, 55).

In spite of these problems, schooling remains a key factor in the development of children and society. Schools and teachers can be sources of joyful, safe, and effective learning, overcoming restrictions of poverty and minimal facilities.

Can School Mix with Work?

Since many advocates and reputable scholars claim that work hinders formal schooling (e.g. R. Ray, 2009), we take this claim seriously. In this section, we consider whether and how work detracts from formal schooling, and whether there is a role for work as part of children's education, broadly defined. We first want to emphasize that there is little evidence to support the common notion that the effects of work on schooling are similar and generalizable, especially across societies. A common-sense reading of the vast literature suggests they are largely situational. David Post tested the idea of cross-national commonalities by comparing work and school relationships, and the family and other social and institutional factors shaping them, in Chile, Peru, and Mexico. He found major differences between the countries in why and how children related school and work, and how the societies dealt with this interface. He showed that policies appropriate for dealing with the issue in one country would not necessarily be equally reasonable in the others (Post 2001).

There are three ways in which work might interfere with schooling. First, work might prevent or hinder attendance at school. Second, work might take time away from school-related work. Third, work might hinder school performance. We address each of these in turn.

Does Work Affect School Attendance?

The assumption that work keeps children from school appears at first to be supported by statistical studies showing inverse correlations between school attendance and work. One study covering five Latin American countries (Brazil, Colombia, Ecuador, Guatemala, and Peru) showed the problems children have in balancing school and work: there was a clear inverse correlation between school attendance and outside work. The authors argued, however, that the failure of the educational system to offer adequate, stimulating, and affordable schooling encouraged children to drop out in favor of paid work, which appeared to offer advantages more relevant to their everyday lives (Salazar and Glasinovich, 1998). A recent ILO study, using surveys from 34 countries between 1998 and 2006, shows overall negative correlations between work and school attendance (Allais and Hagemann, 2008).

There is also some contrary evidence. Some studies show working children to have slightly higher attendance rates than nonworking children (Edmonds, 2008, 3641). A Kenyan study showed that children working over 24 hours per week were likely to have a school attendance record as perfect as those of children working only seven hours a week. Ranking of states in India with the highest levels of "child labor" does not correlate with ranking of school attendance (Krishna, 1996, 99). A Sri Lankan study showed nonworking male students missing school more often than their working counterparts (Guarcello, et al., 2005, 14, 25). Other studies suggest that part-time work has little if any effect on school attendance. Indeed, income from work sometimes covers school expenses and makes schooling possible.

We question the usefulness of summary statistics from studies—like the ILO study by Allais and Hagemann (2008)—that take no account of particulars such as school availability and quality or the situations of particular children, and yet make sweeping assertions of a generalized causal relationship. Labor-force and household surveys typically do not include information that could inform researchers about school availability or quality, or the experiences of the enumerated children in their schools. In such cases, researchers do not have enough information to determine whether working causes children to miss school, or whether a poor learning environment at school leads children to search for other activities.

When work becomes full-time rather than part-time,[6] there is a dramatic reduction in numbers of children who continue to attend school. Whether the work in question is labor-force work or household work, long hours of work are associated with lower school attendance (Edmonds, 2008, 3641, 3944). Again, the challenge is to figure out what causes what. We will return to the question of whether these working children are not in school because they have full-time jobs outside, or whether they find jobs because they are not in school. Case studies point to causality working in both directions (e.g., Lieten, et al., 2005).

In some situations, studies show convincingly that necessary work keeps young people away from school. In chapter 2, we mentioned caring work, which is particularly widespread in countries affected by the epidemic of AIDS. Other studies have indicated that heavy involvement in domestic work, particularly by girls, can interfere with education (Levison, et al., 2001; Assaad, et al., 2010). Seasonal work on family farms or caring for livestock may keep children from school on an occasional or temporary basis, and in some cases such work prevents schooling altogether. Waged work can have a similar effect: in Muranga, Kenya, when a quarry opened and employed children, 20 percent of pupils dropped out of the local primary school within weeks (Andvig, 1998, 339). But enrolment rates were dropping in Kenya generally at that time, which suggests that available schooling was losing its perceived net value, making alternative occupations more attractive.

We presented evidence in chapter 4 that children are particularly likely to be withdrawn from school and pushed into waged employment when the family suffers a crisis, such as the permanent or temporary loss of a bread-winner, or the destruction of crops by drought or some other hazard. The following case illustrates this point.

Catherine was eleven years old, and had dropped out of school to run a stall on the streets of Harare, Zimbabwe, for which she started work at six in the morning. She was living in two rooms with her elder sister, who had one more year to complete in secondary school, and her mother. They had fled an abusive father, and her mother had been supporting the family through a small fruit and vegetable store, which she ran near a bus terminus in the city center, until she became seriously ill and bedridden. Catherine agreed to stop her schooling to run the stall and enable her sister to complete her examinations at secondary school. Then her sister would be able to support Catherine through school. At this time, Catherine was the bread-winner for the family, helped by her elder sister when she was free, and occasionally by her mother when she was able. She also acknowledged the support of women with stalls near hers, commenting, "These women are like mother hens to me" (Bourdillon and Rurevo, 2003, 42–45).

In the short term, Catherine perceived her family's needs as more important than her schooling. Barbara Rogoff has pointed out that in Appalachian communities in the United States, commitments to other people frequently take precedence over school, and in hard times youth may leave school to help to hold things together (Rogoff, 2003, 23). Here, as many studies have shown elsewhere, school is valued, but in difficult circumstances other things take precedence.

Among marginalized groups in India, although rates of attendance at school are relatively low, nearly all parents say that they value education for their children, very few of whom have no schooling at all. But many children drop out, a quarter to a half of these for work or economic reasons, and many others because they had failed or were no longer interested in school (Nambissan, 2003; Sanon, 1998, 95; Nangia and Khan, 2002, 328). Dréze and Sen point out that in India exclusion from school is far more extensive than "child labor," and argue that it "would be quite wrong . . . to view the average out-of-school child as a victim of rigid work responsibilities" (2002, 157). Generally, poor school performance can result in lower attendance at school (Bhalotra, 2003, 42). Surveys of children in eleven countries showed only a minority of children giving work as the reason for their failure to attend school (Dorman, 2008, 26–27, table 12). A study in Egypt showed that children with greater achievement in school tended to stay longer in school (Hanushek, et al., 2006, 27). Many studies have shown children dropping out of school because of costs or for some other reason (see, e.g., Prakash, 2002, 276).

Several studies confirm that incentives for children to attend school (like the PROGRESA program, above) result in fewer children in full-time work, and less time spent in part-time work. In Bangladesh, for example, a program to provide stipends for children attending school resulted in a large increase in the number of children attending school, and a small but statistically significant reduction of children's paid work (Ravallion and Wodon, 2000). The converse, however, has not been shown to be generally true: we know of no study that shows children entering school simply because they are barred from paid employment.

In summary, part-time work does not necessarily keep children away from school. Although full-time employment does compete with school, frequently this provides an occupation for children already out of school for other reasons. In certain situations, economic or domestic work is deemed essential to livelihood and therefore more important than school; in these cases it seems more precise to say that poverty (or another difficulty) was the impediment to school, rather than blaming the work.

Does Work Take Time Away from School Work?

When school pupils take on part-time work, is it appropriate to assume that this takes time from school work? Some research supports this assumption. A study in India shows that domestic and farm chores of marginalized children sometimes interfere with time available for school. Children arrive late after attending to domestic animals and attend irregularly during peak harvesting seasons (Nambissan, 2003, 122–123). A study in Tanzania suggested an overall trade-off between hours of study and hours of work (including domestic work), although the two are not always directly related (Akabayashi and Psacharopoulos, 1999, 133–134).

Nevertheless, careful research, such as the *Youth Development Study* in the U.S.A., which we discuss below, shows that school and work are frequently not in direct competition for time. Adolescents found time for jobs by spending less time on such passive activities as watching television or "hanging around," and teenagers negotiated with employers to ensure they had time for schoolwork when they needed it (Mortimer, 2007, 97–110, 177–178). In a Scottish study, part-time workers were slightly more likely than nonworkers to miss an occasional lesson or day of school, but no more likely to skip school for days or weeks at a time (Howieson, et al., 2006, 39). As in the Bangladesh study described above, a reduction in the costs of schooling in Pakistan showed an increase in school attendance and a smaller reduction in paid work, suggesting that school takes time from leisure activities as well as from work (Hazarika and Bedi, 2003, 55). Overall, it is too simplistic to assume a one-to-one relationship between time spent working and time in school and studying. The actual relationship depends at least on the type of work and the context of the work.

Does Work Affect School Performance?

Even when outside work does not keep children away from school, it might sap their energy or deprive them of sleep, resulting in poor school performance. Several studies have looked at the relationship between part-time work and school performance and found links between them. Results vary with context, particularly between countries. Studies in Britain and the U.S.A. suggest that up to ten hours of work a week do not normally adversely affect the performance of children at school, and can sometimes even enhance it (Stack and McKechnie, 2002, 99; Post and Pong, 2009, 112). The effects of larger amounts of working time remain disputed and depend on circumstances, particularly the kinds of work available and the flexibility of the school system.

A study in Turkey showed working children to be more likely than their nonworking counterparts to achieve "unsatisfactory" marks in mid-term examinations (Guarcello, et al., 2005, 32). A Tanzanian study suggested an inverse relationship between hours of work (including such domestic work as collecting fuel and water) and skills of reading and writing (as assessed by household heads) (Akabayashi and Psacharopoulos, 1999). Data from Bolivia and Venezuela showed working children to be more likely to be failing in school (Psacharopoulos, 1997). Other studies suggest that all work, including the housework of girls, has such effects (Guarcello, Lyon, et al., 2007, 68).

On the other hand, a Brazilian study showed working children performing better than their nonworking counterparts. In Sri Lanka, work appeared unrelated to performance in mid-year and end-of-year examinations. In Brazil work appeared to have little impact on how tired children felt in class, and in Kenya nonworking children were more likely than their working peers to report often feeling "tired" in class (Guarcello, et al., 2005, 8, 25, 1). A study in Scotland showed little difference in pupils' involvement in part-time work according to their Standard Grade level. It also found that pupils who were positive in their attitudes toward school were more likely to have a part-time job than were pupils who were more negative about their school experience (Howieson, et al., 2006, 44).

Problems of Causality

Although we cannot generalize, in specific situations several statistical studies have shown significant inverse correlations between work and school attendance and/or performance.[7] When a particular study shows that children who spend more time in paid employment do less well on average in school, and those who do well in school spend on average less time in employment, this does not necessarily mean that the work causes children to do badly at school. Researchers who assume the conventional wisdom that work stops children from attending school or performing well at school fail to consider that children may be driven to work by failures in the school system.[8]

Although a correlation between two variables cannot on its own indicate a causal relationship between them, consideration of further variables may sometimes allow reasonable inferences about causality (Pearl, 2000, especially 41–64, chapter 2). One way statistics can establish a connection between school performance and outside work is to control for variables that might relate to both, such as poverty or education of parents, which have been shown to correlate both with performance at school and the incidence of work. When good information is available it is possible to compare these various relationships, and where the relationship between school performance and outside work cannot be fully explained by other factors, this suggests a more direct link between them. But it does not indicate how the link works.

Some researchers, however, have questioned the direction of causality between work and educational outcomes. A simple way to do this is to look at specific variables. For example, Pedro Goulart and Arjun Bedi controlled for interest in school. They reasoned that when children had little interest in school, poor performance is likely to push them into work outside school; but that when they were interested in school, they argued it was work that caused poor results (Goulart and Bedi, 2007). Some children, however, may be interested in school, perform badly for a variety of reasons, and subsequently seek more positive experiences outside school, so still there is no certainty of the direction of causality.

A more complex statistical technique tries to establish the direction of causality through the use of "instrumental variables." The mathematical procedures can be left to experts, but the logic and validity of an instrument are easier to follow and to scrutinize. Variable A (say, work) relates to variable B (say, educational achievement). We suspect that work is related to achievement, but we do not know whether the relation is causal, and, if so, in which direction causality works. So we take variable C, which must fulfill two conditions. First, C must have an effect on child work (but not vice-versa). Second, C cannot affect educational achievement directly in this context. So if a correlation is established between C and achievement, it can only be by means of a causal chain through work.

We take one example by Kathleen Beegle and her coauthors, who use two instruments in their study of data from two Vietnam surveys five years apart (Beegle, et al., 2005). They argue that children's work does not affect rice prices, but that higher prices can affect their work. High prices result in more rice being grown; this could mean more work for children, or the greater income from rice could mean less compulsion for children to work. Either way, there should be a one-way causal effect. Thus, rice prices meet the first condition for an instrumental variable. The authors argue that rice prices meet the second condition as well, since they do not affect school attainment in any way except through work; they controlled for structural features that they thought might link rice prices to school attainment (p. 13). Natural disasters—the second instrumental variable—can affect the productive work for children by disrupting productive technology, or by disrupting household economies in ways that lead them to rely to a greater extent on children's work. The authors argue that the natural disasters occurring at the time were transitory and unlikely to affect school attainment directly. Since these two instruments are linked with lower school attainment, the authors argue that this can only be the result of children's work. They conclude that work lowers attainment at school for a significant number of children.[9] This is a creative way of getting around the difficult problem of what causes what, although of course any conclusions drawn from this kind of study cannot be stronger than the validity of the instruments used.

The Youth Development Study in the United States

Another way of determining the effects of work on children's educational attainment is through panel studies that collect information on the same children over a number of years. For the past twenty years, Jeylan Mortimer has led the *Youth Development Study*, which followed the same children as they grew from early teens through to adulthood, a procedure that is expensive in time and resources and takes many years to complete.[10]

Mortimer and her team selected a random sample of about a thousand boys and girls attending the ninth grade in the city of Saint Paul, Minnesota. In early

1988, they started collecting data about these students—then aged fourteen to fifteen—and her survey team has continued to collect further information from them and their families every year or two since then. The students were similar to students around the United States with respect to demographic, economic, and work-related characteristics. Three-quarters of the original sample were still being tracked at the time of the reports we use, sixteen years after the study started. Among other things, the team collected details about the jobs the adolescents had, how many weeks they worked in those jobs, how many hours they worked, their other activities, and background information on home and school. They heard what these young people themselves had to say about school and their jobs. The research also followed the students' educational progress, their jobs as young adults, their earnings as they matured, and many other aspects of their lives (Mortimer, 2003; 2007).[11]

Mortimer emphasized four areas in which the information collected in the study challenges the conventional wisdom of experts.[12] We considered one of these in chapter 5, namely, the concern that teenage work can create stress: the other three follow.

Some experts have argued that teenage jobs are usually dull and repetitive and offer little opportunity for learning, and that this kind of job does nothing to encourage a positive orientation toward work (e.g., Greenberger and Steinberg, 1985, 125). The *Youth Development Study,* however, showed that teenagers usually move from initially simple jobs to more complex and responsible work as they gain in experience. They generally have a positive attitude to their jobs and most claim to learn something from them. As they grow in experience of paid work, they become aware of different kinds of rewards from it, such as opportunities to be useful and to express their interests.

Another conventional assumption challenged by the *Youth Development Study* is that teenage work interferes with high-school achievement. The researchers examined all of the children's activities, and noticed how children changed the amount of time spent in these as they grew. As pointed out above, time for jobs came largely from passive activities, and adolescents ensured adequate time for school work. The study found no evidence that jobs generally took time away from school-related activities.

Furthermore, when account is taken of academic performance prior to working, and their social background, there was no evidence that work—even intensive work—lowered academic achievement. Indeed, for one group, namely white males, those who had regular jobs during adolescence were more likely than others to end up with a university degree (Mortimer, 2003, 187).

The third article of conventional wisdom challenged by Mortimer's study is that teenage work has a negative impact on socioeconomic attainment in adulthood, or at least early adulthood. The study indicated that those who engaged in regular jobs in adolescence were more likely than others to settle quickly into career-oriented work, and experience less unemployment. The experience of combining paid work and school seemed also to pay dividends in helping them to cope with college education, especially when they had to contribute to its costs through their own earnings (Staff and Mortimer, 2007).

Mortimer's work has important practical implications. As a recognized expert in child and youth development in the U.S.A., she was invited onto the Committee on the Health and Safety Implications of Child Labor of the *National Research Council* and *Institute of Medicine*. When the committee gathered to make recommendations on how many hours of paid work is typically problematic for adolescents, a common view was that more than twenty hours per week of work should not be allowed for school pupils under the age of eighteen. Some findings of the *Youth Development Study*, however, led Mortimer to block a unanimous recommendation.

Mortimer's study included students who benefited from steady jobs occupying more than twenty hours per week. Although these were a small minority when children were younger, they comprised about a quarter in their final year at school. These youth had on average poorer grades than other students, and they sometimes admitted that their jobs hindered their school work. But the study showed that they were achieving low grades before they found employment and that their grades did not deteriorate further,[13] suggesting that paid work was a response to, rather than the cause of, poor performance at school. This group, like most children, valued what they learned at school, but they usually also had a very positive attitude to their jobs, saying that these taught them things they did not learn at school. They were generally able to settle quickly into their careers after leaving school: four years later, they had the highest average incomes—although those acquiring professional qualifications overtook them later (Mortimer, 2003, 56, 76, 192–196). Mortimer argued that for youth who enter high school "with little educational promise, . . . little interest in school, relatively poor achievement, and lower educational aspirations," steady paid work, even if relatively intensive, seems to provide the motivation and skills that they need to complete high school and sometimes to continue with higher education (Mortimer, 2007, 121). She was afraid that some of these, already disadvantaged in a system where childhood is focused on formal schooling, would drop out of school altogether if their hours of paid work were limited.

The *Youth Development Study* underscores that young people have different needs and characteristics. The study showed different responses to paid work among girls and boys: boys tended to work more hours, earn more, find more challenging jobs, and have more stress from work than did girls (Mortimer, 2003, 55, 68–69). Minority status decreased the likelihood of a steady work pattern in high school (perhaps because of discrimination by employers), as did having parents who were less educated or families that were not "intact" (Mortimer, 2003, 123, 128). Children differ in needs according to competencies and age. When policies are applied in a way that ignores such differences, some children are likely to be deprived of useful opportunities—and often those in most need of support suffer the greatest loss.

Mortimer came to this conclusion:

> Almost all adolescents in the United States do paid work for considerable periods of time while attending high school. . . . Students seek these jobs so they can have their own spending money, save money for college, and engage in sometimes expensive adolescent lifestyles. Some are helping to support their families. Most American parents encourage their children to work because they think that employment has benefits for them that are not usually obtained in school. Most important, they believe that working will teach their children to be self-reliant and to obtain general knowledge about the workplace (how to act at work, what to wear, the need to be on time, etc.), pertinent skills (especially "people skills" fostering smooth interpersonal relations), and positive work orientations (a positive work ethic and recognizing the importance of being able to take responsibility when others depend on you) that will enable them to participate effectively in this sphere in the future. (Mortimer, 2007, II.)

This depicts steady work outside school as part of the formation of adolescents—education in its broadest sense.

Mortimer's findings from the U.S.A. cannot be transferred to other countries with their very different conditions of work, education, and childhood. Nor do they tell us about the effects of work on younger children, which are also a concern of this book. But it does show that we cannot simply assume that time and energy spent on work detracts from education. It also alerts us to the need to consider the benefits of different kinds of work, and not to focus only on potential harm.

Combining Labor-Force Work with School

Akram was around twelve years old. He used to work in a garment factory in Bangladesh, cutting loose threads, because his parents could not afford school expenses. After being fired from the factory as an under-age worker, he was placed in a school to accommodate children who had lost their jobs, and received a subsidy of about half of what he had been earning. He made up the difference buying eggs wholesale and selling them at a profit, which he gave to his mother for food for the family (keeping a little for pocket money). He said this was better than his previous work, because he could work at his own pace, no one scolded him, and he could combine it with school (Bissell, 2005, 377–378). We shall discuss the intervention in Bangladesh in chapter 9.

In practice, most of the world's working children also receive at least a primary education. Thus for most children, productive work and schooling are already compatible in practice, although not always easily so. This partly depends on the nature of work and the flexibility of the school system. In France, a primary school child is likely to leave home at 8:30 and return at 5:00, and a secondary school child might leave an hour earlier and return an hour later, taking up over ten hours of the day. In other countries, primary schooling takes up less than four hours a day. In Vietnam, more than 90 percent of children in rural areas attend schools operating in shifts with an average class time of only 3 hours and 10 minutes per day (Glewwe, 2004). Secondary schooling may occupy half a day, leaving plenty of time before or after for other activities. In countries with rigid educational systems, it is more difficult to combine work and school than it is in countries with more relaxed and flexible systems.[14]

Work and school can be combined more systematically. At the beginning of this chapter, we described earn-and-learn schools in Zimbabwe, where schooling is connected to work. In other contexts, employers have provided education for their child workers (we shall present examples of this in chapter 9).

Many young people have to earn money to see themselves through school. In a survey of working children in Ibadan, Nigeria, 46 percent said they were working to help their families, and 43 percent said that they were working to earn money for school (Omokhodion, et al., 2006, 284). In Madagascar, those who have no secondary school near their own homes have to travel to the towns, perhaps on a weekly basis, and support themselves through school. Leslie Sharp (1996) describes how three young school pupils ran a bread stall to maintain themselves through secondary school, eventually learning how to manage their business to allow sufficient time for schoolwork. While teachers regarded such workers as uncommitted to schoolwork, these working pupils were highly respected in their own communities for saving their parents the humiliation of seeking subservient employment to cover their children's expenses.

We have suggested that society has an obligation to provide appropriate education for children who have other important demands on their time. In practice education for working children has largely been instigated in informal schools, outside the state educational system and sometimes cooperating with it. We believe that the state has an obligation to provide appropriate education, and that appropriate schools should be incorporated into the formal system.

There are numerous examples of appropriate education, with content and times adapted to the needs of working children.[15] Talib shows how schools in rural India can be flexible to allow children to continue with necessary work for their families and still receive an education (Talib, 2003). In Bangladesh, a nonformal system of education produced good results from negotiating the hours of schooling with parents: it provided many working children with education and fed some of them into the formal system (Chowdhury, 2003). In India too, informal schools cater to working children and provide a bridge to formal schooling (e.g., Rajagopal, 2003; CINI-ASHA, 2003). Informal schools can, in some cases, produce results that match those of formal schools. The MANTHOC project in Peru organized schools operating near where the children work, with hours suitable to them, and operating a module system that enables the children to progress at their own pace even if they miss some classes. In these schools, teachers incorporate and build on what children learn through their work, producing positive learning results in the children (Delap, 2004, 7–9). Such an educational system, targeted for working children, can teach protection from abuse and hazards at work and it can be combined with social support for the children.

Part-time education has disadvantages. Informal schools may divert attention away from the exploitation of children, or even appear to justify such exploitation. Another danger is that these schools may simply be inadequate, illustrated by evening schools to accommodate working children in Bolivia (den Berge, 2004, 111–116). The facilities were poor, teachers did not always attend, and they did not always respect the children. They were supposed to cover the standard school syllabus, although children only attended for two hours an evening and many repeatedly missed classes on account of their work. This alternative education was simply poor education. On the other hand, where the formal system is poor, informal schools can be an improvement: a study in Pakistan showed children in informal schools being livelier and more alert than their counterparts in formal government schools (Khan, 2007, 185).

Learning through Work

In chapter 2, and more systematically in chapter 5, we pointed out that children learn through work. In many communities, working alongside adults during the school-age years is the only available way to learn farming and craft skills that are needed for access to livelihoods upon completion of school. In certain Mexican communities, children are introduced to the wider world through work with parents in seasonal employment (Bey, 2003). Child street traders in Nigeria acquired knowledge of their socioeconomic milieu and useful interpersonal skills; they were dominant in leadership roles in their schools (Oloko, 1993; 1989, 21). Child street workers in Guatemala City claimed to learn entrepreneurial and social skills that would enable them to improve their incomes and social standing in the future (Offit, 2008, 162–3). Children often claim to pick up many skills through part-time employment. For some children, what they learn through work may be at least as important as their grades in academic subjects, and rewards received from such learning are usually more immediate.

Co-operative Education

In many industrial countries, such learning is incorporated into the formal school system in what is called "co-operative education": schools arrange with employers to take on pupils in various kinds of safe work, under the combined supervision of employers and teachers and as part of the school curriculum. In the United States, many schools require unpaid work in community service before pupils graduate. A report on part-time employment of pupils in Scotland recommended that instead of ignoring the work experience of children, teachers should incorporate and use this in the overall education of their pupils, a recommendation that had general support from pupils and their parents, teachers and other educationalists, and employers. Too close a link, however, between productive work and school may interfere with the effectiveness of independent work experience (Howieson, et al., 2006, 227, 230–231).

We mentioned education-with-production schemes in the 1970s and 1980s. In southern Africa, there were several successful programs for learning through productive work. The best-known case was the "Swaneng Hill model" in Botswana, which organized students into "brigades" to generate both learning and income. Program sustainability, however, required incorporation into the government educational system, which in turn put pressure on the work-with-study brigades to adapt to the study-only model of formal Western education. Incorporating productive work into an inappropriate formal education framework proved too difficult for educational bureaucracies. It was a problem in trying to adapt an African approach to a colonial institutional model. The effort collapsed (Myers, 2001b, 324–325; Gustafsson, 1987).

Work can be the means for learning the particular skills of many crafts or trades. Academic schooling is not always the best way to provide opportunities for future employment, whether because of the quality of the schooling, the aptitudes of particular pupils, or the nature of the local employment market. Some people instead opt for some kind of vocational training, which involves a strong practical element (Whitehead, et al., 2007, 29). Indeed, vocational schools have sometimes been established in an attempt to reduce youth unemployment (for brief pointers to some examples, see Winrock International, 2008, 115–143).

Apprenticeship

Individuals may learn a particular trade or career through formal or informal apprenticeship, in which the student moves from observation and peripheral participation to full and guided participation in the activities of the craft under the guidance of an established master. In chapter 5, we mentioned apprenticeship as a model for learning. Although apprenticeships do not always exclude girls, they typically cater to boys.

To illustrate informal apprenticeship, among the Kyrgyz nomads in Central Asia, a child might become a tent maker by watching and helping a master, who may be his father or some other relative. The child learns how to care for the trees that provide the wood, how to form the wood, and how to make the roofing. It takes only a month to make one tent, but the apprentice must stay with the master for a year, at the end of which he will be given equipment and told to work on his own (Bunn, 1999, 80).

Historically in Europe, the apprenticeship system provided training in skills by a master craftsman in exchange for labor. In spite of some decline in the nineteenth and twentieth centuries, the system remains in a modified form in Europe (H. Hansen, 2004; Aldrich, 1999). In Germany, the current apprenticeship system links into the system of formal schooling. Typically, the apprenticeship starts at the age of sixteen or older. The apprentices receive a low wage for their work, which underscores the fact they are still primarily learners rather than workers. While they receive training at work in a particular occupation under an experienced craftsman with teaching qualifications, they also spend one or two days each week in school. The state pays for the apprentices' schooling and the salaries of their teachers (D. M. Hansen, et al., 2001, 133–136).

Elsewhere, apprenticeships are not so well controlled. While the tradition of apprenticeships provides an avenue for admission into a career, or at least a job, it is often also a means of exploiting cheap labor. In chapter 1, we introduced young girls apprenticed into the textile industry in Morocco, who were supposed to have limited hours of work, training in their work, and time to attend classes; these rules appear to have been largely ignored. In West Africa, common forms of apprenticeship for girls include sewing, embroidery, weaving, tailoring, and knitting; boys apprentice in mechanics, carpentry, welding, and other forms of metal work, fishing, tailoring, and as assistants on trucks (Riisøen, et al., 2004, 22). Apprentices are paid little or nothing: typically, the families of an apprentice pay a fee to the teacher for the training. Sometimes they have to buy their tools, which they are not always allowed to keep, and there may be further payments to be made for the receipt of a certificate of qualification and release from the master. Sometimes they receive accommodation and meals, both of which vary in quality. Apprentices are often treated with scant respect and are frequently beaten. Rarely are their tasks clearly defined, and include cleaning the workplace, watching over it during the night, and often performing domestic and even agricultural work for their masters. Most apprentices start in their middle to late teens, for a period of two to three years, but there are wide variations, depending on teachers and local cultures (Morice, 1982). In Senegal, apprenticeship for tailoring can last up to ten years, starting as young as ten years old and excluding formal schooling (Bass, 1996).

The apprenticeship is sometimes subsumed into a form of fostering, in which the master takes responsibility for the apprentice. Indeed, in many situations learning a trade is subsumed into joining the household of the master. In Nigeria, parents try to find people to whom they can foster out their children, as a way of finding them an urban footing and learning a trade (Bass, 2004, 23–34). For all their potential shortcomings, apprenticeship systems can be an effective way for children to learn a trade, enter a network of trading contacts, and ensure gainful employment in adulthood.

Conclusion

The world, governments and civil society alike, should be embarrassed by its failure to educate so many of its children. The evidence on the whole, however, does not support the assumption that children's work generally is hindering the achievement of the Millennium Development Goal of education for all. To achieve this, it is necessary to improve the quality and accessibility of schools to meet the appreciation and expectations of the vast majority of children and their parents.

By "educate" we do not refer only to formal schooling. While school work is the dominant means of acquiring knowledge to participate in the modern world, it is not the only, nor always the best, means. A narrow focus on academic schooling sometimes diverts attention from general life-skills education—the broad development of the child to his or her fullest potential.

Effective education requires a combination of school, work, and play. It cannot be assumed that work necessarily interferes with schooling. In those situations where school and work appear to be in tension, the benefits of each should be assessed to establish priorities. Rather than focusing on the elimination of work, intervention would better serve children's interests by ensuring that schools attend to education in its broadest sense. For this, they must accommodate other needs of children, including the need to work, and they must become places in which children want to be and to learn. In particular, education should empower children to take control of their lives, first by understanding the situation in which they live and then by finding ways to improve it. This is the subject of the next chapter.

7

Children Acting for Themselves

Thembisa was thirteen years old, living in South Africa with her younger brothers aged seven and two. Their mother worked away from home and returned only once a month for a weekend. This is how Thembisa described her life.

> In the morning I wake up and make the fire. I warm up the water and then bathe my youngest brother. My mother is away working: she comes at the end of the month. Then I go take my brother to a neighbor and I go to school with my other brother. After school I fetch my little brother and then go home and collect water, make a fire and wash the clothes and clean the house and cook supper.
>
> I like to wash the dishes. I like washing the clothes and cleaning the rooms. I don't like to look after children. Looking after children makes me not to have time to play.
>
> I feel not good about the children, if they are sick then I have to take them to the clinic. I do it after school. But all the time I am at school I do not manage to concentrate because I am thinking. But there is nothing I can do because I need education. My brothers don't cry for my mother as they are used to this life. My mother only manages to come at the end of the month. (Clacherty, 2002, 37.)[1]

Here we find a child who is supported economically but takes responsibility for running the household. She is constrained by her mother's means of livelihood to perform various tasks, but within the constraints she is constantly responding to situations that face her. She makes many responsible decisions, but her life choices—her agency—are severely restricted.

In chapter 2, we pointed out that children often choose their work. Chapter 5 showed how children grow and learn by actively participating in actions around them. The previous chapter pointed to education as empowerment through understanding. Repeatedly, we see children not as passive victims, but as people who, from a very young age, engage with the situations that face them and with the people they meet. This chapter focuses on the agency of children, by which we mean their capacity to choose and act on the world around them. We consider agency and its limitations in three areas in which children act on their own: children living on city streets, children traveling on their own away from home, and children's organizations. We then go on to consider ways of empowering children by encouraging their participation in making decisions that affect their lives.

Agency of Children

Chapter 5 shows how children develop by doing things, by reacting to their social and material environment. Agency refers to the ability of people to make effective choices, particularly in responding to opportunities. Social structures and the physical environment limit the possibilities open to an individual, who might still exercise agency in responses to such constraints. Agency can be limited by constraints and structures, but only in extremely debilitating cases is it removed entirely. Thembisa, introduced at the beginning of this chapter, had little choice about her overall situation, which was largely decided by her mother, but Thembisa still exercised some agency in the responsible decisions she made in running the home and caring for her siblings. An issue is how to allow children to be proactive in developing their lives rather than simply reactive, how to empower them in the fuller exercise of agency.

The Romantic view of childhood as a time for freedom from responsibility and for instruction from adults denies the possibility that children may choose how to develop their lives. Agency is ignored when it is assumed that children have no role in deciding whether or not to work. Many studies by economists, for example, assume that decisions about dividing children's time between work, school, and play are rational responses of "households" or parents to particular situations (Levison, 2000). Applied economists, who typically take quantitative data collected for other purposes and then use that data to study children's work and schooling, do not have information on children's actions and preferences.[2] Moreover, abstract economic theory provides very limited direction for actors in real situations of complex, repeated bargaining—like negotiations among family members. Organizations, like the ILO and the World Bank, that rely heavily on such theory often pay inadequate attention to children's agency. Such neglect of children's contributions to their own lives is contradicted by situations in which children are compelled to fend for themselves.

There are demographic factors that make it difficult for children in low-income countries to rely on adult support. In these countries, 31 percent of the population were younger than fifteen in 2005 (and 41 percent in Africa), compared with 17 percent in high-income countries.[3] The populations of sub-Saharan Africa's countries are increasing at a rate of 2.5 percent per year[4] (that is, doubling in 28 years), imposing severe challenges to economic development in general and to education in particular. Many children are without adult support. Sub-Saharan Africa had just over forty-eight million orphans under the age of eighteen in 2005. Of these, just over nine million had lost both parents, approximately one in forty of all children (from UNICEF, 2006, 36, table 2), resulting in large numbers of child-headed households in many countries. The devastation of HIV/AIDS means that many other children live with incapacitated parents, becoming effective heads of household and the principle breadwinners for their families.

When children do not have adequate adult support, they must do more for themselves. Judith Ennew, a leading expert on research with children, has pointed out that in any work with children, a significant barrier is often the attitudes of adults, and "the main resource in any project is the children themselves" (Ennew, 1994a, 7). Rescue that fails to engage the children and offers them no chance to exercise agency can itself be traumatic. On the other hand productive work can enable them to establish some control over their lives in contexts where the world of adults has failed to provide for them. A thirteen-year-old orphan from the Mozambican civil war had this to say about what he had missed most during his period of traumatic bereavement, displacement, and "rescue" in a refugee camp in Malawi: "The thing I hated most in Malawi was that I had no garden. I had no place where I could go and dig up my own food; but now I have a field and I have planted it with sugar cane and cassava . . ." (Gibbs, 1994, 272.)

Street Children

Research on street children in the 1970s and 1980s showed them finding ways to deal with the oppressive environment in which they lived. The fact that many children chose to live in the street challenged common assumptions that all children lived under the protection and control of adults and could generally be regarded as passive victims (Hart, 1997, 14–15). These children have been badly failed by the adult world and have taken their lives into their own hands.

Some young people living and working on city streets have homes to return to occasionally, or periodically, or regularly. Some receive emotional and practical support on the streets by older family members, who are themselves impoverished and homeless. Some have been orphaned or deserted by their families. Many have made their own decision to leave home, often because of extreme poverty or violence and abuse at home (Felsman, 1984; Tyldum, et al., 2005, 37–41). A small minority flee tensions at home created by their own deviant behavior, or are drawn by an illusion of free and exciting life on the streets.

One reason for young people to come onto the streets is to find a space where they can exercise choices free of the adult control that dominates schools, clubs, and families.[5] They come onto the streets to associate with peers and to play, to work, and even sometimes to live (Connolly and Ennew, 1996a, 135). In some cases, they may even emphasize the marginalized and dangerous character attributed to them by wider society in order to protect their space from intrusion and interference (Davies, 2008, 320–321). The boundary between children who spend much time working and playing on the streets and children who live on the streets with no other permanent home is not always clear: children can drift between spending more or less time on the streets.[6]

While children may exercise some agency in deciding to go onto the streets, they can lose control over their lives in conditions of extreme degradation. Older persons may exploit children, demanding a share of income—or sexual favors—in exchange for support or protection or to be allowed to work a particular patch. Street children suffer harassment, violence, even death, from others on the streets, including other children, and sometimes from officials.[7] Many find themselves powerless to change their situation and resort to crime to stay alive, or destroy themselves with drugs (e.g., Gigengack, 2006, 200–213).

Others learn to cope, perhaps with the help of peers, or older kin, or adults. They find work that provides income and may eventually enable them to move off the streets. Paid work is necessary for survival, but can also provide a sense of accomplishment. Carrying goods for shoppers and for others at terminuses is a widespread activity. Polishing shoes is common, for which the child needs to be established with a stand and basic cleaning tools and polish. In Lima a low-income and low-status form of work is washing car windshields and requesting payment; children prefer to work on well-kept cars that need little if any cleaning, whose owners are likely to be wealthy and generous (Invernizzi, 2001, 45). Such work may earn a little capital to allow the young person to establish a more lucrative trading enterprise. In Belgrade, children and even adults cleaning windshields bring young children into their teams to gain sympathy and larger tips (Žegarac, 2007, 107). Some children simply beg for an income, perhaps utilizing and coordinating even younger children to gain sympathy. In some African cities, children and youths earn an income by guarding parked cars, sometimes demanding payment for unwanted services and ensuring custom by vandalizing cars not entrusted to their care.

Children achieve areas of competence that enable them to survive on the streets, while they remain incompetent in skills that might otherwise be provided by school and a secure home (e.g., Baker, 1998). Children working the streets of Hanoi, Vietnam, took pride in their independence and maintained a level of professionalism in their work. Some said that by leaving rural homes and working city streets, they acquired skills as well as material benefits for themselves and their families (Burr, 2006, 114, 72; also on Guatemala City Offit,

2008, 162–3). Survival skills are illustrated by a study in Nepal that showed street children to be stronger in indices of growth and nourishment than children in impoverished homes or children in a remote village (Baker, et al., 1996, 177–178).[8]

Between those who are destroyed on the streets and those who succeed is a wide range of situations, which engulf children or through which children pass. Children who are denigrated on the streets may be held in high esteem in their rural home communities when they earn enough to send home support for younger siblings (e.g. Burr, 2006, 106).

In some environments, street children fall outside traditional moral values and social structures, and develop violent and illegal strategies to survive (Droz, 2006, 352). Street children in Hilbrow, Johannesburg, on the other hand, largely upheld the moral values of the communities they came from, even if they were not always able to live by them—if you are hungry you may have to steal or prostitute yourself although you would prefer not to. These children showed themselves capable of acting with a high degree of altruism particularly in supporting each other (Swart, 1989, 74–77). A comparison between children doing similar street work in Brazil shows that those working from home usually maintain the values of their families, while those living on the street are more dependent on peers for support and more likely to get involved in criminal activity (Campos, et al., 1994). Different contexts produce different results.

Children usually team up with peers on the streets, forming supportive gangs, under the leadership of an older person, sometimes on a passing and temporary basis, and sometimes forming relatively stable relationships. A study in Colombo, Sri Lanka, showed children finding in group leaders and companions the care that they had lacked at home (Hanssen, 1996; see also Burr, 2006, 113, 115–116). The social support of peers enables them to acquire competence to live on the streets and can provide feelings of self-esteem and well-being. In the absence of other supportive social networks, children on the street often provide each other with concern and affection, sometimes developing into sexual relationships and forming young families. They provide company and moral support, as well as protection against bullying by other children and against extortion from predatory adults such as petty criminals, exploitative employers, and violent or corrupt authorities. These relationships often result in altruistic activities benefiting others, when, for example, children care for sick friends. The relationships in these peer groups can help provide children's lives with meaning, order, and self efficacy that they do not receive from adult society; on the other hand, some behavior that seems maladaptive to outsiders, such as taking drugs, may be perceived by the children as adaptive strategies to maintain relations with a support group (Ennew, 1994b; Aptekar, 1989, 79–114; Swart, 1989, 74–77; Gigengack, 2006, 232–293; Kombarakaran, 2004). To disrupt the social support network of any child can be traumatic: street children are particularly vulnerable since their empowering support networks go largely unrecognized, whether they involve peers or other adults on the streets.

Social services, whether by government or NGOs, frequently focus on rescue, ignoring what children do for themselves with support from their networks. Often, service organizations do not have the conceptual framework to handle the different relationships and life styles that young people develop on the streets. Adults may regard relationships with street peers as problematic, hindering "rehabilitation." Common forms of rescue can cause further stress by cutting children off from their supporting networks. Gigengack reported on Lupita, a teenage street child in Mexico City, who once complained that Padre Oberón[9] was willing to baptise her two toddlers only if they were placed in one of his baby centers, if Lupita herself would enter a foster home for girls, and if Julio, her husband, would go to a shelter for boys (2006, 87–88). Such interventions diminish the agency of children and fail to respect their experiences and efforts to improve their lives.

Children may, nevertheless, utilize services for temporary relief from stresses at home or on the streets. The security provided by shelters compensates— at least for a time—for the rules that must be observed (Aptekar, 1989, 38; Gigengack, 2006, 89). Indeed, some shelters provide support while respecting the autonomy of children and their reasons for being on the streets (Baufumé, 2001). Other initiatives provide support—particularly schooling, skills training, and education in rights—that fits into the street life of the children (see Volpi, 2003).

Street Kids International (mentioned in chapter 3) provides an example of intervention that respects the agency and achievements of the children. It arose out of supporting street children in Khartoum, Sudan, by helping them establish reliable and regular incomes, and establishing schools they could attend in the evenings. The organization's policy is to encourage street educators to engage children on their own turf and to support them in transforming their own lives.

Independent Migration

Migration for economic or social purposes is another way in which children evidently exercise agency—to be distinguished from "trafficking" in which they have no agency. In many situations, young people migrate without accompanying adults, in search of better incomes, better lives, better schooling, or simply for broader experience. Such movement may take place between rural areas to gain access to the better resources of a particular area, including better agricultural conditions and food security. More frequently, movement is from rural to urban areas. Sometimes it crosses international boundaries.

In situations of dire poverty, parents might encourage, or even demand, the child to earn money away from home. We find accounts of children being sold to traffickers for domestic service or abusive work in the fishing industry or small cocoa farms in West Africa and elsewhere (Riisøen, et al., 2004, 28–31; Blanchet, 2005; Ould, et al., 2004). In a region of West Java (Indonesia), teenage girls from land-poor families are under great pressure from parents to go abroad to earn money in the sex trade, entertainment industry, or domestic service. One sixteen-year-old singer said, "Perhaps economic hardship or envy of the material success of their neighbors makes parents regard their daughter as a commodity" (B. White, et al., 2009, 16). Sometimes children are simply abducted (Human Rights Watch, 2001; Ould, et al., 2004, 49–51). Younger and more inexperienced persons are particularly vulnerable to exploitation and abuse when they have no supporting adults around them (Dottridge, 2004, 19–20).

On the other hand, many children are willing migrants. Many children give as their reason for travel a chance for a better future through income, experience, education, or other training. In a Bangladesh study, over half the child migrants asserted that they had decided to travel, and only 19 percent said the decision had been made by their parents (Whitehead, et al., 2007, 24). In a study of child migrants in Karnataka state in India, 26 percent (mostly boys aged thirteen and above) left home with little or no parental cooperation, and three quarters of these suggest conflict with parental wishes (Iversen, 2002, 821). In a Ghanaian study, the majority of migrant children had instigated the move themselves or were happy to cooperate with the suggestion from their parents. Children sometimes have to negotiate permission to migrate, especially when their desire for life elsewhere conflicts with the need for their labor at home (Whitehead, et al., 2007, 23). In practice, we find children being forced into labor migration by adults, children running away against the wishes of their guardians (who sometimes try to trace them and bring them back), and a majority of situations between these extremes, where there is negotiation and agreement between adults and child migrants, with the initiative coming from either side.

In some cases children are constrained by need. Some children speak of being neglected by their parents, sometimes meaning that their parents cannot afford to provide what they need or want. Sometimes, the movement of children between friends and kin is a strategy to overcome food insecurity, due to local failure of harvests or the need for parents to leave home for income (Waal, 1996, 43–45): fear of being separated from family can nevertheless increase the stress of children already under threat of hunger from poverty or drought (Babugura, 2008, 141). The loss of a parent leading to financial crisis is a frequent reason for a child to move (Whitehead, et al., 2007, 11). The loss of both parents is more disruptive: a study in Kenya showed orphans adapting to their situation and avoiding dependence on kin by taking up paid work, often moving away from home to do so (Nyambedha and Aagaard-Hansen, 2003). In these constrained circumstances, travel provided an opportunity to exercise agency and take some control of their lives. The collapse of local economies in Zimbabwe and Mozambique has driven many children to undergo dangerous and illegal journeys to South Africa, where they risk harsh treatment and arrest (Staunton, 2008).

Even when the need is not dire, young people might be attracted by better living standards away from home. While some suffer disappointment and disillusionment when they travel (as we point out below), many claim to profit from the experience. A seventeen-year-old who had migrated to Bangalore, India, four years previously commented, "The advantages of life as a migrant include good food, life in the city, increased income, business contacts and the opportunity to search for alternative options in the future. There are no disadvantages" (Anarfi, et al., 2006, 24).

Occasionally, movement for work provides relief from a harsh or abusive environment at home (Tyldum, et al., 2005, 37–41).[10] Tension at home might encourage a child to leave: the study in South India showed that discord in the household significantly increases the chances that a son will leave (Iversen, 2002, 828). But this does not necessarily mean a permanent break with parents: tension might arise over a particular incident such as scolding for failure at school, and contact is renewed and relations improve while the child is away.

A study in Burkina Faso shows teenage boys leaving home to work, often without parental permission, partly to attain a degree of independence and to escape oppressive control and workloads imposed by adults at home. Migrating also allowed them to negotiate a new status in their families through their financial contributions. While the initial move might be made without parental permission, it was sometimes motivated by an intention to improve the homestead and the standing of the family, which in turn brought approval for their actions later (Thorsen, 2006). In several cases, children returned home at the request of a parent to fulfill a particular need at home. Child migration, therefore, does not necessarily disrupt family relations, either immediately or subsequently (Thorsen, 2006; Whitehead, et al., 2007, 7).

Sometimes children move in the hope (not always realized) of continuing their education when this is no longer possible at home, perhaps for financial reasons. They might look for experience and training that will enhance their future prospects, particularly when they see little use in the schooling available to them. Sometimes too, they migrate to earn money for the education of younger siblings (Whitehead, et al., 2007, 28–33). In some societies, or some sections of societies, it is culturally expected that children travel for work and to gain experience (Iversen, 2002, 828). Moreover, poor rural areas may offer little to engage adolescents who are not in school. When children have nothing to do at home, especially if they are thereby getting into trouble, they may be encouraged by parents to go and find work elsewhere.

Movement often involves the cooperation of extended kin, even sometimes against the wishes of the parents. Children may travel with kin or call upon kin to provide accommodation near the place of work. In particular, children who have been orphaned may travel in search of support from a network of kin and acquaintances (Whitehead, et al., 2007, 7–9). Especially where there is a cultural tradition of children migrating to work, there is often a network between the places of work and the home community, even crossing international frontiers, which informs prospective migrants on what to expect, provides helpful contacts to make the trip a success, and enables them to keep regular contact with their homes.

Sometimes, however, the decision to move can arise from unrealistic hopes of a better life elsewhere and a lack of awareness of the risks involved. Such hopes may be fanned by false promises of access to goods and a better life by the traffickers who wish to exploit the children (Human Rights Watch, 2001, 2). Young people who have dreams of possessing luxury material goods are particularly vulnerable to such persuasions (Ivanova, et al., 2007, 43–45). Some migrants fail to achieve what they had hoped, making it too embarrassing for them to return home. In this way, many children from poor rural areas can end up struggling to survive on city streets. Since lack of knowledge—and particularly unrealistic dreams—is a key feature of those most at risk, children and communities have suggested that the most important means of preventing trafficking is to provide information to children and their families, and raise awareness of the dangers through the media (Ivanova, et al., 2007, 55, 68).

Migration from home, even when voluntary, often removes young people from their normal supportive networks, and can make them vulnerable to exploitation and abuse. When they move outside the network of acquaintances or kin, they have little chance of contacting their families or escaping harmful treatment (e.g., Human Rights Watch, 2001; Asghar, et al., 2005; Riisøen, et al., 2004, 62–69). Even the presence of kin is no guarantee of safety: a study in Ghana showed migrant children as likely to complain about their treatment when working for kin as when working for others (Hashim, 2006, 11).

Such disruptions, however, are not confined to the work situation. Even young children are sometimes removed from their homes and placed in boarding schools. Children may be removed from abusive situations at home and placed in "places of safety," which can in turn raise different problems for the children that leave them still vulnerable (e.g., Ivanova, et al., 2007, 87; Kovačević and Mirović, 2007, 112). In situations of war or natural disaster, communities are broken up and children may have to survive without the support of their families. To judge what is in the best interests of such children, we have to take into account their total life situation and available opportunities.

In practice, children have both positive and negative experiences of working away from home. We mentioned children who improved their lives and the livelihood of their families by leaving rural homes for city streets. Children who returned home after years of work away sometimes express a desire to travel again to a more fulfilling way of life (e.g., Anarfi, et al., 2006, 21). Even when they are abused away from home, they may still consider the benefits worth the suffering. Amin Hashim describes interviewing a young girl of eleven or twelve who was living away from home with her half-sister, and who burst into tears at recounting the beatings she was receiving—but she wanted to stay to earn and buy things to take home (Hashim, 2006, 17).

Children become particularly vulnerable when they move illegally across international frontiers and do not have the means to return home. The United Nations adopted in 2000 the Palermo Protocol,[11] which responds to reports of children (as well as adults) being abducted by traffickers and taken away from home on hazardous journeys to work in harmful and exploitative situations. In the case of all persons under 18, the Protocol forbids "the recruitment, transfer, harboring or receipt of a child for the purpose of exploitation"[12] even when this does not involve "the threat or use of force or other forms of coercion, of abduction, of fraud, of deception, of the abuse of power or of a position of vulnerability . . ." which are considered the defining conditions of trafficking applying to adults as subjects.

Children's experience of migration is clearly affected by whether it is undertaken willingly for a purpose, or whether it is forced and undertaken under deception. While the Palermo Protocol gives overdue attention to a serious problem, it sometimes creates further problems by focusing only on victims of trafficking while failing to consider the agency of children in migration and the reasons for which they might wish to migrate. Since it focuses only on protecting children from harm, it does not recognize the possibility that it may deprive children from low-income areas of benefits from travel. Since exploitation is not clearly defined, and since willingness of a minor is not accepted as a criterion of legality, the Protocol fails to offer a way of distinguishing those who traffic in children from those who help children to travel, sometimes for a fee. This can drive children to find more hazardous and less trustworthy means of traveling, especially those children who have no means of securing legitimate cross-border travel (O'Connell Davidson and Farrow, 2008, 10–11; Busza, et al., 2004, 1369–1370; Hashim, 2006, 17–18; Huijsmans, 2007).

Organizations of Working Children

Children can be rendered powerless away from home, on the streets, or in the workplace, and their agency is restricted by the structures in which they live and by the domination of adults. They can, however, acquire some power by coming together in small informal groups or in larger organizations. While adult workers can join trade unions to protect their rights against powerful employers, child workers are usually denied this right—even by trade unions and federations, often on the grounds that those below the minimum legal age of employment cannot be recognized as workers (Ennew, et al., 2005, 33, 53 note 4). Even those legally permitted to undertake "light work" sometimes receive no union protection. Since child workers are often refused entry to organizations supposed to protect the rights of all workers, they sometimes form their own unions. Some working children and their allies point out that the right to organize is a recognized basic human right extended to all functioning workers without exception, a claim difficult to deny (Weston, 2005, 433).

Since early in the industrialization of Europe and North America, working children have organized themselves in their own defense (Nasaw, 1996, 158–166; Liebel, 2004, 20–32). When American child newspaper sellers mobilized a hundred years ago to protect their economic interests and to pressure city authorities to grant their legitimacy, their resourceful actions stirred trepidation and admiration from the public, grudging acceptance from authorities, and consternation and resistance from adult activists campaigning for the elimination of child labor (Nasaw, 1996, 167–186). Working children's initiatives continue to meet similar mixed reactions today.

Children's organizations are often initiated by adults, and may be either formal or informal. Since the early 1970s, a standard method in social work for approaching and serving children working in streets and other accessible workplaces has been to gather them together in locations near their workplaces to converse with them collectively. Older youth and adults are routinely recruited and trained (as either volunteers or paid employees) to establish contact with working children and befriend them. The children are encouraged to form groups based on location or occupation, and then address their problems, both personal and occupational, through group discussion and activity. Adult facilitators guide the children in working and discussing together, paying attention to the views of all members. In the process, the children acquire identity and self-respect and develop working children's solidarity, awareness, and problem-solving skills (Myers, 2009). In various places, programs using such informal methods of organization have been effective in protecting working children, promoting their psychosocial development, and even in catalyzing social change (Overwien, 2001; for an overview of early initiatives and the formation of movements of working children, see Swift, 1999).

The early initiatives in Latin America arose largely in a tradition of empowering the poor to help themselves. Concerned adults realized that they often did not understand the problems facing children and decided that the best form of support was to facilitate the formal organization of working children to deal with problems themselves. Movements of working children spread from the Caribbean and Brazil to other countries in Latin America. They arose independently in Asia and in Africa, where they are now widespread. Representatives from movements in different countries have met regularly on regional bases, and occasionally internationally. Having their own organization gives working children opportunities to speak and act without interruption from better-educated peers, who often dominate other children's organizations.

It is not clear how prevalent are these initiatives, in what regions they are most common, or what proportion of working children participates in them. It does appear that the phenomenon is largely urban, although most working children are rural, and that many children work in occupations or conditions that do not allow for such organization.

Bhima Sangha is one such organization, started in Bangalore, India, in 1990. When child workers attended union meetings for the catering industry, adults formed an organization, The Concerned for Working Children (CWC), to provide them with support, establish part-time schooling, and encourage the establishment of a working children's organization, Bhima Sangha. CWC facilitated its spread to rural areas, where it gained respect through its initiatives to improve the situation of communities generally. This became a broader movement in which children learned to identify their problems, collect accurate and persuasive information, and create initiatives to alleviate them. After fifteen years, virtually no children in Kundapur District are involved in harmful work nor deprived of education,[13] making the working children's organization superfluous (though it continues in the city).

Empowerment requires knowledge and understanding. In Bhima Sangha and many other movements the spread of information, through newsletters and other means, is an important activity. Education is given importance by all movements, though not necessarily a simple endorsement of local formal schooling. MANTHOC, a Christian-based movement in Peru, emphasizes information about society and skills that are useful in the particular situations of the children (Miljeteig, 2001, 119). The African Movement of Working Children and Youth asserts the right to learn to read and write, and to receive training in skills that will be useful to them to earn a living later.

The principle focus of activity of working children's organizations has been at the local level. Their main function is supporting each other in coping with their daily lives. Initially, they were active in improving conditions for working children, and had some success, particularly in reducing hours of work and in improving wages and prices for children's work. They achieved this through negotiating with employers and enabling child workers to speak about their conditions (Black, 2004, 18; Swift, 1999, 36). They have also raised awareness of employers who do not treat their child workers properly. However, in the face of a mounting campaign against "child labor," some have found it difficult to draw attention to working conditions. When they raise these, a common result is not that the children have their complaints addressed, but rather that they are removed from work as "child laborers," making their situation worse.[14]

Some working children's organizations have succeeded in organizing literacy and skills training for their members. In West Africa, the movement has also been successful in obtaining health facilities. Sometimes the members co-operate in obtaining materials needed for their work. They often take on wider issues than simply their own work and interests, trying to improve the situation of their communities and to relieve poverty. They frequently campaign on behalf of children's rights and promote their own right to play a significant part in their communities. They thus reject discourse that treats them as passive victims, in need of rehabilitation (Miljeteig, 2005).

In several countries, organizations of working children have been able to influence policy at the local level. They have been able to negotiate with police to reduce harassment, and with local authorities to improve services to children, such as transport and the quality of teaching (Black, 2004, 13–14, 18). In Lima, Peru, a contract with the city authorities gave paid work under dignified conditions to a few hundred children over 12 years old (Liebel, 2003, 280). In Kundapur, Bhima Sangha contributed to establishing elected child councils that have created initiatives and frequently contributed to decisions at the level of local government (Swift, 1999, 36–37; Ratna, 2000).

Occasionally, children's organizations have been able to influence policy at the national level. In the 1980s, the Movement of Working Children and Adolescents in Peru persuaded the Ministry of Education to develop a new curriculum for working children, and the explicit right of children over 12 to work in dignified conditions became law (Swift, 1999, 21; Liebel, 2003, 280). Proposals from working children were incorporated into the Honduran national plan of action against the worst forms of child labor (Black, 2004, 25).

There have been several international meetings, facilitated by adult supporters but conducted and controlled by elected representatives of the organizations. The first, in Kundapur, India, in 1996, was followed by the children's participation in international adult forums on "child labor," after which a senior UNICEF observer commented, "Working children, with their organizations and networks, have today entered the public stage of discourse on child labor and have come increasingly to be recognized as key social actors to be taken into serious account in policies and interventions on child labor." (Karunan, 2005, 304.) Nevertheless, it has in recent years been difficult to find forums at which the movements can make their views felt. Even when they are invited to attend international meetings of adults, this is no guarantee of effective influence (Ennew, 2008), in part because of resistance from adults, notably trade unions and some governments and multilateral agencies.

Occasionally, however, children's organizations work together with trade unions and ILO bodies when their interests coincide. In Senegal, the African Movement of Working Children and Youth is an official partner of the ILO's International Programme for the Elimination of Child Labour in its campaign against the worst forms (Miljeteig, 2005, 127). In Nepal and Zimbabwe, specific adult unions have supported working children's organizations.[15] In Bolivia, the central trade union organization enrolled shoe-cleaners, child traders, and other child workers, pledging to work for their better conditions (Liebel, 2003, 280).

More frequently there is tension or even open hostility between children's organizations and adult trade unions, which together with the ILO regard children's organizations as controversial (e.g., ILO, 2006, 77). Unions and the ILO tried to keep representatives of working children's organizations out of, or peripheral to, international adult forums discussing "child labor" in the 1990s. This is partly due to emphasis of children's organizations on dignity for working children and their work, in opposition to discourse on "abolishing child labor." There have also been specific criticisms of some organizations of working children. Organizations have been criticized for failing to change the working conditions of children, a difficult task when neither they nor their work are regarded as legitimate. They are sometimes said to be dominated and manipulated by adults. The question has been raised of whether or not they adequately represent all working children (see, for example, the essays in Zweegers, 2005).

Autonomy of Children's Organizations

Are working children's organizations manipulated by adults? Such organizations claim that they promote the autonomy of children and youths to initiate their own aims and activities (Miljeteig, 2001). In this they differ from traditional organizations such as the international scouting movement or Boys Brigades, which are controlled by adults, and which have often failed to attract working-class children unless they offered material benefits (see Childs, 1992, 14). Organizations of working children also differ from the Global March against Child Labour, which is presented by some as an exemplary contemporary movement of children concerning child labor,[16] and which has received extensive funding and publicity. Although this movement involves children, it is explicitly under adult control and adults determine the policy and agenda of the movement. Susan Levine described the selection and preparation in South Africa for an international meeting within this movement. Children initially indicated that they did not want to be stopped from working, but took up slogans for the abolition of child labor when they realized this was required for selection as a delegate (S. Levine, 1999, 151–152). Here, children did not make decisions about policy, but participated in activities controlled by adults.

Even where children control their organizations, however, autonomy is limited. Children's organizations depend on adults for financing and training, and this dependence can give adults within these organizations a controlling influence. Even if a children's organization should be financially independent, with members contributing and controlling their own funds, they may still need the help of adults for access to legal and financial institutions, which are often not available to children. Children's organizations usually depend on adult facilitators to help maintain continuity and cohesion (Invernizzi, 2007). Members, and leaders in particular, reach an age at which they are no longer eligible for the organization, and adult support is often necessary to maintain continuity. Tensions can arise between adults and children, especially when the children perceive the adults to be too intrusive. Tensions can also arise between older—or more assertive—and younger members of the movement, with the former dominating discussions (see Rodda, 2007).

For international meetings, children do not have direct access to the funding necessary for travel, nor to administrative necessities such as visas. They do not have the experience to handle accommodation and catering for large meetings. Adults are needed to interpret for children speaking different languages. Adults are also sometimes needed to organize meetings with adult bodies and to negotiate spaces in which the children can express their views.[17]

Facilitating adults are needed to train children, both in the skills of running an organization and in other life skills. Children often need more experienced people to help put their ideas and initiatives into practice. In some places, the children decide on the roles of adult support and vote for the adults who will support certain activities. Elsewhere members of the children's organization endorse the appointment of supporting adults and the terms under which they are employed.

Our experience of meetings of working children is that while the children are ready to accept help and advice from adults in formulating their decisions, they insist on expressing their own ideas. Nevertheless, children are certainly influenced by supporting adults, especially when the latter play a training role. Although children are competent to express and reflect on their own experiences, they are usually dependent on information provided by others for knowledge and understanding of the wider world. We have observed disagreements between groups of working children that reflect disagreements between supporting adults. The Brazil National Movement of Street Boys and Girls, for example, became marginalized from other movements in Latin America because the Brazil movement supports a minimum age for employment, reflecting the policies of adult supporters. Notwithstanding such influence, children do think for themselves and reflect on information that they receive. In our experience, when they are given freedom to express their own ideas, they do not simply repeat what adults tell them.

Representation

Do leaders of children's organizations represent all working children? Many working children are confined to factories, homes, or farms, or reside in rural areas, and are unable to participate in the activities of the organizations. Others seek security of anonymity and avoid the publicity that movements may entail. Certain organizations appear to comprise relatively elite groups, since the most marginal working children have no time to participate in meetings and in the movements' activities (Invernizzi and Milne, 2002, 420). In some cases, leaders have continued to dominate the organization after they have reached the age of majority. It is argued that these elite leaders cannot speak for all working children.

In fact, virtually all working children's organizations have leaders elected by their peers. Those who are elected are likely to be those who show particular initiative and power to speak, and so are not typical of all child workers. The elected leaders in some cases have less experience of work and more education than many of their peers. There is no guarantee that each will remain true to his or her constituents. The partial failure of individual leaders, however, does not invalidate the system of governance, any more than it does with adult organizations.

Adolescents often come together to challenge adult dominance over their lives. The issue is not whether this happens, but whether adults can gain sufficient trust of the children to help them develop their combined power constructively. How can adults learn to respect young people as citizens and help them to develop responsibility and competence as their autonomy grows? This leads into the topic of child participation in making decisions that affect their lives, of which organizations of working children offer good examples. Such participation is central to children's agency.

Child Participation in Making Decisions

A study of young people, aged eight to fifteen years, in a British hospital for orthopaedic surgery, explored the extent to which children were informed and consulted, and their views respected (Alderson, 1994, especially 60–61). It was often assumed that young children would not be able to understand the issues. Some adults thought it unkind and unwise to expect children to share in making major decisions and did not consult them. Coercion was sometimes justified on the grounds that children are not competent to make such decisions and need to be treated with firmness. If a child does not agree to invasive medical treatment, is his or her right to bodily integrity to be respected as it would be in the case of an adult? There is a danger that the child can experience treatment as an assault.

Although a few children preferred to leave final decisions to adults, even the young children wished to be informed and consulted. Those health practitioners and guardians who did not dichotomize between competent adults and ignorant children took care to inform the children of the situation and options, and to take the children's responses seriously. When children were informed and expected to be competent, even young children showed an understanding of the proposed treatment. Usually adults and children agreed on the course to take, and occasional differences could generally be overcome by discussion and compromise.

What is child participation, and how does it affect children and work? Article 12 of the UNCRC states, "States Parties shall assure to the child who is capable of forming his or her own views the right to express those views freely in all matters affecting the child, the views of the child being given due weight in accordance with the age and maturity of the child." Section 2 of this article refers explicitly to juridical and administrative proceedings concerning children, but the article has been widely interpreted more broadly to include decisions on policy and strategy, including the design and implementation of programs. In this way, advocates of child participation have taken the concept beyond what the Convention explicitly demanded, making it a fundamental issue in all dealings with children. While participation does not mean that children necessarily make decisions, it does mean that their opinions should influence decisions. Here we are not concerned with children taking up activities planned by adults, even taking up causes under the direction of adults.[18] Participation in decision making can be considered as parallel to children's participation in other activities, discussed in chapter 5: children move from observation at the periphery to participation under guidance as they develop the capability of making responsible decisions on their own. Participation concerns partnership between adults and children, which involves sharing power and transferring it to young people as they grow. It also concerns the differences between children in age and maturity.

The right to participation is one of the most far-reaching rights in the UNCRC and has been the subject of much discussion.[19] On the one hand, it has been argued that participation is a gloss over the Convention's failure to address the political rights of children (Ennew, 2000a). In discourse on human rights, where adults usually have the right to choice, children may have the right to be heard, and yet not to make the final decision (Archard, 2004, 64). Even among adults, however, men often have rights of choice while women are constrained by decisions of men: women often have to struggle for the dignity of controlling their own lives. Similar problems face children. In practice, many children on their own have to make important decisions affecting their lives, and there is no evident reason why those who show such competence should be deprived of the right to do this.

On the other hand, even this limited right to participation has caused considerable difficulty in its application. Pressure to encourage child participation often comes from international agencies, whose local employees or NGO partners may fail to understand it or regard it as an imposition from outside. These local-level professionals sometimes perceive child participation as taking away or intruding upon rights of families and communities, and emphasizing instead the individualism of the West (see Burr, 2004), or of failing to understand cultural hierarchy in families (Naker, 2007, 147). Some adults argue that children do not have the experience for long-term decisions on such matters as children's work and that these should remain the responsibility of adults, who have access to the resources necessary to put decisions into practice (Burra, 2003, 90–91; Hemrica and Heyting, 2004, 457; G. K. Lieten, et al., 2005, 28, 159). Some hold that children should be protected from the responsibility of difficult decisions. Why is participation so important?

Rationale

The right of children to have a say in decisions that affect them is grounded in the fundamental right of any persons to control their own lives and is linked to the complex notion of "citizenship," which includes membership and rights in a society, and responsibilities toward it. There is a conundrum in the participatory rights of children, since they depend in turn on the children's capacity to be participatory citizens (Lister, 2008, 11). The conundrum is resolved in practice by pragmatic judgments on the evolving competencies of the persons involved. Such judgments can be helped by considering the practical benefits to children and to society of involving children in decisions, as well as the problems that sometimes arise.

There are pragmatic reasons for involving children in decisions that affect them. The field of development studies has long recognized that people more readily cooperate in projects if they have some control over them, and especially if they exercise ownership of the project. Community control of projects accords with democratic principles.[20] Similarly, when children are involved in deciding and planning a program, they are more likely to accept it and cooperate with enthusiasm.

Child participation offers the best protection for children, since they sometimes see problems that are overlooked by adults. More so than adults, children are often aware of those in serious need, and are better able to win the confidence of vulnerable children (Groves, 2003b, 9). When organizations involve children in planning and executing interventions, this ensures that adults take full account of how children see the projects and how the lives of children may be affected. It also ensures that children's interests are kept to the fore and not overridden by such adult concerns as fear of scandal (Thomas, 2000, 183). Consultation with the children is particularly important in evaluating the implementation of projects (Iyer, 2001).

Child participation in decisions has been shown to bring social and psychological benefits to the children involved, even to very young children (Lansdown, 2001, 4–10). They learn to reflect on their situation, to seek solutions, and to operate on their own behalf to improve their situation for the future. It gives them confidence and improves their social and political skills, often enabling them to speak out about issues that affect them. Participation enables young people to establish meaningful relations with adults, in which they see themselves as contributing persons and not simply passive dependants (Sabo, 2001).

All of these points are aptly illustrated in organizations of working children discussed above.

When children successfully address issues that affect themselves and their communities, it improves their standing in their own eyes and in the eyes of others. Studies have indicated how such action improves children's sense of responsibility, and consequently their relations with their families and communities (Lansdown, 2001, 4–8). Involving children in collecting information about their lives and their social and physical environment can help them to understand their problems and seek appropriate help. This can be an important intervention for marginalized children who have lost confidence in social relations with adults (Clacherty and Kistner, 2001).

Child participation can therefore help to bring about better cohesion between adults and children in society. In practice, children, and especially adolescents, create their own worlds of meaning and relations, just as they come together in groups. If adults exclude them from decisions, they may decide that the only way to get noticed is through destructive action (perceived by adults as vandalism—e.g., Morrow, 2005, 65). When adults adopt a policy of child participation, they gain an opportunity to work with children and a chance to influence the way young people develop (Percy-Smith and Malone, 2001).

Many initiatives have seriously involved children in defining their problems and seeking solutions to them, enabling them to take responsibility for the development of their communities to the benefit of all.[21] Such consultations can also serve to raise awareness among the children and their communities of children's rights, and to determine where these rights are being seriously infringed.[22] Far from supporting individualism, participation encourages young people to see themselves as fully part of a larger community to which they are responsible and from which they can expect respectful support. What then are the problems?

Difficulties in Applying Participation

Consulting children is not straightforward. When an issue affects large numbers of children, a representative sample may be needed. Consultation requires that children be provided with appropriate information in a manner that is intelligible to them; they must have the opportunity to reflect on relevant information in an appropriate environment; they must be free to express their views; and they must have guidance and practice in forming responsible views based on information. Discussion and expression of views may require creative facilitation, especially for younger children, using games, drama, drawing, and other forms of expression. This takes time and resources (illustrated in the Egyptian case in chapter 9). The larger question is how to treat children's opinions once they are obtained.

TENSION BETWEEN EMPOWERMENT AND PROTECTION. In the next chapter, we shall introduce cases in which children wish to undertake work that adults deem to be seriously harmful or hazardous to them. Some decisions can result in irreversible harm to a child's physical or social development and adults have a responsibility to protect children from such harmful decisions. It has been argued that children's right to be protected from exploitation overrides their right to have their views on work taken seriously. On the other hand, in chapter 5, we pointed to the danger of stifling children's development by protecting them from all risk. Children sometimes perceive "protection" negatively, as excessive restriction by adults (Sinclair, et al., 2002, 8).

There are numerous situations in which reasonable adults are divided on whether children should be prevented from incurring risks of which they are well aware, when there are clear benefits that the children wish to pursue. For example, tree-climbing teaches children physical dexterity and strategic thinking, besides being fun, but many parents will not allow their young children to climb to the top of a tall tree, and the height at which they will say "stop!" will vary substantially. To what degree should children be allowed to risk hazards in the workplace when they perceive the work as providing opportunity for long-term benefits (such as training)? There is no simple answer to this kind of problem, and it remains a constant matter of negotiation with children. It partly depends on how one judges "age and maturity of the child" (UNCRC, article 12, 1).

COMPETENCE OF CHILDREN. Gerison Lansdown (2005) considers the evolving capacities of children in different situations and in different cultural settings, and points to large variations and the difficulty in finding reliable and universal criteria.

Age is a simple and frequent criterion for legal assessment of competence, to vote, for example, or to drive a car, or to marry. While this may be justified for convenience on issues affecting a large population, age is not on its own reliable in assessing the competence of individual children to make important decisions (Lansdown, 2005, 24–26; Mantle, et al., 2006, 503–506). As we pointed out in chapter 5, theories of natural and universal stages of child development have largely been discredited by cross-cultural studies. Development of competence varies with the training children receive, social expectations placed upon them, and personal characteristics (which in turn depend largely on their particular experiences).

A common-sense approach to assessing competence also has dangers. One study of children in institutional care showed that children were assessed as competent when their opinions were broadly in agreement with the views of adults (Thomas, 2000, 178–187; see also Eekelaar, 1994, 56; Invernizzi and Milne, 2002). A study of children's councils in Norway commented that children were praised when they acted like small adults and criticized when they did not (Begg, 2004, 131). In practice, adults often base (perhaps subconsciously) their judgments on their own childhood experience and on their conceptions of an ideal childhood as a time without responsibility (and therefore implicitly of powerlessness). The expressed wishes of children might consequently be suppressed or overridden by adults in what they judge to be the children's interests (A.L. James, et al., 2004, 192, 194).[23]

Competence may be assessed on whether the child has goals that are realizable (Eekelaar, 1994, 56–57). Recent academic discussions on consulting children regarding their custody in cases of parental divorce in England and the Netherlands suggest that the competence of children can be assessed in rational terms. It is argued that children's competence in these situations depends on the degree to which they are able to understand the reasons on which a decision about them should be based and possible consequences (Hemrica and Heyting, 2004, 458). Similar criteria could be applied to decisions about work. There is no simple way to assess competence, but it is possible to devise criteria.

While children are conceptually and legally dichotomized from adults, the criteria will be devised and applied by adults, and it will be difficult to ensure that the opinions of children will be given due weight (A. L. James, et al., 2004, 201–202). When children are perceived as citizens, decisions about competence and the weight given to their views can be a matter for negotiation.

The implementation of child participation can easily degenerate into manipulating children to perform roles that satisfy adult organizations. In Bangladesh, for example, Amra was a group of working children with adult facilitation, developed to discuss and face their problems. As the group moved into advocacy, their presentations became known and some group members traveled widely and received allowances: travel and payments were incidental to the motivations of the adults but central to the interests of the children and aroused conflicts over access to these. Meeting the models of child participation set by international organizations and dominated by middle-class adults disrupted relations between the children (S.C. White and Choudhury, 2007). Such agendas take participating children out of the contexts of their daily lives and place them in contexts (such as meetings and workshops) which are clearly distinguished from the world of adults but ultimately under adult control. In particular, they can become exclusive, allowing certain children to participate while detaching them from excluded peers.

Another way in which children can be manipulated under the umbrella of "participation" is by setting up councils of children to form specific tasks assigned by adults. These often mimic adult institutions with little effect on policy (Thomas, 2007, 206–207). In effect they become a way of isolating children from important discussion.

A tension appears between the idea that children should be recognized as social agents and young citizens, and the dominant idea that they should be regulated and controlled. For example, school authorities may decide which children sit on school councils and their agenda (e.g., Morrow, 2005, 62–63). Even when the adults are genuinely interested in having the children discuss issues of policy, such as the school curriculum, it is not always easy for children to have confidence that they understand and can contribute to such issues (e.g., Wyness, 2005). An overview on the involvement of young people in public decisions in Britain showed some schools having established pupils' councils that are effective in bringing about improved policies, while pupils' councils of other schools ceased to meet for want of results. In area-wide strategic planning, there had been much consultation of children, but this had little influence in policy (Perpetua Kirby and Bryson, 2002, 15–18; see also Stafford, et al., 2003, 371; Sinclair, 2004, 113). A study in Pakistan showed some appreciation of children's councils in school and some skepticism of how much power was actually ceded to them (Morrow, 1999, 160–161).

A policy of child participation can become an end for adult organizations, losing focus on the interests of children and their development.[24] Handing decision-making processes over to children can be a form of abrogating responsibility for guiding children in their development and for supporting vulnerable children (Nieuwenhuys, 1997; Garbarino, et al., 1992, 13).

Partnership

Children's human right to have some control over their lives cannot be confined to occasional decisions when adults deem this to be appropriate. Children's participation is something that should permeate all relations between adults and children, a matter of partnership requiring constant renegotiation (N. Reddy and Ratna, 2002). In particular, working children have a right to form associations to defend their interests, and they have a right to have a say in what kinds of work they do, indeed in whether or not they are to work.

In this chapter, we have shown ways in which children sometimes exercise agency—make choices to improve their lives—in their homes, on the streets, away from home, and in organizations; and we have pointed to ways in which their agency may be constricted. The right to participation in decisions that affect their lives can be seen as a right to allow their agency to grow. The next chapter, in which we discuss how to assess harm and benefits in children's work, further emphasizes the choices and perceptions of young people as fundamental to their growth and development.

8

Assessing Harm against Benefits

As we have explained in the introduction to this book, we believe that it is not work as such that should be the focus of concern and the target of policies on children's work, but rather the forms and conditions of work that may harm or abuse children. The question of defining and assessing "harm" thus becomes a key issue. Earlier chapters have given much attention to benefits of work to children, many of them often overlooked, to counteract widespread assumptions about the harmful nature of work. We have also considered how work relates to poverty and can sometimes impede education. In this chapter, we explore the various kinds of more direct harm, or the risk of such harm, that comes with working, and that needs to be assessed against possible benefits. Such assessment is not a straightforward matter. Most work that children do has both positive and problematic aspects, in both the long and the short term. But with the exception of some extreme and obvious cases, we know very little about the physical or psychosocial impacts of work; research on the topic has been relatively neglected, regarding impacts to both physical (Fassa and Wegman, 2009) and psychosocial (Woodhead, 2004) health and well-being.

We first illustrate some of these issues with a discussion of domestic work outside the child's own home. This shows how a type of work that is in itself potentially benign—work that is done every day by literally billions of women and children, and some of the world's men, in and around their own homes—can be rendered harmful by the social relations and conditions surrounding it, and how potentially harmful work situations can benefit disadvantaged children when surrounding relations are supportive. This suggests that work often cannot be dichotomized into "good" and "bad." We then consider how to assess harm, examining first the most harmful forms of work. We indicate a way of assessing psychosocial benefits and harm arising from work, which is often more important than physical hazards. Finally, we consider what might be meant by protection from "exploitation."

Child Domestic Work: Pros and Cons

Child domestic work,[1] both in and beyond the child's own home, is dominantly girl's work,[2] although in some cultures boys engage in it as well. Employment in child domestic work covers a range of situations, from visiting a home in the neighborhood to work for a few hours, to living in the employer's home in a far-away city and working full time. Paradoxically, the most damaging situations, as well as the most significant potential benefits, are found in full-time, live-in employment.

What Is Wrong

On October 16, 2006, a ban in India went into effect against employing children under the age of fourteen as domestic workers or in related work such as catering. This was welcomed by some as a step toward protecting children.[3] Some NGOs, however, pointed out that this ban would result in half a million children being deprived of their means of subsistence.[4] Since domestic employment involves tasks that children often fulfil in their own homes, what, these groups asked, is so wrong with it to provoke this kind of protective legislation?

Harmful effects of child domestic work have been widely documented. While some child domestic workers (CDWs) may take pride in the work they do—as expressed dramatically by the Senegalese girl whom we quoted in chapter 1—CDWs notoriously have low self-esteem (Blagbrough, 2009; Zaman and Blanchet, 2003, 7). A study in Kenya found that CDWs, more than other children, showed symptoms of psychological problems such as bedwetting, insomnia, nightmares, frequent headaches, withdrawal, regressive behavior, premature ageing, depression, and phobic reactions to their employers (Bwibo and Onyango, 1987). Children long in domestic work in Indonesia, unlike most other child workers, were unable to imagine that they could do anything other than to continue life in domestic service (Blagbrough, 1995). This kind of work has been called a violation of human rights, with many practical characteristics of child domestic labor having features "akin to slavery" (Black, 2002, i–ii; Rani and Roy, 2005). Why does apparently benign work have this kind of result?

Certainly, domestic work may entail certain hazards, as when children have to cook over an open flame or use electrical appliances without adequate training or safety precautions. They may have to deal with dangerous chemicals in the house or garden. They may be required to go on errands in dangerous times or places. But for the most part, the work is physically not more hazardous than are many legitimate children's activities.

The more fundamental problem lies not in the work itself but in work relations, in the status of the child worker in the employer's household. Relations between employers and employees always contain elements of inequality, but in the case of domestic work these are often seen in extreme form. Children are in a weak position in relation to adults: when the adults who dominate their lives are also employers, the children's position is weaker still. Girls are further undermined by gender inequalities. CDWs are thus frequently at the vulnerable end of three cross-cutting hierarchies of class, age, and gender. A study in Bangladesh shows some people taking in young girls not only for convenience but also to emphasize their status as people who can afford a maid; the maid is required to show her lower status in her dress and behavior (Blanchet and Zaman, 2004, 29–30).

Partly as a result of this low status, a degree of bad treatment in child domestic work is the dominant experience in many countries, and probably the majority experience everywhere (see Black, 2002, 4–7). CDWs are frequently forced to work long hours (Jacquemin, 2004, 385; M. Ray and Iyer, 2006, 8–9; Oyaide, 2000, 42). They are routinely insulted and scolded by their employers. Mistakes are often punished by physical beating and sometimes deprival of food.

Sexual abuse is common. A study of employing families in Lima, Peru, showed that 60 percent of males had their first sexual experience with domestic workers (Boyden, et al., 1998, 8). A study in West Bengal showed over 20 percent of girl domestic workers saying they had been forced or tricked into having sexual intercourse, and many others had been sexually abused in other ways (M. Ray and Iyer, 2006, 14–17), as experienced by this fifteen-year-old Indonesian CDW: "I felt uncomfortable when [my employer's husband] would be naked outside his bedroom. . . . I started getting really scared whenever the children would go to school and the employer would leave, and I would be left alone with him. . . . He'd ask me 'Do you want to see [my penis]?' He would do this every day that we were left alone. I wanted to tell the employer but I was scared we would get in a fight" (Human Rights Watch, 2009, 15).

Frequently, live-in CDWs are prevented from socializing with their peers. Even visits from family may be discouraged. Occasionally, CDWs are incarcerated in the employers' homes, perhaps under the notional justification that it is for their own protection (Jacquemin, 2004, 385). The national labor laws of many countries exclude domestic servants from the standard protective coverage of minimum wages, maximum working hours, and various benefits, on the grounds that domestic service is more akin to a family relationship than a labor relationship.

A large majority of child domestic workers do not have access to formal schooling.

Why Do Children Choose This Work?

Although there are reports of CDWs being compelled to work by their parents or guardians, sometimes as bonded labor (e.g., Rani and Roy, 2005, 17), many child domestic workers insist that they chose to work. Some children had left school before entering domestic service; they had wanted something to do as well as to earn an income (Bourdillon, 2006a, 35–38; also on Philippines,

Camacho, 1999, 70). These children often actively sought employment as CDWs, using networks of relatives or friends.

Many of the reasons why children choose any job, outlined in chapter 2, can apply here. Although wages are normally low, children paid to work as servants may contribute significantly to the incomes of very poor families (Rani and Roy, 2005, 10, 15, 22). Children from impoverished families may find better and more secure nutrition working and living in the home of a wealthier family. The influence of a wealthy employer may also extend to better opportunities later in life (Sommerfelt, 2003a, 56; Camacho, 1999, 70; UNICEF, 1998a, 14; Smucker and Murray, 2004, 27). In some cases, employers have taken in a young person as an employee precisely to provide dignified support and even schooling (e.g., Ravololomanga and Schlemmer, 2000, 301–302; Bourdillon, 2006a, 25–27).

Although many child domestic workers are deprived of schooling, others enter service precisely to pay for their school expenses, or for access to schooling that is not available in their home rural areas. In some situations, employers may feel an obligation to send teenage employees to school in the evenings (Blagbrough, 2009; Black, 2002, 7; Bourdillon, 2006a, 58–60; Smucker and Murray, 2004, 22–23). In Côte d'Ivoire, those traveling to work in urban households were more likely to receive schooling than the siblings they left behind (Ainsworth, 1992).

For children, especially girls, growing up in isolated rural villages, going into domestic service may provide an escape from a stifling environment with few opportunities. Domestic work in a city may also be a way of saving a child from heavy agricultural work in her home area (e.g., Sommerfelt, 2003a, 49, 55). Rural children who must run errands while living in a town or city learn to navigate urban life.

A Mingling of Benefits and Harm

Employment in domestic work can bring benefits and harm to children, which cannot always be separated. This is illustrated by a fourteen-year-old girl in South Africa, who was sent to stay with her aunt because her parents had no food and could not afford her schooling. She complained about being made to get up at four in the morning to clean the house and fetch water before going to school while the aunt's daughter did nothing. Moreover, she was constantly afraid of being beaten. But her father insisted she stay at her aunt's house for the food and education she received there (Clacherty, 2002, 25–27). As a result of the research she and her family received support that ensured she was not compelled to return to her aunt's house.

Even when children are not treated well, they still sometimes prefer to remain in employment than to return home. In a Zimbabwean survey, the majority of child domestic workers were critical of their work situation; but 12 percent did not mention anything they did not like about their work, some commenting that they liked everything about it, and only a third of the children wanted to give up their employment altogether. For the rest, the available alternatives seemed worse (Bourdillon, 2006a, 13–14). Even young maids who are critical of the institution of domestic service may declare that they would rather continue to work than return to their poor rural communities (Sommerfelt, 2003a, 26, 33).

A further complication is that domestic employment sometimes merges with traditional practices of rearing children in which responsibilities for children are shared within the extended family. Thus, in Côte d'Ivoire in 1985, about one fifth of non-orphaned children between the ages of seven and fourteen were not living in their parental homes, and were largely providing domestic service and other work (Ainsworth, 1992).[5] Girls stay with relatives, or perhaps others known to their families, and work without payment. But they are fed and clothed, provided with necessary medical attention, and receive substantial gifts at the end of their service to set them up in adult life (Jacquemin, 2004, 384). Freedom to choose which kin to live with, and consequently where they work, gives children a degree of negotiating power over how they are treated, which is especially important for orphaned children.

Fostering practices can, however, be exploitative as well as beneficial for children (e.g., Hashim, 2006, 20–23). Wealthy relatives may take in poorer kin, claiming to help them according to kinship obligations, but in practice obtaining cheap and uncontrolled domestic labor, and perhaps freeing their own children to focus on schoolwork (Kielland and Tovo, 2006, 19). When children move away from their homes to live with relatives or other acquaintances, these adults do not always adhere to promises of payment and education (Anarfi, et al., 2006, 4–5, 36–39; Bourdillon, 2006a, 20–21). The notion of helping poor children and "giving the child a home" may mask employment to avoid implications such as the right to compensation for labor and the determination of working hours and benefits (Black, 2002, 2; Blanchet, 1996, 102–103). In Bangladesh, some people foster children precisely to acquire their service: children adopted when very young may become servants of their adoptive parents when they grow into adolescence (Blanchet, 2004, 3, 8).

Some argue that if children are to undertake this kind of work, it should be openly recognized as such with a formal contract and clear rights for the worker (UNICEF, 1998a, 15). On the other hand, several studies have found correspondence between worker contentment and the degree in which they are incorporated into the employers' family activities and treated as family members, sharing meals and entertainment and receiving emotional support (Jacquemin, 2004, 393–394; Sommerfelt, 2003b, 33–34).

What Can We Learn from Child Domestic Employment?

The effects of domestic employment on the children clearly depend on the context and particularly the social relations surrounding the work rather than the nature of the work itself. Some relatives help poorer kin and some exploit them; many mix help and exploitation. Some employers help child employees to get to school and some prevent them. Such individual behavior is affected by social and cultural contexts, which determine common expectations of relations between employers and workers, and between adults and children in general: sexual abuse, for example, appears to have been institutionalized in some Peruvian communities, while it may be rare in other places.

Another factor in assessing harm is the material and social alternatives available to the children. A homeless child, or a child from an abusive home, or even a hungry child, may rightly see herself as benefiting from a dull, poorly paid job under an indifferent employer in the absence of better alternatives for her support and protection.

Much may be missed by focusing only on harm suffered by children in employment. A report on child domestic work in Morocco by Human Rights Watch (2005) focuses on children whose situation is intolerable as argument for the implementation of the legal minimum age of employment. A report by an anthropologist, Tone Sommerfelt (2003a), also points to the abuse and suffering of child domestic workers in Morocco but notes that some girls, even very young girls, feel they have benefited from employment and have no desire to return to their rural villages. This report pays attention to the views of employers and families as well as those of the girls. It points out that intervention on behalf of the girls should not make their situation worse by antagonizing employers or distancing the girls from their families.

Child domestic work, thus, covers a range of situations. At one extreme, when the child is badly abused and virtually imprisoned, urgent rescue and criminal proceedings against the perpetrators is the only reasonable response. At the other extreme, a very deprived child finds security, education, emotional support, and self-esteem in the employer's home; in this case encouragement of child and employer is a more appropriate response. Between are situations that confer benefits but may also damage the child. Often the employers mean no harm but simply follow local practice, without thinking of the damage it can do.

Policy and advocacy responses of interveners vary equally. Some focus on the damage and seek to ban all child domestic employment as a matter of child protection: although this may be justified in specific situations where child domestic workers are routinely abused, a ban on its own does not guarantee that the majority of ex-workers, or indeed any of them, are better off as a result. Interventions that provide support and education for older workers and remove younger workers from employment mean in effect that younger children, who most need support, are prevented from seeking it if they wish for any reason to remain in employment (Jacquemin, 2006, 398). Programs can focus on opening up new opportunities rather than restricting old ones, providing counseling and education for workers, and financial incentives to leave their work (e.g., Groves,

2003c). One program, Shoishab in Bangladesh, while supporting child domestic workers with educational and other activities, engaged with employers and communities, who agreed on a code of ethical practice providing rules and guidelines for the treatment of young domestic workers, and several employers actively contributed to support and education programs (Black, 2002, 48–49). This proved beneficial to the children and appears to be sustainable.

A Continuum of Harm and Benefit

Domestic work cannot simply be classified as good or bad, and neither can most specific situations of child domestic employment. More generally, it is not useful to classify forms of children's work as either "child labor" that is bad and to be abolished or "child work" that is good and to be allowed. It is more realistic and more helpful to see children's work as lying on a continuum (figure 8.1). At one end is work in conditions that are not susceptible to efforts at humanization and improvement, which are so harmful that there is no alternative to removing the children involved and preventing the employment of others in the future, as a matter of urgency. At the other end, there is work that is so beneficial that it should be encouraged. In between, there are kinds of work which in their present conditions are harmful or hazardous, but which also confer benefits and can potentially be made less harmful through efforts from above (regulation) and below (popular pressure) and which potentially can be combined with school or continuing education; there are also kinds of work which are "neutral," that is, neither particularly harmful nor particularly beneficial to children (B. White, 1997, 15–17). For these "in-between" categories in particular, there are degrees of both benefit and harm, which have to be balanced against each other (see McKechnie and Hobbs, 1998, 40–42).

Placing any particular work on this continuum may not be straightforward, since high levels of benefits do not necessarily correspond with low levels of harm. Dull, poorly paid, part-time work may contain no hazards and limited benefits. Work that has high benefits in terms of pay, status, or experience may be harmful in terms of the time it occupies or hazards involved. A child sport or media star may obtain international prestige and great financial gain, but at great disruption to social life.

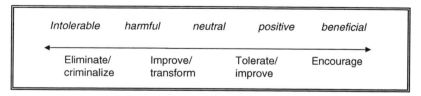

FIGURE 8.1. A continuum of child work

"Continuum" and "balance" models do not solve any problems in them-selves, but they can help us think more carefully about what it is that makes different kinds and conditions of work more or less problematic for children, and about the possibilities of addressing and overcoming those problems. Is it, for example, the physical nature of the work itself that makes it harmful or danger-ous? Or aspects of the work relationship, which make it abusive, humiliating, or exploitative? Or the indirect harm that comes from what is foregone as a result of work (for example, through long hours that prevent the child's access to edu-cation, recreation, or social life)? Or a combination of any of these?

In chapters 2 and 5, we focused on work lying at the positive end of the con-tinuum. Now we attend to the problematic and intolerable end. In chapter 3, we saw that the ILO's Convention 182 on the worst forms of child labor (1999) defines "worst forms" in two ways: first, the "unconditional worst forms"; and second, the "hazardous forms," that is, all forms of child work which "by its nature or the circumstances in which it is carried out, is likely to harm the health, safety or morals of children." We explore each of these in turn, in the next two sections.

Intolerable Forms and Conditions of Work

Convention 182's unconditional worst forms—those considered harmful to chil-dren and society under any conditions—include slavery and similar practices, such as the sale and trafficking of children, debt bondage, forced or compulsory recruitment of children in armed conflict and the use of children in prostitu-tion, pornography, or illicit activities such as the production and sale of drugs.

The urgency of ending the abuse of children in these "unconditional worst forms" is not a contentious issue that requires much discussion,[6] so long as it is recognized that children may see even very harmful and morally repugnant work, under certain conditions, as preferable to available alternatives. In such cases, any form of rescue must be accompanied by provision of better alterna-tives, in consultation with the children.

Where Children Have No Choice: Slavery-Like Practices

While the majority of working children have some choice in their work, albeit often under duress, there are situations in which children have no choice at all. One is where children are trafficked and enslaved,[7] where rescue is usually the only option.

While the term "slavery" is sometimes rhetorically used to refer to all kinds of abusive child work (e.g., Lee-Wright, 1990), actual enslavement of children (whose persons are traded as chattels) still exists in a number of countries (Bass, 2004, 149–152 for some African examples). Bonded labor is a more common (although often illegal[8]) institution, particularly in southern Asia. When a fam-ily is in critical need of money (perhaps to overcome a critical shortage of food or to pay medical costs), they may obtain a lump sum by bonding a child to an employer for a specified time, which may be as much as ten years, starting sometimes at five or six years old. Often further debts are incurred before the initial debt is paid off, sometimes through fines resulting from mistakes made by the worker (Gulrajani, 2000, 57–58).[9] Parents may sometimes be partly motivated by the hope of establishing a long-term relationship between their child and the employer, and of acquiring some training for the child (Bonnet, 2000, 183). While bonded child laborers are occasionally able to exchange employers by finding another willing to take on the debt, children rarely have any say in the work they are required to do, and the debt can only be repaid by the child's labor (Human Rights Watch, 2003, 16–17).

Cultural practices can also force children into conditions akin to slavery, as in the Trokosi tradition of southern Ghana, where thousands of girls as young as four may be betrothed to fetish gods to atone for transgressions of a family member, when families are unable to raise money to buy the necessary cattle to atone for the offense. The Trokosi girls are deprived of freedom and education, suffer inhumane and degrading treatment, and have to work for the priests as cooks, farmhands, cleaners, and mistresses (Quashigah, 1998; Bass, 2004, 151–152). In Senegal and Gambia, *talibes* aged between seven and thirteen are placed with a quranic teacher by their parents or guardians, who are usually poor and illiterate. The children beg on the streets for many hours a day, giving proceeds to their teachers, and study the Quran. They sometimes have to work in their teachers' homes and farms. The teacher is supposed to provide shelter, clothes, and food, but these are often inadequate (Bass, 2004, 204; Riisøen, et al., 2004, 19–20).

Included in practices akin to slavery is the sale and trafficking of children. In the previous chapter we discussed the independent migration of children, and how vulnerable children become when they are away from home. In extreme cases, children are sold by their families, or are abducted or deceived, and taken to places where they are exploited and abused with no support and no possibility of returning.

We also pointed out how difficult it can be to distinguish such trafficking from the voluntary migration of children for economic and educational purposes. Independent child migration and child trafficking are two extreme ends of a continuum. As we pointed out in chapter 7, this is not adequately reflected in the UN Palermo Protocol (2000) against the trafficking of persons.

Armed Conflict

ILO Convention 182 includes the compulsory recruitment of persons under age eighteen in armed conflict as a practice similar to slavery. The UNCRC demands that state parties should not recruit anyone under the age of fifteen into their armed forces, and should ensure that no one of this age participates directly in armed conflicts (article 38, 2 and 3). Some children are kidnapped or otherwise compelled to join fighting groups, typically boys to be soldiers and girls to be servants and wives of leaders.[10] They may be inducted into an armed group to perform chores like taking messages and carrying loads, to be incorporated into fighting activities later (Shepler, 2004). Even when children have joined an armed conflict willingly, they may be coerced to remain in the forces against their wish to leave. Extreme measures may be taken to break down children's values and to commit them to the armed group, including beating and killing peers—perhaps even a sibling (Blattman and Annan, 2007; forthcoming). In any case, child soldiers commit the violence on others that war entails, sometimes of a criminal nature. They may find it difficult or impossible to return to their communities, and rehabilitated children may revert to a life with guns as the only kind of life they know (e.g., Akello, et al., 2006).

Children involved in armed conflict almost always miss out on education. When former child soldiers in Uganda were interviewed, a minority showed extreme symptoms of distress, but many more boys were very worried about the interruption of their education and employment (Blattman and Annan, 2007, 7–8). Paradoxically, as education possibilities are disrupted in combat zones, some children opt for recruitment as a means to acquire skills and competencies that can help them build a better future, as explained to Michael Wessels by a sixteen-year-old Sierra Leonean girl, a former commander with the Revolutionary United Front: "I'm proud of what I learned—how to speak to groups, organize people, command, use weapons. I never got this from [the] government. How else am I supposed to have a future?" (Wessells, 2006, 50).

While some youth are forced to participate in armed conflicts, others take part willingly, perhaps in a struggle for national liberation, out of patriotism, or to avenge death or dishonor to kin or friends. At different times and places their right to do so has been recognized.[11] Youth may also choose to join armed conflicts when they are frustrated by their prospects in their own society (e.g. on Sierra Leone, Fithen and Richards, 2005). They may take up arms simply because it appears relatively safer than the powerlessness of unarmed noncombatants in a war zone.

Only when we learn how children understand their recruitment can we responsibly position ourselves to prevent child recruitment and to support the reintegration of former child combatants (Wessells, 2006, 223–224; Akello, et al., Honwana, 2006, 104–134).

Sex Work

A variety of factors can put pressure on children to engage in the sex trade. Desperate poverty can drive children into using sex as a means of survival. In Russia, minors are present in all forms of prostitution, partly as a result of collapsing economic and welfare systems (Save the Children Sweden, 2001). Parents in parts of Indonesia may put pressure on their children to enter the sex trade not through desperate poverty, but in order to finance improvements to the house or the costs of a sibling's education or support of a disabled parent (B. White, et al., 2009).

Usually, children in the sex trade are powerless, disparaged, and physically abused, both by the people who control them and by their clients. They have little control over their lives, live in fear, and are stigmatized socially, making it difficult to break out of this form of work and improve their situation (e.g., Barnes-September, et al., 2000, 121–124; Woodhead, 1998, 23). Not all underage girls in the sex trade fit this stereotype. There is a difference between prepubescent children who are literally trafficked into the sex trade or pornography and those older adolescents who are in a position to make choices on the matter. Appropriate intervention is urgent for both groups, but come in different forms (Black, 1995, 86).

Although such choice is usually constrained by poverty and absence of alternatives, in some cases sex work may be freely chosen, often under the influence of peers and perhaps linked to a desire for alcohol or other drugs (e.g., Powell, 2007, 34, 36; Barnes-September, et al., 2000, 118). A frequent factor behind such choice is the experience by these children of sexual abuse in their own homes (Barnes-September, et al., 2000, 32–3). Girls (and sometimes also boys) on city streets may exchange sex for protection, or for warmth at night and a place to sleep (Bourdillon and Rurevo, 2003; Riisøen, et al., 2004, 47–48; ZARD and MAPODE, 2001, 27; Human Rights Watch, 2001, 24; Johnson, et al., 1995, 59). Girls may choose to work in the entertainment industry, which often leads to trading sex, for better pay and conditions than they had in previous work, such as abusive domestic employment (Black, 1995, 30). Sex may be perceived simply as a means of quick and easy money (e.g., Ivanova, et al., 2007, 68).

Among minors who migrate into the sex trade, we can distinguish three major categories (as we can among adult women). Some are misled into thinking they were moving into some other occupation, only to find themselves pressed into the sex trade. Others travel in search of other work and are unable to find it. Yet others choose the sex trade because it is more highly rewarded than other occupations, because they see it as the only way out of poverty, or because treatment at home is even worse (O'Connell Davidson, 2001, 11; Ivanova, et al., 2007, 50–51; Riisøen, et al., 2004, 47).

Not all young sex workers feel exploited and abused. Montgomery argues that although children are harmed by prostitution, they weigh this against the economic benefits to be gained, which are often used for what they consider to be very moral purposes of family support (Montgomery, 2001, 95, 156–159). In Bangkok, sex workers in respectable cafes have freedom to choose or reject customers. They point out that the income is good, the hours are short, they stay indoors and out of the heat, their skin remains pale, and they have time to socialize with friends. Ex–sex workers are not stigmatized and are able to marry.

Girls find sex work a convenient way to earn an income and provide filial support to their families, and less degrading than outdoor agricultural work in the sun (Rende Taylor, 2005, 416). Some young children do not see themselves as victims of adults, but rather as performing filial obligations to support their mothers, establishing long-term relationships with wealthy adults whom they speak of as supportive friends and to whom they sometimes supply sexual services. While unfamiliar to Westerners and many others, such relationship patterns have been carefully studied and documented (e.g., see Montgomery 2009). The question is how to deal with them.

An issue here is that not all cultures share moral disapproval of extramarital sexual behavior. When there are fundamental differences in cultural values, it becomes especially important to be precise about the harm, both physical and psychosocial, to children that is to be prevented. A Western understanding of child protection based on cultural perceptions of morality is unlikely to be helpful to these children (Montgomery, 2007; Child Workers in Nepal Concerned Centre, 2003; Equations, 2003).

Illicit Activities

Although there has been little research on children involved in illicit activities, Dowdney's study of children in the drug trade in Rio de Janeiro, Brazil, warns of the complexity of such situations. Children move into the trade through social association with dealers on the streets, and through lack of alternative prospects to improve their lives. They often enter full-time employment between the ages of ten and fifteen.

The children are drawn into dealers' gangs, which give them an identity and status in an organization, together with some excitement. Although drug traders claim that children should not carry weapons, their perception is that some children mature at an early age, and children as young as thirteen often carry guns. They become involved in gang control of their communities and in battles with the police and rival gangs, whom they are indoctrinated to hate (Dowdney, 2003, 125–127). Once employed in the trade, children are considered legitimate targets by rival gangs, even when not armed (Dowdney, 2003, 154). In the fourteen-year period from 1987 to 2001, 3,937 persons under age eighteen were killed due to injuries related to guns in Rio de Janeiro.[12]

Dowdney points out that this involvement of children takes place in communities in which there is limited government presence, in which social control is exercised by persons outside government, in which access to formal labor markets is limited (particularly by inadequate education), and in the context of repressive and corrupt policing. He argues that the problem cannot be dealt with simply as a criminal matter, nor is any intervention that directly confronts the drug traffickers likely to succeed. Rather, an approach is required that provides children with alternative perspectives from a very young age, including alternative cultural activities, alternative youth organizations, better education, and improved and realistic prospects to improve their lives in other ways (Dowdney, 2003, 22).

Assessing Hazardous Work

ILO Recommendation 190 (1999, section 3), which accompanies Convention 182, provides guidelines on the definition of the "hazardous forms" of children's work, suggesting that they include work that exposes children to physical, psychological, or sexual abuse; work underground, underwater, at dangerous heights or in confined spaces; work with dangerous machinery or tools; work that involves handling or transport of heavy loads; work in an unhealthy environment; and work under particularly difficult conditions, such as work for long hours, during the night, or where the child is unreasonably confined to the premises of the employer.

Considering how such a list might be translated into solution-based action raises a number of issues. First, while some of the hazardous conditions are relatively unambiguous (such as work underwater or underground—although we assume the latter does not include the basement floors of shopping malls!), many of the others are relative matters on which further judgments have to be made. At what height does work (and work of what kind?) become too dangerous to be permitted? When is a closed space too confined? When is a load too heavy? How unhealthy is too unhealthy? What are too long hours? And how can all these questions be answered for children of different ages? Second, even if science or (more likely) political consensus provided answers to all these questions, which could then be translated into precise regulations and guidelines for employers and labor inspectors, the result is likely to be an increasingly complex set of unenforceable rules. In the Netherlands, for example, government guidelines provide nineteen pages of detailed information on what kinds of work are and are not permitted for children of different age groups (12, 13–14, 15–16, and 17–18), for how many hours and at what times of day during school terms, and which of these may only be undertaken in the presence of adult supervision; another lengthy guideline explains what is and is not permitted during school vacations (Ministerie van Sociale Zaken, 2009a; 2009b). Yet even in this relatively well-regulated society, various studies have shown that the great majority of employers of working children are in one way or another in violation of these rules (White, 1994).

A third issue is the static nature of the Recommendation, in which all kinds of work are on one side or another of the "hazardous" definition; it offers no guidance on how hazards might be diminished or removed in order to make work more acceptable. Finally, it ignores the need to ensure that removal from (or prevention of) work results in an improvement in the situation of children. We illustrate the last problem with reference to underground mining.

The employment of children is rare in large, highly capitalized mines. It is more common in small-scale mining, where working conditions are poor and unsafe and there is little legal control. At a workshop in Harare, Zimbabwe, representatives of young people working in informal mining pointed out that they had to take on this work or starve, and they appealed to be allowed to work in the larger mines, where pay and safety are so much better. To the children, formal-sector underground mining looked good compared to what was available to them (Save the Children U.K., 2000, 1).

In Colombian coal-mining areas, children are employed in a variety of tasks in small-scale mines, and twelve- to fourteen-year-olds are preferred for work in the small shafts underground. They typically work four to six hours in the early morning, while it is still cool, before going to school and working on family farms in the afternoons. In spite of the danger, some of the children want to work longer in the mines, because they are paid well and they consider school useless (Sastre and Meyer, 2000, 88–89). Neither children nor adults should be working in dangerous informal underground mining, but they will continue to do so until they have better alternatives. ILO Recommendation 190 says that the design and implementation of programs should take into consideration the views of the children concerned. But what should we think when children are aware of the risks but still see this work as their best option, or when their perceptions of harm differ from ours?

Children's Perspectives on Harm from Work

There are many ways in which children's perspectives on harm and hazard can differ from those of adults, exemplified by the following case.

In the late 1980s, Indian newspapers repeatedly exposed the sorry plight of girls from the southern state of Kerala working seasonally in prawn-curing factories in Gujarat and Maharashtra, thousands of kilometers away from home. They were said to have been crudely exploited, working in squalor late into the night. To sleep, they were locked up in a hall without beds.

The anthropologist Olga Nieuwenhuys (2000) knew the fishing villages from which some of the girls came. She was surprised that fathers allowed their daughters to travel away from home on their own, and interviewed some of the girls. A different perception emerged. The girls had been attracted by accounts of friends who earned money from this seasonal work to help their families and for their dowries. They persuaded their reluctant fathers to allow them to travel together on the annual trip, often starting in their early teens. They spoke of their pleasure at the train journey through India, at working with their peers, at watching videos on weekends, and at gaining respectability in their families. Since they traveled to make as much money as possible and were paid piece-rate, they wanted to work long hours. One described the dormitory as a safe and convenient place to stay.

At home, the girls had little chance of earning money on their own, and were involved in the heavy domestic work of poor homes. Most also worked at home alongside their mothers making coir yarn for fishing nets: while a woman spins, two girls work at peeling and beating coconut husks, winnowing, and turning the spinning wheel. Although the income from such work is low, it contributes to feeding the family. Girls might also help when their parents hire out a daughter's services to a neighbor, perhaps in payment of a debt. The girls saw seasonal work in distant prawn factories as a better opportunity. Whose perception was right?

Children are not in a position to establish empirically the long-term effects of different kinds of work, many of which are also not well understood by adults. Street vendors or garbage scavengers, for example, are unlikely to be aware of the dangers and the long-term consequences of lead pollution (see Ide and Parker, 2005). Children may also not be fully aware of long-term benefits deriving from schoolwork.

Children's views often largely tally with what adults say about harmful work. The priorities of children and adults, however, sometimes differ, as do their perspectives on protection from abuse. One study that sought Australian children's (aged eleven to seventeen) opinions about child abuse revealed their concern about the power and control of adults, and the emotional stress in children when adults appeared not to care about their feelings and opinions. They saw physical abuse as resulting from this power and lack of care. An occasional beating was considered a small price to pay for the care they generally received from parents (Mason and Falloon, 2001).

Working children surveyed in Bangladesh listed many things they did not like about their work (longer than the list of things they liked), including long hours that hamper schooling and play, irregular and low wages, lack of leave even when sick, compulsory overtime even at night, verbal and physical abuse, lack of contact with home, lack of freedom, physical dangers, lack of facilities, and the fact that nobody listened to their views. They showed more concern for adequate pay than for workplace hazards, and they wanted to be treated fairly by employers. They complained about the extension of apprenticeships and about job insecurity (exacerbated by moves to remove them from their jobs). They pointed out that it is particular tasks and conditions that should be targeted as harmful rather than entire occupations or sectors (Groves, 2003b, 7). Children in the Philippines considered work "unacceptable" (a term they found more intelligible than "intolerable") when it forces them to leave school, to enter prostitution, or to deal with drugs. They also considered work at home abusive when it is demanded unfairly, as "when a child works like a slave at home when the youngest sibling is not given work to do" and when "a child is not through doing one chore and is already asked to do another" (Rialp, 2005, 191).

Another concern is violence in the workplace, both physical and psychological. A study in Nicaragua, El Salvador, and Guatemala shows children linking violence by employers with violence by the public and by authorities who harass working children on the streets. Working children were critical of how many adults "make fun of us, or insult us, humiliate us, treat us disdainfully, or make advances to us" in the street (Liebel, 2001b, 55). Some issues raised by children are missed by adults. Children from Bangladesh said that being confined indoors and forced to be stationary was worse than being able to move around out of doors (Groves, 2003a, 3). Bhima Sangha raised the matter of violence against children working in the streets or on their way to work, and particularly harassment of girls. They were also concerned about the absence of saving facilities for their money, which is particularly necessary in context of street bullies: normal saving and banking facilities are not available to minors (Bhima Sanga, 2005).

Occasionally children have been asked about what work is not acceptable to them. The children of the Balkur Panchayat in Karnataka State in India produced a booklet outlining the tasks around the home that they considered appropriate and inappropriate at different ages, based on their experiences of what adults sometimes required of them (Children of Balkur Panchayat, 1999). They considered certain light tasks, such as watering plants in front of the house, appropriate for children as young as three, and many household chores, such as sweeping and swabbing of floors, appropriate for nine-year-olds and older, but not younger. Responsibility for looking after the home, cooking, milking cows was considered appropriate for those aged fifteen. The children listed some work, like rolling tobacco, harvesting sugar cane, or employment in a hotel away from home, to be harmful to anyone under eighteen. Sometimes, the children reflected cultural assumptions, as when they said that girls lack the ability and strength to repair bicycles, work that they considered appropriate for boys over fifteen. There was a constant insistence that work must not interfere with schooling, and that the amount of work should be limited according to the child's age. Occasionally, they distinguished between chores in one's own home from working in the homes of others. Generally, however, they were concerned with the work and the hours, and had little to say about the social relations surrounding it.

Most adults would sympathize with all of the points raised by working children in the examples provided above. Adults have the further responsibility of guiding children on hazards that may not be evident to the children, and adults have to make laws and formulate policy. The children bring out both psychosocial and physical problems they encounter in their work, without always distinguishing the two. We consider them separately, taking physical hazards first.

Physical Hazards

Many concerns about physical hazards in children's work relate to health and safety standards in the workplace generally. Many "worst forms" involve conditions of work that no one should experience, children or adults.

Some factors, however, relate particularly to children. Fassa and Wegman summarize characteristics that make young people more susceptible to work hazards. They distinguish three categories of hazards: exposure to toxic substances; exposure to excessive heat and noise; and ergonomic hazards linked to repetitive motion, high force, and awkward posture at work, the latter including mismatches between children's small body size and the machinery, tools, workstations, and protective equipment they may have to use. They note the striking "lack of scientific evidence that addresses the susceptibility of youths to the wide range of risks that exist in their places of work" (Fassa and Wegman, 2009, 129).

Considerations of work's impact upon health and growth illustrate the difficulty in producing effective general rules. Attempts to establish the effects of work generally on children's health and growth have produced inconsistent results (Levison and Murray-Close, 2005) and seem to be largely biased by prior judgments about whether work as such is good or bad (for a review of recent research, see Dorman, 2008, 29–46; Parker, forthcoming). Nevertheless, the effects of particular types and conditions of work on health and growth can sometimes be assessed and may require urgent attention. Some studies have shown poorer health and slower growth related to particular work environments (e.g., Boyden, et al., 1998, 96–97; Ambadekar, et al., 1999), and there are a number of evident health hazards posed by certain kinds of work (Forastieri, 2002).

Parker (forthcoming) points out that, in addition to acute trauma (injuries, illness, and death) that occur in part when children's work takes place in chaotic or hot environments, or with machinery, equipment, and tools designed for adult use, some kinds of harm from work may have chronic or have latent onset. For example, silicosis (leading to tuberculosis) is associated with stonecutting and pottery work in India, but the disease may develop only after twenty years. Ergonomic stress due to repetitive work involving high force and awkward positions can have long-term consequences. A study in rural Vietnam showed no immediate impact of agricultural work on the health and growth of child workers, although child workers were more likely to develop health problems five years later (O'Donnell, et al., 2004). Particularly dangerous for children are hazards from chemicals, such as insecticides in agriculture, toxins in manufacturing, and other pollutants in the workplace (Dorman, 2008, 30–33). Some work has mixed effects on health. Scavengers in Manila, Philippines, had higher levels of lead, but lower rates of anemia than school children in metropolitan Manila (Ide and Parker, 2005).

Hazards in work do not necessarily result in actual harm to children (see Boyden, et al., 1998, 79). Some children manage to avoid danger and some respond with resilience to potentially damaging situations. Consider the possibilities of physical harm on the job. A boy wielding a machete to cut brush has a lower probability of cutting himself if he has been trained in the use of the machete, and if it is the right size for a person of his stature. How likely is it that he will

cut himself, and how seriously? The possibility of accidents is not in itself sufficient ground to ban an activity; if it were, nearly all children's sports would have
to be banned. Even children at play take risks; it is impossible—and developmentally problematic—to remove all possible hazards from children's environments. The question is how much risk is involved, and is the level acceptable in
relation to benefits and when compared to other activities of children. In the
U.S.A., one study showed agriculture to be a particularly high-risk employment
for adolescents, with many accidents due to the use of machinery (Wilk, 1993).
This does not mean that they should not work in agriculture—children's work is
legally allowed on family farms throughout the world—but it does mean that
more care needs to be taken when young people come near machinery.

Psychosocial Considerations

Psychologist Martin Woodhead (2004, 324) has pointed out that children are
often aware of hazards, but weigh these against the benefits that work conveys to
them, and argued that assessments of hazards would be misleading if they did
not include psychological, social, and economic rewards from working, such as
the status and self-esteem they acquire from contributing to their families.
Psychosocial factors are related to what the UNCRC is concerned with when it
requires protection from work likely to be harmful to a child's "mental, spiritual,
moral or social development" (article 32). There is widespread agreement among
researchers, program staff, and children's advocates that these are at least as
important as physical factors in assessing the impact of work on children.

We listed some principle psychosocial factors in chapter 5. There is much
anecdotal and case study literature describing positive psychosocial effects of
work as well as instances in which negative psychosocial effects of work on children have been observable and serious. But these are hard to measure, and a lack
of suitable methodological tools for applying research findings to practical situations has prevented these factors from receiving as much attention as physical
ones. Martin Woodhead (2004) has now produced a useful framework for analyzing the psychosocial impact of work on children. At the center of his system
and argument, Woodhead proposes grouping impacts into five important psychological and social "domains" that need to be investigated in respect to children under study. These domains represent clusters of topics on which there is
substantial psychological or other social science research. For each domain, he
lists generalized indicators for both positive and negative impact, insists that
both need to be analyzed, and summarizes what needs to be considered for each
of the five domains. The result is a comprehensive map of issues presenting an
empirical basis for guiding research and policy, as shown in table 8.1.

Woodhead makes two further points worth special attention. First, children's self-image is of central importance to their mental health. Work, or interventions in work, that damage their sense of identity and self-esteem not only

TABLE 8.1

A framework for assessing psychosocial well-being among
working children

Broad domains	Major positive indicators	Major negative indicators
Cognitive abilities and cultural competencies	Intelligence, cognitive, communication and practical skills, culturally valued	Delayed development, narrow range of cognitive, technical, and communication skills, maladaptive for future prospects
Personal security, social integration, and social competence	Secure attachments, positive adult/peer relations, social integration/adjustment, moral reasoning, and behavior	Insecurity, inhibition, low social confidence, conflictual relationships, social exclusion or rejection, deviant or antisocial behavior
Personal identity and valuation	Positive self-concept, high self-esteem, self-worth, personal pride	Feelings of worthlessness, fear of failure, self-denigration, negative social comparisons, shame and stigma
Personal agency	Self-efficacy, internal locus of control, autonomy, responsibility, positive outlook, motivation	Learned helplessness, external locus of control, hopelessness, apathy, fatalism, feelings of confusion, betrayal, abandonment
Emotional and somatic expressions of well-being	Subjective well-being, stability, general health, growth, and development	Stress, trauma, fear, anxiety, depression, anger, distress, despair, disturbed sleep and eating, substance abuse, self-harm

Source: Woodhead, 2004, 348

seriously undermine their mental health, but may amplify other forms of harm as well. This facet is often ignored in traditional interventions into children's work, and is perhaps a source of considerable harm to children.

Second, Woodhead points out that work may be an important "protective factor" boosting children's ability to cope successfully with adversity. Far from being a cause of trauma to children, as is frequently assumed, the engagement of children in work may in fact often be a factor preventing trauma. There is some recent research evidence that even exposure to risk and to stress, in moderate amounts and in situations in which it can be handled by the children, may help to equip children with coping skills useful more generally (Werner and Smith, 1982, 136, 163, 158; Legault, et al., 2006; Caldwell, et al., 2004). Work may be an important mechanism of this learning (Boyden, forthcoming).

Weighing Harm against Benefits

It is useful to compare the way we think about work with the way we consider other childhood activities. In the case of most sports, the benefits accruing to children are considered to outweigh the risks involved. When a child suffers from bad relations with teachers or peers at school, or excessive stress at examination time, appropriate solutions focus on improving the situation or coping skills of the child. When a child suffers from abuse or excessive work at home, social workers try to find ways of improving the situation of the child and only in extreme cases do they recommend removal of the child from the home (see e.g., Dearden and Becker, 2004).

Similarly, when children are exposed to harm or hazard in the workplace, it is not always necessary, or the best available option, to remove the children from work. It is often more useful and respectful to them to focus first on the precise nature of their problems in the contexts of the children's lives. Extra income for food might be extremely important for a child who would otherwise be malnourished, but insignificant to a child from a middle-class home. Feelings of competence arising from productive work may be insignificant to a child who is excelling at school, but may be very important for the self-esteem of a child humiliated by poor school grades. A child in a secure home is likely to develop resilience to cope with adversity, while a child without this security may learn to cope only through successful work. Abusive supervisors may be more threatening to girls than to boys. Young children might suffer more through separation from their families than do older teenagers. While no list of potential workplace benefits and harm can be all-inclusive, we suggest here a summary of common points to be considered (table 8.2).

A Note on Exploitation

The UNCRC requires that children be protected from "economic exploitation," a term often used with reference to children's work, but rarely defined.[13] In common English usage, the term suggests taking unfair advantage. Karl Marx defined exploitation in terms of surplus value: capitalist employers pay workers much less than the added value generated by their inputs in production, and so

TABLE 8.2

Potential benefits and harm in children's work

	Potential benefits	*Potential harm*
Physical		
Health	Improved nutrition—for worker and other children in family	Unhealthy environment Tiredness from excessive work or lack of sleep
Growth	Exercise	Excessive work hindering growth
Working conditions		Excessive hours, poor lighting, excessive noise, cramped conditions
Hazards	Learn to deal with dangerous situations	Toxic chemicals Air polluted by dust or vapors Dangerous equipment Abusive punishment
Income		
	Improved livelihood—for worker and other children in family Growing autonomy Rights in family resources	None or inadequate remuneration Remuneration taken by guardians or others
Psychosocial		
Learning	Life skills, trade skills Learning to interact with adults, customers, etc. Experience for future labor-force work	Prevents or hinders schooling
Responsibility	Develop a sense of responsibility	Anxiety from excessive expectations
Agency	Growing autonomy Sense of purpose, especially for those out-of-school Develop resilience by dealing successfully with stress Discipline, learn to manage time	Forced to work with no choices Lose control over life in an abusive work situation Loss of confidence after failing to cope with excessive stress Loss of opportunity for creative activity

(continued)

TABLE 8.2

Potential benefits and harm in children's work *(continued)*

	Potential benefits	*Potential harm*
Relations	Broadening of relationships with adults and peers	Independence and loss of adult guidance
	Relief from tension at home or school	Harmful relations in the workplace
	Shared experience with working parents	Disrupted relations when away from home
	Improved relations in the home	Social isolation
		Tensions in the home
Self-esteem	Sense of achievement, status	Denigration, work not appreciated
Status	Status in family and with peers	Loss of freedom, dignity
	Empowerment	Gender discrimination, sexual harassment
	Improved status for girls	
Recreation	Escape from a dreary home	Loss of leisure

are able to keep for themselves the surplus value generated during a part of the working day. This use of the term is widely accepted in social studies, although the boundary is not always clear between acceptable returns on investments (without which capitalists will not invest) and exploitation of powerless workers. In the case of adult workers, combating the exploitation of labor means ensuring they are properly rewarded and working under tolerable conditions, not normally forcing them to stop working. This may be seen in the efforts of both organized and unorganized labor to achieve better wages, reduce the hours of work, and improve working conditions.

With respect to children, however, "exploitation" is often used to refer more broadly to harmful work,[14] or sometimes to any work below a certain age, changing the meaning of the term from its use in adult contexts. Some people assume that any child who undertakes productive work outside the family must inevitably be exploited (e.g., Schlemmer, 2000, 12).[15] The definition of "exploitation" is thus stretched (we believe incorrectly) to apply to any situation in which children enter the labor market.

"Exploitation"—like many other terms discussed in this chapter—is a relative term, and as such is easy to recognize in its extreme forms (such as slavery and forced labor) but difficult to pin down in other contexts. What is a fair wage for a child when adult wages are unfair? Underpaid work of children is often part of a general situation of inequality, in which rich and powerful nations, social classes, firms, or individuals increase their profits or standard of living by paying minimally for the resources and labor of members of poorer communities. In this perspective, the work-free childhoods of wealthier people are linked to the exploitation of children in poorer communities, and the exploitation of children is seen as part of a wider exploitative situation (Nieuwenhuys, 2005; Bey, 2003).

Protection from exploitation requires that children are properly rewarded for their work. But what is proper? Even with respect to adult labor, what is acceptable—and what can realistically be achieved in collective bargaining and labor struggles—depends on local economic and political conditions, on available technology, and on local expectations. When children are paid on a piecework basis at the same rates as adults are paid, they are not being exploited *as children*, although they may experience the problem of the general exploitation of labor.

If children are paid lower wages than adults for the same work, does that automatically constitute age-based exploitation? With respect to time-based wages, children often receive lower wages than adults, and this is sometimes established in minimum-wage regulations. In the Netherlands, the minimum wage is scaled according to age: there is no minimum wage for workers below the age of fifteen (although various kinds of paid employment are permitted from age thirteen), and a fifteen-year-old is entitled to only a third of the full adult minimum wage, gradually increasing to the full adult minimum wage at the age of twenty-three.[16] Similarly in Britain, the National Minimum Wage Act (1998, chapter 39, 1, 2, c) does not apply to those below the age of compulsory schooling (sixteen): in 2009, the hourly minimum wage was £5.73 for an adult, £4.77 for those under twenty-two, and £3.53 for those under eighteen.[17] In these countries, therefore, age-based discrimination in wages is sanctioned and regulated.

Paid employment is not the only context in which children may be exploited. Unpaid work in the home can be even more exploitative than factory work (Nieuwenhuys, 2000). We have pointed out that children can become effectively full-time but unpaid domestic servants within their extended families, and that children's work is sometimes part of an exploitative situation affecting the whole family or community. Adults sometimes demand that children work to provide adults with (relatively) more leisure, as women and girls are sometimes compelled to contribute long hours of reproductive work compared to men and boys.

At the very beginning of this book we clarified our standpoint, stating that "we condemn the exploitation and abuse of child workers" and "we support the UN Convention on the Rights of the Child, including the right of all children under 18 to 'protection from economic exploitation.'" While "exploitation" in its extreme forms—which typically include non-economic coercion of some kind—may be easy to recognize, the above note shows the great difficulty of using "economic exploitation" operationally as a criterion for intervention.

What Does This Mean in Practice?

The evidence and arguments presented in this chapter suggest that it is probably impossible, and in any case of doubtful value, to develop a set of clear, objective, and unambiguous criteria to distinguish between "intolerable," "harmful/hazardous," and "neutral/positive" forms of children's work, covering all situations and contexts. Where certain clearly harmful situations are common in a particular type of work and environment, more general rules may be necessary. Abuse of child domestic workers, for example, may be so common in a particular social setting that minimum-age regulation may be justified. Generally, local communities, in consultation with the children concerned, are better able to assess such situations than international or even national bodies, both in terms of relative harm and benefit to children and in terms of available alternatives.

This task does not lend itself to bureaucratic judgment and classification, such as by government ministries. This task is best accomplished through consultative procedures in which the observations and opinions of children, parents, employers, and outside observers are taken into consideration. For this reason, approaches involving community consultation have evolved in various places for making decisions about the appropriateness of children's work and possible interventions in it.

In some places, consultation has been formalized in some sort of "council" mechanism. A 1995 report from UNICEF on what then were considered new approaches to "child labor" described two of these (Boyden and Myers, 1995). In the Philippines, protection of working children was overseen by local councils bringing together local civil society groups involved in social services and advocacy of many different kinds. The participating organizations brought a variety of viewpoints and priorities to the table, where they pooled observations and agreed on where attention was needed for the benefit of children. This example was largely driven by "grass roots" initiatives and organization, and supported by local and national government (Rialp, 2005).

In Brazil, a similar system of independently formed local councils was subsequently formalized in national law, and expanded to take in a broader spectrum of child protection issues. All municipalities were mandated to form councils for child rights and protection, with equal participation from civil society and local government. While national government provided a legislative framework of procedural law and principles, the local councils joining government and civil society were empowered to decide priorities and actions appropriate to local situations and the specific children involved. This system emerged from extensive positive experience with cooperation between local programs dealing with "street children" and other working children. The expansion was based on the finding that problematic situations in children's work tended to be linked to many other social and economic conditions also requiring attention, making it necessary to approach the issues from a perspective much broader than just that of "child labor" (Boyden and Myers, 1995, 11–29; Myers, 1988).

Experience also has made clear that one starting point of any consultative process should be the observations and opinions of the children concerned. They provide good sources of information and often new insights into the positive or negative aspects of different kinds of work and work situations. Like many adult workers, they do not always have the knowledge and experience to appreciate long-term hazards, and often they do not have experience to extend their observations to situations very different from their own. Nevertheless, they are in a good position to assess kinds of work situations in their local context most in need of attention, and the kind of attention that would be helpful.

Consultative processes are necessary and productive in part because they help refocus the terms of discussion away from abstract ideological positions and toward the particular facts and problems of actual children and situations. Experience strongly suggests that while it has been next to impossible to annunciate rules that successfully apply everywhere, it is in fact not so difficult to discern at the local level what specific work situations are damaging to children and require urgent attention, and to devise interventions specific to local context that effectively work for children. "What is important is that concrete, feasible decisions be made about which child work problems require the most urgent attention, and that these decisions enjoy at least a modicum of social credibility and legitimacy. Fortunately, the task of designating children at high risk usually turns out to be easier in practice than in theory . . . it is a question more successfully lived through in practice than intellectually agonised over beforehand" (Bequele and Myers, 1995, 26–27).

The next chapter looks at specific interventions and illustrates the importance of balancing harm against benefits in children's work, and the damage that can result to children's well-being when this is not done. It shows further how children's interests are enmeshed in larger national and international interests.

9

The Politics of International Intervention

The discussion to this point has focused primarily on how work, and interventions in work, affect children as individuals. This chapter expands the optic to consider how national and international policies, institutions, and interventions governing children's work play out in the national and international politics of "child labor." The Méknès case, with which the book opened, presented a close-up study of how irresponsible coverage by British media of a small number of teenage girls working legally in a Morocco clothing factory rebounded disastrously on the girls. We heard them relate the devastating impact of being dismissed from their jobs as a result of uninformed foreign pressure based on unjustified stereotypes and assumptions about "child labor." Subsequent chapters have deconstructed these notions, indicating why they should not serve as the basis for dealing with issues of child work, criticizing interventions based on them as empirically unjustified, and suggesting other approaches that we believe would be more protective for children. Now it is time to consider the much larger-scale penetration and impact of ideas about child work when they are applied nationally and internationally as policies and are infused with the power of the state and economic globalization. We look to see how working children and their rights fare when subjected to the "pressure cooker" of international power politics and economic interests.

This chapter begins with two cases from South Asia, one in Bangladesh and the other in Pakistan, in which outside political and economic pressure on these countries to implement child labor policies in their export sectors forced strict compliance with ILO Convention 138. We present these relatively well-known and well-documented cases as examples of good intentions gone seriously awry, and we discuss how that happened and some implications for rethinking children's rights and policy governing the work of children. The Pakistani case shows how the lessons that should have been learned from Bangladesh were ignored a few years later. We then consider a case from Egypt in which an approach is taken to issues of child work that we believe to be far more likely to benefit the children. The chapter ends with some general conclusions and suggestions.

We ask the active reader running through these cases to be awake to two issues that are of paramount importance in considering international policy and politics governing the work of children. First is the question of how to balance the application of universalized international standards with contextualized understanding of children's specific needs and situations in particular instances. What are the fundamental differences between intervening in child work primarily on the basis of international norms and intervening primarily on the basis of empirical understanding of children and their situation in particular instances? This issue is important because the two approaches generate very different definitions of the problems, actions to solve them, and results for children. Can they be reconciled, and if so, how? The second issue is that of accountability, especially to children's best interests, in the face of great power inequalities. What is the proper use of political and economic power in promoting children's rights and well-being, and what constitutes the abuse of power? What should be done when international standards and children's welfare seem to conflict? Can insisting on the application of international standards constitute an abuse of power? How can inequities between rich and poor countries be managed to ensure that raw political and economic power does not overwhelm the best interests of children and drown out the voices of the vulnerable and powerless?

The Case of Child Garment Workers in Bangladesh: Tragedy or Scandal?

One of the most visible and heated current debates about child work concerns whether goods produced with the participation of child workers should be excluded from international trade, whether by governments through law or by consumers through boycotts. It is also a discussion of whether children should or should not be allowed to work in businesses producing goods for export. By extension, this debate now has become something of a battleground between defenders of an abolitionist approach seeking to remove "underage" workers from their economic activities and proponents of less draconian interventions seeking first to protect children in work they want, coercively removing them only when required for children's own protection. The first position is today especially associated with ministries of labor, trade unions, and the ILO. The second has widespread (but not universal) support among NGOs that work with children, child rights and protection specialists, academics, and UNICEF.

To facilitate understanding of the complex issues involved, this chapter presents a now famous (or infamous) Bangladesh case in which some tens of thousands of children were forcibly removed from their jobs in the export garment industry. It first recounts how American ideas and politics resulted in massive coerced retrenchment of working children in a faraway country, and then describes the effects of the retrenchment on child workers and a program attempting to mitigate the worst effects on some of them.

Historical Background

In 1992, Bangladesh was one of the world's poorest countries, desperately short of revenues and foreign exchange required to invest in the most basic physical and human infrastructure for development. Its agriculture had very limited possibilities, but the country had found a workable, productive niche as a producer of clothing for export, and it became one of the world's leading manufacturers of ready-made garments. By far its largest market was the U.S.A., and ready-made garment exports to that country provided roughly 40 percent of all Bangladesh foreign exchange earnings.

The garment industry was even more important as a source of employment. The government calculated that every job in the ready-made garment industry generated about nine more jobs elsewhere in the economy, which meant that the roughly 1.4 million workers directly in the industry generated jobs for as many as ten million more.[1] Moreover, these were modern sector jobs that provide for more upward mobility and the creation of a more skilled workforce than do agriculture, crafts, transportation, and the other prominent forms of employment. Most of the direct benefits were to women, providing them with access to regular wages, relative independence, more influence in the household, and increased choices in how to live their lives. Although work in the garment industry can be hard and unpleasant, various studies of women workers in this industry have shown that they view their work as one of their few available routes to improve their lives (Paul-Majunder and Begum, 1997; Kabeer, 2001). Benefits to women were known to convey especially important nutritional, health, educational, and other benefits to their children.

Child workers had been present in the Bangladesh garment industry since its inception, but were never a mainstay of its workforce. Although there has been no enumeration of the garment industry workforce according to age, estimates from the most qualified observers placed the percentage of child workers at no more than 15 percent of the total workforce prior to retrenchment. The industry was never really dependent on child workers for its survival, but did find them useful as a reserve labor force that could be hired at times of peak demand, such as for the pre-Christmas rush. Most child workers were girls twelve years of age and older who worked in safe entry-level tasks (such as handing materials to sewing machine operators) as "helpers" for a few months at a time, entering and leaving the workforce or moving between employers at will. Those who stayed with an employer for a year or so as a helper generally were promoted into more skilled and higher paid positions when they attained the legal working age of fourteen (Zohir and Paul-Majunder, 1996; Paul-Majunder and Chowdhury, 1993; Paul-Majunder and Begum, 1997).

Children did not generally consider work in the hot and crowded garment factories to be pleasant. They kept the same hours as did adults, and in seasons of peak demand might put in eleven or more hours per day, and although their work was not strenuous, it could be stressful. Children complained that they were often shouted at and humiliated by supervisors for even minor mistakes and infractions, and sometimes were physically abused, usually in the form of slaps (e.g., Pelto, 1997).[2] Such treatment, however, seems to have reflected how Bangladeshi children were generally supervised and corrected everywhere—in school and home as well as in employment. In studies of current and former child garment workers, half or more of the respondents felt they were treated better in the garment industry than they would have been in other kinds of work realistically open to them (such as domestic service or manual labor).

There were tangible advantages to a job in the garment industry. In 1993, a survey[3] of working children drawn from a sample of 500 households in Dhaka areas known to provide workers for the garment industry found that children working in the industry were earning more,[4] eating more nutritiously, and making better use of health services than were children either not working at all or working in other jobs. But child garment workers were not generally attending school, although most had received some education before working. No respondent in this sample had returned to school upon leaving the garment factories, largely for reasons that excluded them from schooling in the first place. Another study of the same period found that three-quarters of a sample of 100 child garment workers had attended school up to at least the third year, but few of them had learned to read well enough to pass a simple literacy test (Rahman, no date). Children reported that most other work open to them paid less, and was more dangerous or otherwise less appropriate for them.[5] Observers agreed (Zohir and Paul-Majunder, 1996; Kamal, et al., 1993). In the extreme poverty of Bangladesh, many children did not have the option not to work and instead to attend school full time.

The U.S. Movement to Ban Importation of Products Made with Child Labor

Starting in late 1992, tens of thousands of child workers from Bangladesh export garment factories were dismissed from their jobs as the result of pressure from the United States. The immediate cause was proposed (but never enacted) legislation in the United States Congress that would have denied goods made with participation of child workers access to United States markets. This legislative project, properly known as the Child Labor Deterrence Act of 1992, was commonly called "The Harkin Bill," after United States Senator Tom Harkin of Iowa, one of its most prominent sponsors. It was strongly and aggressively backed by

United States trade unions and a coalition of forty United States nonprofit organizations known as the Child Labor Coalition.

The purpose of this legislation and the support for it was in dispute. Various Bangladesh accounts from the time suggested it was at least in part trade protectionism to shield the United States textile industry, masquerading as child protection. United States government, trade unions, and civil society activists hotly contested this view and insisted that their interest in child labor in the Bangladesh garment industry was motivated entirely by broader social justice and child welfare concerns, of which Bangladesh happened to be a particular case. A report by Sarah Bachman, a well-qualified United States journalist familiar with labor issues, addressed this issue.[6] She pointed out that the Harkin Bill essentially updated the foundational Fair Labor Standards Act of 1938, which among other things prohibited the interstate transport or sale of domestic products made with child labor, by expanding this prohibition to goods imported from outside the U.S.A. She found no hard evidence of protectionism as the driving motive, although general concerns about "leveling the playing field" for United States exports were current at the time.[7] The language in and surrounding the Harkin Bill also suggests that it was intended to improve the lives of children by freeing them from factory and other production work in order to attend school.

In December of 1992, only months after the introduction of the Harkin Bill, a major television network in the United States broadcast an investigative report showing that America's largest retailer (Wal-Mart Stores) was selling clothing labeled as made in the USA, but actually produced in Bangladesh with the involvement of child labor. The resulting uproar attracted both political and public support for legislative action to ban imports made by children, and some organizations threatened a consumer boycott.

Afraid of a boycott in the country providing the biggest market for their goods, and anticipating an American demand that all products be produced exclusively by adult workers, some Bangladeshi garment manufacturers began to divest their operations of the youngest workers. Buyers for clothing retailers also began to insist that Bangladeshi suppliers rid their factories of underage workers if they were to keep their sales contracts.[8] Under trade union pressure, the United States Government also became involved and aggressive. Widely articulated threats from the American ambassador and the local office of the Asian-American Free Labor Institute[9] inflamed Bangladeshi fears of an imminent United States consumer boycott. This caused a near panic, and the industry abruptly increased the rate at which it was dumping young workers into the street, sometimes without paying them back-wages already earned.

The desperate situation of children suddenly bereft of income began to overwhelm local and international organizations concerned with child rights and welfare issues, and they raised the alarm of a massive emergency. It remains far from clear just how many children were laid off (retrenched), since they just disappeared from view and there was no way to count them: a general magnitude of 40,000–50,000 has been adopted as a consensus guess. It was observed that the retrenched children were not returning to school as the United States campaigners against child labor had expected, but were instead showing up in other types of work still less appropriate for children than garment work[10]—such as chipping bricks into aggregate, maid service, and even prostitution.[11] A subsequent systematic tracer survey[12] of former child workers in export garment factories suggested that a large number found new jobs in non-export clothing factories where pay, working conditions, and opportunities for advancement were notably inferior to those in the factories producing for export. This survey found that retrenched child garment workers experienced a significant reduction of both income and quality of life. Their diet deteriorated seriously, and they used health services much less. Very few of them returned to school.

It became clear that even the well-meaning U.S. champions of clearing child labor out of the Bangladesh garment industry had seriously miscalculated what would happen to retrenched children. How could such a blunder have happened? There is no record of Senator Harkin, or any member or staffer of the United States Congress, having visited Bangladesh or any other developing country to consult in advance with local experts on the expected social results of legislation banning the importation of goods produced with the participation of child workers. The whole episode was based on United States suppositions and assumptions that apparently were never even questioned until they provoked a disaster among the children of Bangladesh. Those assumptions were the same ones behind ILO Convention 138, and it now seems evident that United States actors simply assumed that the reigning ILO international standard to protect against child labor would be good for children everywhere. The only issue they saw was implementation, in this case by imposition. Few among the American actors questioned the competency of the standard itself, even though the United States declined to ratify Convention 138 because of problems it recognized in respect to its own children and society. Many noted that that the U.S.A. was using its immense political and economic power to apply to Bangladesh an international standard it would not accept for itself.

Mitigating the Tragedy

Early in 1993, when retrenched children were appearing on the streets but before the worst wave of uncontrolled dismissals, some concerned NGOs and UNICEF in Dhaka had begun looking at the problem from a perspective of child rights. Although UNICEF recognized ILO Convention 138 as a valid guideline for intervention—which implied approval of removing underage workers from the garment factories and placing them in school as the alternative to work—it also called attention to the UNCRC requirement (Article 3) that children's best interest be a "primary consideration" in "all actions concerning children, whether undertaken by public or private social welfare institutions." This opened the door to a UNICEF suggestion, eventually backed by the ILO and the United States and Bangladesh governments, that the garment manufacturers contribute to a fund to provide education, welfare, and other support necessary to ensure that underage children removed from the industry would benefit rather than be left worse off.

This proposal was not well received at first, and it took over two years to convince the various parties and move them to an agreement in principle to assist retrenched children, and it took still another year to negotiate an agreed plan of action,[13] by which time the vast majority of child garment workers had already been retrenched by the factory owners and had disappeared from view. The program simply came too late for most of the children affected by the United States pressure to eliminate child labor from the industry.

Two intervention models were formally proposed for consideration. One followed the model of the Harkin Bill and ILO Convention 138, and entailed removing children from work and placing them in school. This approach was supported primarily by the ILO, the United States Embassy, American pressure groups, and the Bangladesh Garments Manufacturers and Exporters Association (BGMEA), the latter trying to avert the United States threat and still reluctant to foot the bill. They recognized ILO Convention 138 as the universal standard that should be implemented. Activities to protect children according to the UNCRC would have to work within its framework.

The second proposal started from assessment of the specific situation of the children involved, as well as some prior pilot experience in providing education to children in connection with their work. Putting foremost the UNCRC mandate of "best interest," it would leave underage children in the factories, but would seek to ensure them decent workplace treatment and a basic education by structuring combinations of work and school. There would be regular inspection of working conditions, creation of opportunities for advancement, and time off by child workers to attend basic education classes in or near the factory sites. This approach appears to have been favored by virtually all Bangladeshi experts and organizations involved (except BGMEA), together with foreign child defense organizations such as Save the Children. It was also supported by large NGOs with outstanding international reputations for their work in child protection and non-formal education. The idea was imaginative: rather than stripping children of their jobs to get them into school, it would use the concentration of children in factories as a ready-made opportunity to channel education to them without unnecessarily disrupting their lives and source of income. This idea drew on some very promising prior pilot projects in cooperation with progressive garment factory owners. In fact, one NGO had already started such a program with the BGMEA to provide working children with upward mobility inside the industry.

This second model, which local observers thought clearly better for the children, ran into stiff opposition from corporate garment-buyers, who complained that it would be difficult to explain to consumers why children should be left working in the factories. BGMEA would not agree to anything that would put off the buyers and leave the industry vulnerable to loss of its markets. An earn-and-learn approach would not address the purpose of the Harkin Bill, which was to ban the import of goods made with participation of children below 15 years of age. The government of Bangladesh recognized the advantages of an earn-and-learn strategy, but it did not want to run the risk of a boycott that would demolish an industry hiring and sustaining the families of over a million people. It pointed out that the losses of jobs by child workers in factories would cause far less misery among children than would sudden unemployment of a million women with young children depending on them and their wages.

Against the advice of almost everyone who understood and had contact with the situation of child garment workers, the intransigence of buyers, BGMEA, and the United States government killed the earn-and-learn option. That decided, the only issue left was how to move the remaining working children out of the industry with a minimum of harm and bad publicity and get them into school. The difficult negotiations to plan a program of this type resulted in a Memorandum of Understanding (MOU), signed by UNICEF, ILO, and BGMEA, two and a half years after the dismissals started. The stated purpose of the MOU was "the removal of underaged children from BGMEA factories, including subcontracting factories in Bangladesh, and their placement in appropriate education programmes." There were also supplementary activities intended to ease the way from work to school. The main components of the MOU included:

1. Registration by specially trained enumerators of all children under 14 still working in the garment factories.
2. Planned removal of registered children from factory employment and transition into appropriate schools, with provision of a monthly scholarship stipend (amounting to about half what they typically earned as workers), received as long as the child attends school, up to the age of 14.
3. Establishment of appropriate schools readily accessible to all children from their place of residence. Special MOU schools were established in the makeshift *bustees* housing areas where most workers lived and used a curriculum and methods adapted to the needs of the children, most of whom were too old to be accommodated in regular public schools.
4. No new employment of children under fourteen years of age.
5. An inspection and verification system through unannounced garment factory visits by specially trained and hired labor inspectors.

The program proved extremely challenging to manage and was beset by serious problems in almost every activity. The problem was in part the complex model itself, which was aptly characterized by the UNICEF Representative as "a mechanism with too many moving parts and gears that don't mesh." Many factory managers obstructed the registration of their child workers either by hiding them or firing them before they could be registered. Because of long delays, many children gave up, simply disappeared—probably fired, or turned fourteen years of age—before school places could be found or subsistence funds placed into bank accounts. Mobility in and out of the labor market and between factories meant that many children were hard to find; perhaps as few as half the children working in garment factories during the project period were identified and registered. There were problems finding facilities for schools in crowded slum communities where most of the children lived. And so on.

How successful was the whole endeavor? That judgment depends on the criteria applied. One way to assess it is according to its objective—to transfer children out of work and into school. Studies conducted after the program ended suggest that it probably did reduce the number of children found working in the factories in 1995, but of course the vast majority of child workers disappeared long before then. What the project added was credible inspection that could attest to buyers, consumers, and the United States government that factories were reasonably clear of child labor. When it started in 1995, the project found and registered children in 40 percent of the factories, where it calculated they formed about 3.6 percent of the garment industry workforce. By the end of the project in 2001, children were found in only 4.5 percent of the factories, and were calculated to comprise only 0.3 percent of the workforce (UNICEF and ILO, 2004).[14] These figures were accurate only to the extent that inspectors actually found all the children working in the industry, and some observers believed that more children remained in the industry than the ILO and BGMEA inspections reported. As later surveys suggested, a great many children managed to keep on working without interference. Nevertheless, some significant magnitude of reduction probably did occur.

The fundamental objective of the MOU was not only to remove all remaining underage workers from the factories but also to place them in school. Although 336 special MOU schools were eventually established, enrolling about 8,500 students during the life of the project, about half of these students seem to have been from local communities and not the same children identified in the factories for transfer from work to schooling. Follow-up studies strongly suggested that only a tiny minority of children working in the factories in 1995 were successfully identified and moved into education. Once in school, retention became a major problem. A full course of instruction capable of taking a child to literacy was planned for three years, but the vast majority of working children turned fourteen and lost their stipends before completing the course, and so returned to work. However, Bissell's field research found that children who did manage to stay in school reported being happy and learning there. The follow-up study also found former child workers who reported learning much that they found useful, along with feelings of efficacy and self-worth from having achieved literacy. Observers noted that the MOU schools were temporary and only took care of retrenched children without improving the public education system or opening opportunity for future children from the community. Here today, gone tomorrow, the schools were not developmental.

Another way to gauge success is to look at what happened to children in the long run. One of the assumptions behind the Harkin Bill was that working impedes the eventual economic progress of children, and that removing them from work and placing them in school would provide better job and income opportunities in adulthood. By comparison, those who continued to work should in the longer term advance and earn less. To what extent was that true for children working in the Bangladesh garment industry? The tracer study found that five years after the project ended, children who managed to evade retrenchment and continue working in the export garment industry had fared much better economically than had children who were dismissed, whether or not they attended MOU schools. Those who remained in the factories had become more skilled and had advanced normally to better jobs as machine operators or even supervisors. Retrenched children coming back into the industry after turning fourteen years of age had lost their seniority and had to start over at the entry level with lower earnings. While it is possible that children with more education might someday rise higher and eventually recoup the earnings they lost while out of the job market, at least five years afterward this had not yet happened. In the garment industry, experience and on-the-job training were the main channels of advancement, more than the very rudimentary education children received in the MOU schools. This advancement system had long been known by researchers, but it was ignored by planners of the MOU, who did not contest the Harkin and ILO assumptions of the primacy of school education as the passport to advancement.

Another way to assess the MOU would be to evaluate it by the principles of child rights, especially as laid out in the UNCRC. From this point of view it was roundly criticized by a wide variety of both local and international child rights advocates. Some thought the MOU, by acceding to coerced retrenchment and serving so few victimized children and so poorly, was itself a violation of children's rights far worse than was the work that children had been doing. They saw the MOU as more the problem than the solution. UNICEF, as the UN agency entrusted with promoting the UNCRC, came under special attack, for many felt that it had betrayed its role as the protector of child rights and the best interests of children when it supported retrenchment.[15] Indeed, the UNICEF response reflected the focus of its Implementation Handbook on the UNCRC (UNICEF, 1998b), which pays little attention to reaching the Convention's objectives for children and instead emphasizes conformity with other rules set by related international organizations.

But there is a more nuanced and forgiving way of seeing the MOU, and especially UNICEF's role, in a child rights perspective. A terrible situation already
existed, and an emergency intervention was called for in order to reduce its disastrous effects on children. None of the intervention options realistically available at that late point in time were good ones. By that measure, UNICEF and
others undertaking the MOU appear responsive rather than cynical, doing all
that one could under severe and unavoidable constraints. Anything helpful to at
least some children was better than doing nothing. It could be argued that refus-
ing to intervene at all, in the name of purity, would have been a greater betrayal
of child rights and a severe lack of compassion. In kinder circumstances in which
UNICEF and other organizations had the luxury of being able to design and promote an appropriate program prior to an emergency, perhaps the earn-and-
learn or other beneficial options would have been possible, but the pressing
emergency conditions in the Bangladesh case as it occurred did not permit that.

We notice that, despite all that has been documented about the negative
impact of retrenchment on children and the weak ameliorative effects of the
MOU, to this day the ILO continues to portray the MOU as successful and to recommend this model for getting children out of export industries in other places.
That is because it has focused on the objective of removing underage children
from the labor market rather than the objective of leaving children in a better
situation. It is also why it became involved just a few years later in a similar project to eliminate child workers from the football industry in Pakistan, the case to
which we now turn.

Stitching Footballs in Sialkot

This case began similarly to the Bangladesh case. In 1995, an American news
channel attacked the sporting goods company, Reebok, for selling footballs
(soccer balls) made with "child labor" around the city of Sialkot, Pakistan, a
region that was producing almost 90 percent of the world's footballs. In the following year, numerous media reports portrayed children being forced to stitch
footballs instead of going to school. A European and American based "Foul Ball
Campaign" was organized to remove children from this work. It threatened
multinational buyers of the footballs with adverse publicity and possible consumer boycott action (Khan, 2007, 37–40). Many Pakistanis perceived this campaign as foreign aggression and their country as a victim (Khan, 2007, 50–51).

Most stitching took place in homes through a system of piece-work subcontracting: sweatshops were very rare. Working in homes allowed the whole
family to participate and to fit work into other schedules. Women could combine this income-earning work with their domestic work and caring for young
children. Children in the family could help their parents when they were free,
usually in a relaxed and protective atmosphere, and learn the skills required by

participating. Beginners could stitch the simple seams, leaving the more complicated parts to skilled stitchers. This work was not generally viewed as exploitative: a Pakistani child rights activist, Fawad Usman Khan, commented, "If it were
up to me, I would take all child labourers out of the more hazardous professions
and put them into the football industry—there are no chemicals, they are well
paid, and the hours are flexible. The children can work at home in their spare
time, mixing it with housework or after school . . . this is an easy sector compared
to carpets or tanneries" (Khan, 2007, 172).

A study in 1997 by Save the Children showed that child stitchers tended to
come from poorer families than did non-stitchers. Although the majority of
stitchers had dropped out of school, they were nearly as schooled as the non-
stitcher control group (Save the Children U.K., 1997, 18, 23 & tables 3–17). Their
reasons for dropping out of school included negative school experiences exacerbated by lack of support from uneducated parents (Khan, 2007, 181–184: see
chapter 6). Interestingly, the Save the Children study revealed that the percentage of stitchers reaching secondary school (13 percent) was four times that of
the control group, which suggests that stitching enabled them to pay school
expenses (Save the Children U.K., 1997, 35–36, tables 9, 12). It was clear that
these children, like their non-stitching counterparts, should stay in school
longer and receive a better education, but the evidence did not indicate that
stitching footballs was the reason for their not being in school.

Nevertheless, as in Bangladesh, Western assumptions and stereotypes pre-
vailed over local knowledge and perspectives, and again as in Bangladesh, it
appears that no effort was made by the campaign promoters to ascertain the
facts of the situation and the likely effects of the campaign on children. An agreement was reached and signed on February 14, 1997, in Atlanta (Georgia, U.S.A.) by
the Sialkot Chamber of Commerce and Industry, the ILO, and UNICEF, with the
aim of eliminating the labor of children under fourteen in the football industry.
Various NGOs subsequently joined the project. The Atlanta Agreement required
that all exporters transfer football production to stitching centers (factories),
which would operate under minimum standards of wages and conditions, employ
no children under the age of fourteen, and be monitored regularly under the
supervision of the ILO. Manufacturers failing to comply with the agreement
would be struck off the list of approved suppliers to FIFA, the world football
organization and sponsor of official matches.

The Agreement contained a "social protection program," which included
establishing schools for children removed from work, and for other children "at
risk" of being drawn into working. The program offered improved wages and
working conditions to those able to take up employment in the centers, but this
produced winners and losers among the poor. Young men and their families,
and people near the centers, seemed to benefit. Among the losers were the
poorest families, who depended on their children for part of the family income.

It was difficult for women to combine work in the centers with their housework and care of infants. The centers were usually some distance from the poorer districts, requiring greater expense for transport (in cash or time) of workers from these districts. Girls, who were confined to home more than boys, also lost out. Omar, a fourteen-year-old boy, commented, "We used to be able to stitch footballs when we needed to. Now there are no footballs coming to the homes for stitching. Why have they stopped our *rozi-roti* [means of living]? . . . They must hate us. . . . Maybe it is because we are Muslims and people in the West are against Muslims" (Khan, 2007, 53).

Unlike the Bangladesh case, few children moved into more hazardous work. This was partly because parents saw available work outside the home—such as filing surgical instruments, tanning leather, or working in brick kilns—as hazardous for their children (Khan, 2007, 171). At one stage, home-based centers were becoming popular among women, but the ILO monitors found it difficult to ensure children were not involved and so reduced their number (Khan, 2007, 109–131).

When project-supported schools were set up, many children attended them, but it is not clear that removal from their work had much to do with that. They found it advantageous to go to nonformal schools that required no fees or expenses for books and uniforms, and they appreciated that the teaching style and environment were more attractive. They noted that the flexible hours in these schools could allow for part-time work, and they often expressed a desire to combine work with school (Khan, 2007, 181–195). They wished the program had aimed at facilitating a work-study combination.

In summary: the best available assessments of this experience strongly suggest that stitching footballs was not generally harmful to the children, and that, from a child protection point of view, there was no compelling need to remove them from it. This fact could and should have been discovered through field investigation prior to the project. The fact that no such prior field investigation occurred suggests that the real orientation of this project was to protect the markets of football manufacturers and retailers from adverse publicity and possible boycott. Although some children benefited from educational aspects of the program, the most disadvantaged children paid the price through loss of income and opportunity. From the evidence, this project does not seem to have produced a net gain for children. However, it may have saved the football industry as a source of local employment.

What Should Be Learned from These Experiences?

The politics of international intervention involve issues of both policy and organizational behavior. The above cases raise important concerns in both areas.

These two illustrative examples warn against mindless application of universalized international policy standards under the untested assumption that, simply by being followed, they will produce their intended benefits. The world is more complicated than that: principles always need to be sensitively fitted to particular situations and contexts. In the case of ILO Convention 138, however, the issue is more serious. The underlying principle itself—preventing children below mid-adolescence from working—may be flawed. As indicated repeatedly throughout this book, many researchers and practitioners have for some years been signaling unease about this policy, and we have demonstrated conclusively that work within reasonable limits is by no means incompatible with children's education and development, as the policy erroneously assumes. In fact, a review of experience and the literature turns up no credible evidence—such as from the sorts of policy analysis routinely applied to other social welfare policies and programs—that policies banning children from work on the basis of their age have anywhere produced generally beneficial results for either children or society. After over 150 years of being internationally promoted as the accepted policy for protecting children from labor abuse, the national or international impact of this policy has yet to be studied (Bourdillon, et al., 2009). Since there is anecdotal evidence, such as comes from the above two cases, that the minimum-age approach can at least on occasion be counterproductive, perhaps campaigns to expand and implement it should be suspended at least until a proper analysis of its effects can be conducted to determine whether or not, and under what conditions, it is beneficial for children.

Subsequent to the dates of both these cases, the ILO adopted Convention 182 on the "Worst Forms of Child Labour," which targets work that clearly is inimical to children's well-being and development. The arrival of Convention 182 and its quick worldwide acceptance has been interpreted by some as evidence that the ILO and others now understand that Convention 138 is problematic and are moving away from it and toward a more rational strategy (Myers, 2001a). On the other hand, as noted in chapter 3, Convention 138 remains one of the conventions that the ILO considers foundational and obligatory to its members everywhere, and the ILO still seeks to expand its ratification. These conventions are not easily compatible, and in our opinion Convention 182 should supplant Convention 138 as the ILO's policy standard.

Concerning the behavior of countries and international organizations, the Bangladesh and Sialkot cases raise the crucial question of how to make powerful interests accountable. It is possible to argue that children in both places were betrayed and harmed by agencies ostensibly avowing to protect them and guard their rights. Who shall oversee the guardians and make them accountable? These cases validate fear that, in today's globalized economy, the most potent political and economic forces can dictate and manipulate international norms to suit their own convenience and to advance their own interests at the expense of the poor and less powerful. Were not international instruments, intended to protect children in Bangladesh and Sialkot, applied recklessly, even irresponsibly, by powerful groups to serve economic and commercial purposes at the expense of the best interests of children? In Bangladesh, a clearly articulated alternative approach that would have much better served the welfare and rights of children was discarded in favor of one that favored commercial and economic interests and put children at risk. In neither case did the parties depriving children of their work and income undertake prior research, or consult with children, to determine the likely effects of such a draconian measure on the children involved. Even the two international agencies ostensibly protecting children—UNICEF and the ILO—ended up supporting the objectives of economic and commercial interests over the best interests of children. A case can be made for doing what had to be done to keep the clothing and football industries viable as a source of employment—children have strong interest in the continuing employment of their adult family members. But many continue to question whether either UNICEF or the ILO made sufficient effort to challenge the perceptions and assumptions of the powerful before colluding with them to impinge on the rights and welfare of the powerless.

While there may be no easy solutions to issues of either the policy or the political behavior, it seems clear to us that any solutions must lie in the direction of more empirical attention to actual children and the particulars of their situations. Acting on international principles is not a license to ignore local realities. Paying more heed to children's situations and voices could have avoided many mistakes in both Bangladesh and Sialkot. We suggest that policy governing children's work should start with in-depth, empirical understanding of the particular children and specific situations involved. Countries and international organizations should start with, and act primarily on, carefully observed facts of the situation and context to serve the best interests of the children involved. In planning and conducting policies and programs, pertinent international standards such as the UNCRC and ILO Convention 182 should also be consulted as helpful references and guidelines to be utilized as appropriate in furthering the protection and development of children. The next case, a project for working children in Egypt, provides an illustration of what this way of working looks like in practice.

Promoting and Protecting the Interests
of Children Who Work: A Case in Egypt

The creation of employment and the improvement of family income comprise a strong element in most programs supporting small and micro enterprise, and the appearance of new jobs with people actively engaged in production is celebrated. But a recent survey in Upper Egypt showed that about half of the newly created businesses employed children below the age of fourteen years. While most of these children were family members of the business owners, worked reasonably short hours, and continued to attend school, questions arise as to whether specific interventions should be introduced to meet the needs of working children. In addition to these newly employed working children, there are many others already involved in the day to day running of thousands of small and micro enterprises across Egypt (Anonymous, 1998).

This introduction to a report on Egyptian children working in small and micro enterprises under extraneous political or economic pressures, and interest in the report, arose from direct observation of the characteristics and situation of working children in a given place—Aswan and the surrounding area—rather than from abstract international norms. Moreover, unlike the cases of Bangladesh and Sialkot recounted above, the question it posed for action was not how to remove the children from work but how to "meet the needs of working children." Out of this report, and ensuing discussions around it, evolved a project pragmatically espousing child rights and exploring innovative ways to protect working children from unsafe conditions, abusive treatment, and gender discrimination. It was also concerned that working children receive at least a basic education.

This project, called Promoting and Protecting the Interests of Children who Work (PPIC-W), was eventually proposed by the Egyptian Association for Community Initiatives and Development (EACID), an Aswan-based community micro-credit program that had been created to generate employment in the region through provision of credit to small and micro entrepreneurs. Early in its life it had received a grant from the Canadian International Development Agency (CIDA) to create a loan fund to finance women's enterprises. That project had been successful, and EACID was now self-sustaining, with an excellent repayment rate and expanding number of clients. Its founder and president, Dr. Mamdouh Foad, was a long-time community activist promoting local economic and social development. His Canadian partner in developing and organizing the project was Richard Carothers, a specialist in micro-finance with long international experience, including as a teacher at Botswana's Swaneng Hill School (mentioned in chapter 6), an innovator in the "education through production" movement. Through his own consultancy firm, Carothers was connected to a Canada-based NGO highly regarded for its expertise in micro-finance projects. The three organizations were partners in the special project funded by CIDA, which sought in this project to bring together its active commitment to promoting children's rights with its strong priority for local economic development to improve the lives of the poor.

Foundation Ideas and Activities

At the heart of the PPIC-W project was the idea that the rights of working children could be promoted through sensitive use of micro-finance institutions

(MFIs) to convince and enable employers to invest in business changes to improve the safety of children in their workplaces and to ensure that the children would receive an education. Rather than remove children from work, the project would try to make it safe, supportive, and developmental. And the project would do this from the bottom up by changing employer practices voluntarily through education and incentives, rather than from the top down through fiat and law enforcement. The success of the effort was to be assessed not only by improvements in the situation of working children in enterprises receiving EACID loans, but also by the ability of EACID to promote this change without weakening its excellent loan performance. That meant the project had to satisfy objectives of both rights and business. Everyone connected with the project, including EACID loan officers, received human rights training that included not only child rights under the UNCRC but also discussion of gender discrimination and the rights of women, which was especially important since many of the business owners and the child workers were females. At the same time, it was made clear that an active social program financed by EACID depended on a healthy business, on meeting community economic needs and remaining credible and competitive, and on maintaining an excellent level of loan performance. Project staff members were also made cognizant of ILO Convention 182 and the need to prioritize and eliminate the "worst forms of child labor."

This project was of special interest to some in the "child labor" community because specialists had long speculated that economic incentives might be more effective than labor inspection and law enforcement for making children safe in the workplace and allowing them to combine work and school. Incorporating the effort to improve working children's lives inside the operations of a small business loan program provided a chance to test that idea in practice. Whatever the results, they would have wider implications.

The PPIC-W project began by systematically searching out and identifying working children, especially but not exclusively among EACID loan clients, bringing them together in social, recreational, and learning activities through which they could voice their needs and aspirations, not only as workers but also as just children in the process of growing up. This introductory phase, which was under the technical supervision of a prominent Egyptian expert on social welfare practice for children and youth from poor communities, drew on an approach successfully used worldwide to approach and engage street children, adapting it to the situation of children working in shops and stores in Aswan and nearby communities. In this approach, entertaining art, together with recreational and socializing activities that develop solidarity between the children, were used as tools to understand children's lives and to ferret out how children see their world, what they feel to be their major problems and challenges, and what they aspire to become and to do with their lives. Space was opened for children to voice what they needed and wanted, not only in their work, but in their wider

lives that were the context of their work. In Aswan, subsequent project interventions were planned with the input of the children and taking into account
the information from them. This approach rooted subsequent program activity
securely in the characteristics of the children and the realities of their lives. In
the case of Aswan, generally considered a conservative society, children indicated to evaluators that they especially prized the opportunity for socialization
with both boys and girls, and that they gained insight and tolerance from guided
discussions about gender roles and the problems of gender discrimination.

Early on, the project began literacy courses for working children, but from
their feedback it learned that most young workers were in school, and that what
they most wanted and needed was tutoring to help with their classes. The education component was accordingly changed to provide this. Also, girls indicated
that they felt isolated from modern technology and wanted to learn computer
skills they could use for both education and employment, and this also was provided. It is especially interesting to note that EACID found it could fund most of
these educational activities, plus some time from the staff to do social work, out
of the small interest it received for its loans to cover its own operational costs
and expand the loan fund. Spread across a large number of loans, the expenses
of these important activities for working children were affordable.

As direct activities began to expose children's concerns and observations
about their work and working conditions, EACID began consulting leaders
among its client businesses. A group of business owners, with participation from
the young people and EACID staff, was formed to draft a local "code of conduct,"
which could be used as a guide for employers, in improving working conditions
for child workers, and for children, to inform them what they had a right to
expect. The idea was that a code developed by the community in this way would
carry the recognized authority of shared community values, and would therefore
be more readily accepted than were faceless government regulations, which
were anyway less applicable to small business situations. Once completed, the
code was printed for posting in all establishments with child workers.

When a proper foundation had been laid through contacts with working
children and the development of a code of conduct agreed by the community,
EACID exerted friendly pressure on its clients to recognize and deal with the
rights and working conditions of their child workers. Loan officers began to
include in their pre-loan business surveys inspection of working conditions for
children, and to include needed improvements inside the business plan accompanying any loan. The idea was to avoid calling attention to protection of child
workers as a separate and special activity, which could develop resistance to it,
but simply to treat observance of working children's rights and well-being as
one essential characteristic of the sort of well-managed and respected business
that can attract capital. The objective was to build this regard for children's welfare and rights as a self-sustaining feature into the local business culture. This

internalizing psychology is the virtual reverse of the more usual attempts to impose laws and their enforcement on businesses—such as in the above Bangladesh and Sialkot cases. And it led to some particularly interesting controversy about how to handle loans, which, under this project, should have as an explicit objective the improvement of working conditions for child workers.

At the beginning of the program it had been assumed by most non-Egyptian supporters and technical consultants that loans made under the auspices of the PPIC-W project, and using funds provided by CIDA, would be conditional on making improvements in the situation of working children in the businesses. Such improvements presumably would be built into each loan application and contract as a requirement, and the responsible loan officer would inspect the borrowing business to make sure that the promised improvements were made in children's working conditions as a criterion of successful operation of the loan. The leverage for change, by this way of thinking, comes from the business contract. That is at least how a Westerner typically would see it.

But this project happened in Aswan, which shares in the culture of Upper Egypt. In that setting, the strength of personal relationships between participants in business deals is more crucial than it is in the West, and a number of unspoken rules of behavior attend those complicated relationships. EACID originally used the loans not to force compliance through written and signed contract provisions, but to establish and strengthen relationships with business owners, through which the issues of child protection would be raised as a matter between trusted friends and allies. It was felt that trust and a meeting of minds would imbue the final agreement with far more social force than could be imparted by a mere piece of paper. By this model, expectations of action in benefit of children were moved by the financial system into the social system, which is where control of such issues is located in that cultural and social context. This example of radical contextualization of a universal right from a Western to locally valid mode of thinking is virtually the opposite of the impulse behind the Bangladesh and Sialkot cases to resist contextualization and impose international uniformity.

Assessing Success

The PPIC-W project in Aswan was projected as action research, an experiment. One of the open questions was which among the various attempted interventions would produce whatever positive changes that might be observed. The project tried a number of different approaches and activities, and only in retrospect could divine which seemed most productive in causing change. In an evaluation exercise in 2008, the history of the project was broken into three basic approaches: (1) interventions with working children alone; (2) interventions with employers alone; and (3) simultaneous interventions with both children and employers. A systematic sample of businesses involved with the project was drawn, and the owners and children in each business were interviewed by teams of trained interviewers. The objective was to determine what change, if any, had happened in the businesses and how both children and business owners viewed it. The evaluation was especially interested in activities and changes that the working children themselves identified as of value. In addition, the EACID loan offers and social officers relating to these businesses were also interviewed and all records of the transactions studied. A profile of each business based on owner, child, and EACID staff responses was complied, and sorted into one or another of the three approaches. The results of each approach were then analyzed and compared.

If was found that simultaneous activity engaging both children and the employing business owners was most likely to produce changes identified and valued by children. Many of the activities from which child informants reported deriving benefit most directly were the special activities for them, such as classes, discussions, and recreational events. An activity particularly cited by children was their introduction to and mastery of computer- and business-related skills, and they pointed with special enthusiasm to a highly innovative computer game developed by the project to teach basic entrepreneurial strategies and skills. The considerable passion some showed for this business game relates to the small business culture of the area and the desires of young workers to understand better the businesses in which they worked, and some day to own their own prosperous business. Children also placed high value on feelings of support from the project staff as they worked out problems with their workplace employers. Reciprocally, many business owners indicated their approval of outside support and activities for their child workers, some noting better job performance among the children. This perhaps points to a facilitating role that the project played in helping forge open and productive relationships between working children and their employers. A number of children mentioned that, with the support of the project, they found the courage to take their concerns and complaints on such matters as working conditions or remuneration to their employers and get them resolved. While many children also reported considerable benefit from activities specifically for the kids even when there was no corresponding project activity with the employer, the evaluation exercise suggested that workplace changes were most likely when the project was in a position to help facilitate the process from both ends. At the same time, it was clear that activity with business owners alone, involving no contact with the working children in their establishments, was least likely to result in any benefits that children could recognize. This finding presents a special problem in that a program involving activities with both employers and children is necessarily bigger, more complex, and more expensive. Whereas it appears that simple activities for either children or employers probably could be supported sustainably from internal funds of a thriving MFI without recourse to outside funding, the expenses of operating a more complex program involving a full gamut of activities could surpass what such an institution is able to fund on its own. The question is where the difference would come from.

Assessment of the project showed that PPIC-W was no panacea for all ills. Many problems still exist: some employers showed little interest in improving the lot of children working in their establishments, and some children complained they had seen no improvements whatsoever in their situation. At the same time, responses from both children and business owners suggested that very significant progress had been made in many establishments. Through the code of conduct and various other activities, consciousness of the right of working children to protection against hazards and mistreatment is now generalized in large numbers of both adults and children. The most common result of the assessment was the almost universal response of children that they now knew they had rights as children and workers, and that it was acceptable to defend them. Substantial initiatives to improve children's working conditions and facilitate their continued education were documented. Many children indicated that activities for them had expanded their knowledge of the world, their abilities to study or work, and their courage and self-esteem to speak up and negotiate a better situation for themselves. Some spoke of new dreams and aspirations. EACID staff remarked that the day was not far off when many of these same youngsters, now in their late teens and appreciative of interest taken in them while children, would be coming to EACID for loans to start their own businesses as new entrepreneurs. As of this writing, there are conversations under way on how to do a better job of using children's work to train them more systematically in skills they can use in business and in life in the future. This approach shows signs of promoting genuine development in both the individual and economic senses of the word.[16]

Concluding Thoughts

What appear to be mere differences of approach sometimes can be so great as to constitute radical differences in kind. Something like that can be seen in comparing two recent books on "child labor" by scholars of international law. One reviews—in nearly 400 pages of text—the various agreements, organizations, and structures, both governmental and commercial, for eliminating child labor, especially in international trade (Hubert, 2009). It analyzes their relative success or failure in excluding child workers, but at no point does it discuss what happens to the excluded children or how they fare. In this book, children, once "rescued" from their jobs, are invisible, and its recommendations give them no role in the decisions about them. Child labor is treated as a labor and trade issue in which adults are the only legitimate actors. Another book posits child labor as a human rights issue, and children and their well-being are more visible and central in it, especially in the recommendations for action, which call for their participation (Weston, 2005). The strategies for addressing child labor propounded by these two books have little or nothing in common. An approach based on the human rights of children is not at all like an approach aimed at cleaning labor markets of child workers.

That kind of difference also can be seen when comparing the illustrative cases presented in this chapter. In one kind of approach, that taken in Bangladesh and Sialkot in Pakistan, children have no role and are eerily absent except as manipulated victims. In the Egypt case, however, they are at the very heart of attention. There are marked differences between a conventional child labor program based primarily on the provisions of ILO Conventions and a more "children-centered" approach guided by empirical information about local conditions and children and by the UNCRC and other international human rights instruments. They are such divergent ways of approaching the world that they are largely incompatible.

The nature of these differences may help explain why an attempt, based on enforcement of child labor law, to force children out of their work was counterproductive for children in Bangladesh and Sialkot, and why a gentler, more educative approach aimed at protecting and promoting the development of Egyptian children in their work seems to have been beneficial for them. The two approaches started differently. Intervention in Bangladesh and Sialkot was driven by commercial and diplomatic pressures having only partly to do with concern about the well-being of working children, and it applied universalized legal requirements with little empirical local understanding of children's circumstances. Intervention in Egypt, on the other hand, responded to direct concern about the well-being and best interests of the children involved. The project there grew out of detailed observations of child workers in small business and the interest of a local microfinance program that knew the situation intimately. The objective of the conventional child labor approach in Bangladesh and Pakistan was to remove children from their workplace, a highly disruptive and even traumatic event in children's lives. The children-centered approach in Egypt sought to improve children's lives with a minimum of intrusion. Whereas the child labor approach ignored children's protests and imposed its "solutions" on them from above, the child-rights approach in Egypt included ample consultation with working children from the outset, taking their requests and suggestions into account in building up its program. Just these few examples convey the tenor of many differences between these two ways of dealing with child work and working children.

In brief, the child labor approach characterized in this chapter seems much less inclined to base its actions on empirical evidence about what is best for children, and it pays little but lip service to children's rights. We would argue that in these two factors lie the seeds of its dysfunction. A children-centered approach seems to us more productive for children because it values empirical information from and about them and is therefore better able to match its activities to local children and conditions. Its observance of child rights leads it to place its highest priority on the well-being and best interest of children and to view them and their situation more holistically. That, again, provides it with broader perspective and superior information increasing the chances of success. A child-centered program is better focused on child outcomes, is based on better information, has more human resources, and enjoys greater space and flexibility of action than does a conventional child labor program. We conclude that, for the objective of improving children's lives, the child labor approach simply is not competitive with the superior positioning, information, and creativity achievable by a children-centered program.

10

Policies and Interventions

What Should They Achieve, and How?

The long-traditional policy focus on "child labor" narrowly treats children's work almost exclusively as a problem. It is time to replace this focus with a broader and more balanced vision that regards children's work comprehensively and responds to its personal and social benefits as well as its risks. This book shows that such a paradigm change is needed. Experience demonstrates that the current approach is dysfunctional, too often ignoring or harming the children it is intended to help. Moreover, modern research into children and childhood indicates that work plays an important and appropriate developmental role in the lives of perhaps most of the world's children. In growing up, work may be at least as much an asset as a liability, and successful social policy therefore must take both the "rights" and "wrongs" of children's work into account by encouraging in it what is good and discouraging what is harmful.

A new policy framework to implement this expanded vision should be founded primarily on the following pillars:

- Children's well-being and development, defined and evaluated in context and according to rigorous social science standards; and
- Children's human rights, as articulated in the United Nations Convention on the Rights of the Child and the fundamental documents known as the International Bill of Human Rights.

This framework will generate policies and interventions that are more children-centered, taking a more holistic view of children and their best interest than does the currently prevailing "child labor" perspective. The emphasis on children's well-being and development will make policy more effective by encouraging empirical inquiry into the effects of children's work in their welfare and development, and by directing more effort into the assessment of how policies and interventions play out in children's lives. Grounding policy more solidly in properly researched evidence and less in conventional wisdom, ideology, assumptions, and institutional tradition will make it more relevant and realistic. Interventions will better match problems and contexts. The emphasis on children's access to human rights will bring to sectoral and institutional agendas (including the ILO conventions on child labor) oversight, guidance, and support from the most basic and influential instruments for human rights. Strengthening children's rights is necessary both to compel national and international attention to urgent issues on child work, such as those raised by ILO Convention 182, and to reduce instances in which labor, health, education or other sectoral policies intended to help children perversely end up infringing their human rights, as in the case of ILO Convention 138. The combination of increased empirical attention to policy foundations and consequences for children with more sensitive observance of children's rights—both necessarily linked to children's own voices and participation—will provide a high level of accountability to children's welfare and best interest that the "child labor" view of the world lacks. Only a new direction can achieve this.

In order to consider in more detail the elements of a new policy paradigm for considering and governing children's work, we will first summarize key starting points taken from the discussion in previous chapters. Then we will outline basic principles on which policies and interventions should be built, and finally suggest how these might be put into practice.

Starting Points

In the previous chapters, we have presented situations that challenge conventional wisdoms about the place of work in children's development, and we have argued that well-intentioned policymakers and activists often base their efforts on wrong-headed ideas and assumptions that are out of kilter with recent social science research and the lessons of experience. These assumptions are often based on a misinterpretation of the essentials of human and children's rights.

We have seen (particularly in chapters 2, 3, and 5) that all over the world, work has historically occupied an important place—alongside and often combined with play—in children's growth, learning, and development, and that these functions are only partly and imperfectly replaced by systems of formal education (chapters 5 and 6).

We have noted in various chapters (particularly chapter 2) that the world's working children are a large and very diverse group, with diverse situations, diverse interests and problems. A small (but significant) minority of children are engaged in what the ILO calls "worst forms of child labour," in kinds and conditions of work that are generally deemed unacceptable under any circumstances. A much larger group are engaged in work that is not in itself necessarily dangerous, harmful, or morally intolerable but that in its present form (in the words of the UNCRC article 32) "is likely to be hazardous or to interfere with the child's education, or to be harmful to the child's health or physical, mental, spiritual or moral development" or (in the words of ILO Convention 182) which "by its nature or the circumstances in which it is carried out, is likely to harm the health, safety or morals of children." Another very large group attend school and therefore work part-time or seasonally. This includes nearly all working children in industrialized countries, but also a very large number in poor countries.

We have recognized from the beginning that "child labor" is a contentious issue, marked by heated debates between those who believe that children's interests are best served by eliminating all "child labor" and those who believe rather that children should be protected in their work (sometimes referred to as "abolitionists" and "protectionists"). At the same time we have seen that there are many points of general agreement. Few if any would oppose, for example, the view that:

- all children have the right to education, and that this education should be as good as society can provide, or that
- all children have the right to be protected from exploitation or abuse in work, and from any work that is likely to harm them.

Most would also concur with the additional UNCRC principles that:

- all children have the right to express their opinion, and to be heard in all matters that concern the child (article 12, 1), and that
- in all actions concerning children the best interest of the child should be a primary consideration (article 3, 1).

Within these broad lines of agreement, however, there is plenty of debate, much of which depends on how we understand such terms as "child," "exploitation," "abuse," "harm," and "best interests." We have argued (particularly in chapters 2, 5, and 8) that although children can certainly be harmed—and sometimes seriously harmed—by certain kinds and conditions of work, other kinds and conditions of work can have an important and beneficial place in the lives and development of young people. As we have argued in chapter 8, harm, abuse, and exploitation are not mutually exclusive (either/or) terms but refer to continua, where we may easily discern and agree on the extremes (of most harmful and most benign work), but where there is plenty of room for disagreement on the middle ground. People and organizations, therefore, disagree on such issues as the following:

- Whether or not there is a place for work in "good" childhoods, and if there is, what kinds of work are appropriate. This issue concerns the disputed place of work and responsibility in the process of growing up.
- Whether or not work and school can be combined without harming the child. A related question is whether or not a child has a right to work and

to earn money if he or she wants to or needs to, and whether or not this is compatible with the child's rights to education and to protection from exploitation and harmful work.

- The definition of "harmful work" in the context of childhood.
- Whether or not to support prohibitions (by governments) or boycotts (by consumers) on the sale of products made by children.

The examples we have given (in chapters 1 and 9) of attempts to eliminate child employment in export manufacturing industries provided important lessons in how not to intervene. In the export garment industries in Morocco and Bangladesh, and in the football stitching industries in Pakistan—all well-documented cases—children were removed from work in order to protect the industries from international pressure and the threat of boycott. In all these cases, the children opposed the intervention but were not listened to. The entire intervention was planned and designed without the knowledge, consent, or involvement of the supposed beneficiaries. The jobs they were thrown out of—while certainly not without problems—were considered by the children and their families to be not the worst, but the best available jobs, compared to existing alternatives. The great majority of the children removed from work did not re-enter school; many were forced into more hazardous, more poorly paid informal-sector occupations, while others remained unemployed. The removal of children also did not lead to any improvement in the working conditions of the adults who took their place. Meanwhile, campaigners, politicians, and donor organizations considered the mission to have been accomplished, and consciences were cleared.

In chapters 5 and 6, we have argued that it cannot be taken for granted that children are always better off in school than at work, or that they themselves would prefer to be in school, when taking into consideration the extremely poor quality of schools, teachers, and education in many societies and the huge challenge of educational reform, investment, and renewal that will be needed to correct this. This observation in no way dampens our commitment to the right of all children, without discrimination, to as good an education as societies can provide, but it serves to underline that the realization of this right involves much more than simply "getting children out of work and into schools."[1] The persistent failure of so many societies to provide children with good, useful, child-friendly education is simply a disgrace, and under the circumstances it is no surprise that many children find work a more rewarding experience.

We have suggested (in chapters 1 and 3) that in wealthy countries, far from having been eliminated, work (including paid work) is part of the experience of the majority of school-age children before they reach the age of sixteen, and many earlier. What has been achieved in these countries is the shift from work to school as the main (but not the only) activity of children, which has also brought with it the shift from full-time to part-time work and to work that is combined with school attendance. Such longitudinal studies as are available suggest that part-time work of school-going children has not negatively affected their educational outcomes or chances in the labor market. Indeed, the evidence points to a positive influence of combining school and work. We have also noted the important role of work in a broadly conceived education; working, sometimes, can make educational sense (chapter 6).

We have underlined (especially in chapter 7) the need to move away from perceptions of children as passive victims and incompetent social actors, in line with the converging paths of insights from new childhood studies and the global consensus of the UNCRC. Instead, we recognize the need to respect views of children as "agents" capable of analyzing and responding to their situations and problems, as "citizens" with both rights and obligations in society, and as key "resources" in any work we do with children. This does not mean (and this also needs underlining) that children are never "victims" of abuse and exploitation— but it does mean that interventions must move away from victim perspectives and see children as important resources and partners in all interventions involving them.

We have seen (in chapter 3) that the evolution of national legislation and international standard setting on children's work since the late nineteenth century has been dominated by the "British factory acts model" of progressively more restrictive prohibition through minimum-age regulations or conventions, first generally focusing on industrial employment and extending gradually to other sectors, and finally prohibiting the employment of children below a specified age in "employment or work in any occupation" (the phrase used in ILO's Minimum Age Convention 138 of 1973). ILO Convention 138 has been adopted (in 1998) as one of ILO's "core conventions" and the ILO has claimed consistently— even after the adoption of the highly successful "worst forms" Convention 182— that Convention 138 is the central pillar of its work on child labor. Convention 138 (and national minimum-age regulations modeled on it) have never been subjected to rigorous policy analysis, particularly in low-income countries.[2] In our view there are strong grounds for a new debate on Convention 138 within the ILO and its tripartite membership.

We have argued that the UNCRC marked an important milestone in international discourse and consensus on problems that work may cause for children. Besides the UNCRC's important status as the formal basis for the rights-based international discourse on children's issues, it also marked a turning-point in UN discourse on children's work. It defined the problem for the first time in a UN Convention not as "work" itself, but as the harm to children that may result from certain kinds of work, and it established the right of the child to be protected, not from all work or employment, but from economic exploitation and from any work that is likely to harm the child. The ILO itself made an important advance in the same direction when, in the mid-1990s, it decided to develop a new Convention on the "Worst Forms" of child labor, which for the first time would promote a differentiated approach to child work and attempt to establish priorities to deal "immediately" and "as a matter of urgency" with the most intolerable forms.

We pointed out in chapter 9 that certain interventions that have turned out disastrous for children were assumed to be in support of children's rights, particularly rights to education and to freedom from exploitation. These rights are often interpreted as an unconditional imperative to get children out of work and into school, irrespective of the particular needs of the children concerned. We are aware that many development agencies and actors working with children's issues have become weary of "rights" rhetoric, which has often proven empty, unduly legalistic, and/or of limited usefulness in practice. But upholding rights does not have to be rigid and insensitive, as the final case in chapter 9 shows.

In chapter 1, we pointed out that the notion of rights cannot be constrained to what is contained in a formal code of law: "moral" rights extend beyond a legal code. The defense of rights must be sensitive to local values, possibilities, and resources, and to the priorities of the people concerned.

The cases of the Bangladeshi garment industry and of stitching footballs in Sialkot, outlined in chapter 9, show the need to take this point further. We reassert the argument made in chapter 5 that far from trumping all else, rights themselves must be judged by their consequences for children. Rigid adherence to rights embodied in international standards does not necessarily reflect the interests of children in real-life situations. Damaging effects may be avoided if the application of rights is sensitive to local values and to local resources, both of which are likely to affect priorities for intervention. The sensitivity can only come through attention to the views of the people concerned, and their views of what is most urgent to improve their lives. We argue that children's rights should certainly be upheld, but in a pragmatic and sensitive way.

Principles

The discussions in this and the preceding chapters suggest some general principles on which our attitudes, policies, and interventions should be based.

Understand the situation of children and the sources of both harm and benefits of their work. Intervention must start from an understanding of the situation of the children concerned. This means recognition of the following:

a) Children's work and related problems can only be understood in their broader context of persistent global inequality, large-scale poverty, and the webs of power within which children are born and grow up, reflecting inequalities based on wealth, social class, gender, generation, ethnicity, etc.

When excessive involvement of children in work is a symptom of broader problems, interventions that focus only on children's work do not offer effective solutions.

b) Work is one way in which children respond to their situation and develop. Understanding requires acknowledging the agency of children in their responses to both opportunities and problems of work.

c) Work needs to be understood as bringing both benefits and harm to children, and it is necessary to balance benefits against harm, including in policy considerations. Benefits should be recognized and enhanced. Work is normal to childhood and to growing up, although care is needed to prevent it becoming harmful. The appropriate cause for concern and focus of intervention is not work itself, but harmful work, assessed with reference to both physical and psychosocial factors. This is the key basis for prioritizing, in campaigns and other interventions, efforts to focus on the "worst" cases. We understand that this represents a major break from the historically dominant thinking, but, as we have explained, the basis for this step is established in both the UNCRC and in ILO Convention 182.

d) Understanding requires attention to accurate language and concepts, through which we think and communicate. Simple dichotomies between adults and children, or good "child work" and bad "child labor," do not reflect the complexities of growing up and of work, and consequently impede understanding.

e) To incorporate the above principles into the process of understanding children and their work requires the engagement of proper social science research. Agencies responsible for policies and programs usually are not organized, funded, and staffed to conduct pre-program research. This is an activity in which independent researchers, universities, institutes, and others with requisite skills can find many opportunities and make a major contribution.

Respect children, childhood, and children's communities. Implied throughout the UNCRC, and in many recent studies of childhood, is that children and childhood should be respected. Respect for the inherent dignity of the human person (UNCRC, article 31c) is fundamental to all human rights, and should be fundamental to all intervention. Respect includes the following:

a) Respect for children requires recognizing them as persons who can understand their own situations and make choices on how to improve their lives. It requires acknowledgement of their contributions to their own lives and to the lives of those around them.

b) Respect involves listening to children and taking their views seriously. Such respect must also extend to the communities in which children live and grow. This is not compatible with language that denigrates children, their work, their families, or their communities for deviating from some assumed notion of "normalcy" (often Western, urban, and middle-class). Any such denigration "can have the effect of penalizing, or even criminalizing, the childhoods of the poor" (Boyden, 1997, 207–208).

c) Working children are workers, and should be recognized as such. International and national laws should guarantee to working children the right of free association in existing trade unions and in their own organizations. There is no credible justification for excluding working children from guarantees of free association available to adults. Disrespect of, and discrimination against, workers on the basis of age should be no more acceptable than discrimination on the basis of gender.

d) Adults, from within or outside the communities concerned, with concerns for the problems faced by children should not claim to be intervening from a position of moral superiority. Judith Ennew, a leading expert on research with children, has pointed out that in any work with children, the main barrier is often the attitudes of adults, and "the main resource in any project is the children themselves" (Ennew, 1994a, 7). Children have a right, she insists, to be researched sensitively and competently; otherwise, research itself becomes a form of exploitation.

e) Children should be systematically consulted, and space opened for their own initiatives, in the formation, conduct, and evaluation of policies and interventions affecting them. Children are important resources for each other, in work situations and in other aspects of childhood and growing up.

Take child rights seriously and move beyond categorical rights rhetoric to a practical and flexible understanding of rights. We have argued for a flexible, pragmatic, and realistic approach to child rights, which in many situations is more effective than a legalistic approach. This includes the following:

a) Giving concrete meaning to the principle that policy must focus on the welfare and best interests of children. The UNCRC states that in all actions concerning children the best interests of the child shall be a primary consideration (Article 3, 1). Adult economic and political interests should not have priority, and neither should such adult interests as ease of administration and fear of scandal. This principle should be applied to interventions designed to uphold other rights, which should be sensitive to local contexts—social and material.

b) A further principle for intervention is that when children's rights are being violated, action should not be subordinated to political or economic expediency (Weston and Teerink, 2005). Where and when work clearly involves abuse of children, by harming them physically or psychologically, or by depriving them of such rights as education or contact with families, protection of children is a matter of right. Cost-benefit analysis from a societal point of view is inappropriate.[3] Only when rights are taken seriously can we identify those publicly responsible and hold them accountable when children's rights to protection from exploitation and harm are violated.

c) It is the responsibility of adults to help children make the most of their childhood and grow into capable, confident adults, not to overprotect them from every conceivable risk in the wider world (Guldberg, 2009, 179).

d) The right to effective education, by which we mean the best that society can provide within the constraints of available resources, must be taken seriously by national governments, local authorities, and other responsible bodies.

e) A rights-based approach that takes the interests and views of children seriously must be sensitive to the limited resources and possibilities of particular communities, and to the fact that members of communities sometimes have to balance various rights against each other and prioritize them with regard to expenditure of effort and resources. It should also be sensitive to the fact that in daily life, the rights of people, including children, derive largely from cultural values rather than from international conventions. Consequently, any pragmatic rights-based approach must start with an understanding of local conditions and values.

Recognize and strengthen the role of work in learning and development. Interventions should aim not only to minimize harm, but also to maximize potential benefits of work in young people's lives. This is a matter on which young people themselves have clear ideas.

a) Intervention in most cases (barring those involving in the unconditionally worst forms) should focus not on removing children from work, but on making work better for children.

b) The educational function of existing work opportunities should be strengthened.

c) All children (including disabled children and both genders) should have access to safe and educational work appropriate to their age and maturity.

Practice

Putting these threads together, we invite readers to consider the following specific general criteria and pointers for "good practice":

In Education

Exercise pressure on governments, local authorities, and other responsible bodies to get serious about "good education."

The provision of decent schooling free to all is the single best way to prevent children from dropping out of school to work. The aim is to provide, in a safe and respectful environment, all children with free instruction that leads to useful life competencies and that ensures functional literacy and numeracy by the end of five years.

These are the absolute minimum criteria that could be considered consistent with children's rights to at least a basic education under the UNCRC and that can reasonably be expected to hold children in school. In many countries, most children below middle-class socioeconomic status—those most likely to work—do not attend schools meeting even this low standard. In today's world, schooling beyond the primary level has become so necessary that conscientious observance of children's educational rights should include free education for all at least into middle adolescence. Achieving the minimum aims of basic education within five years should provide room for more enriching and challenging further education in subsequent years, which presently are often occupied with correcting the defects of poor-quality primary education. Work that prevents education should not be tolerated, but schools and other education programs should be sufficiently flexible to permit children to engage in part-time work.

As chapter 6 pointed out, research from many places suggests that most children dropping out of school prematurely do so not to work but because of school dysfunctions such as geographical or financial inaccessibility, teacher absence, incompetence of teaching, lack of facilities and materials, and humiliation and other maltreatment of students. That flow can be stemmed only by improving local schools or providing effective educational alternatives that offer children of the poor a quality of education equal to that generally available to students from better-off families. This requires reallocation of resources and the provision of trained teachers dedicated to "joyful learning." It needs to be remembered that the experience of children in inappropriate schools can be as traumatic as that in inappropriate work. Schools and other educational programs need to be places where children *want* to be. Making education compulsory is not sufficient to make it an attractive or effective learning environment. This, rather than chasing children out of labor markets, should be the first and main concern of governments and communities wishing to reduce the number of school-age children, workers or not, who do not attend school. Although other interventions may also be needed, they cannot work unless education is first made accessible, welcoming, and productive for all children. This, and not stopping children from working, is what is needed to meet the Millennium Development Goal of education for all.

Children have a right to education, and schools that merely go through the motions without actually educating the children do not meet that right. Therefore, the language of discourse should separate "education," which is an objective, from "schooling," which is just one instrument, albeit a very important one, for reaching that objective. It should never be assumed that participation in schooling has provided children with education except as can be demonstrated by student performance, such as by literacy testing.

Make more systematic use of work as a source of education.

Far from using schooling to keep children out of the labor force, educators should make productive work a respectable and widely available component of education, such as by placing students in supervised part-time work experience outside the school or by the school itself undertaking to produce goods or services for the community, with students gaining management and work experience. Work may be either remunerated or a form of volunteer service learning. When properly planned and supervised (and safe and non-exploitative) work is available as education, student involvement in it should be open to even young children and should not be constrained by minimum-age laws intended to regulate children's work in open labor markets. Information should be made available about outstanding places and programs that bring work into education, so that others can learn from their experience.

Businesses should offer children apprenticeships or other on-the-job learning arrangements inside many types of economic or service undertakings, seeking public or private reimbursement as appropriate for training they provide beyond their own human resources needs. Where such arrangements are already common for youth, they should be made available also to interested younger children.

UNESCO, perhaps in partnership with UNICEF and the ILO, should place new emphasis on "Education through Work" and its research underpinnings, promulgate successful "education with production" models, and revive and update its earlier campaign to promote and assist the inclusion of productive work in formal and nonformal education, in both rich and poor countries.

In Regulation of Children's Work

Replace minimum age as the foundation of national and international policies to regulate the work of children with approaches based on the effects of work, and of interventions in work, on children and the observance of their human rights.

Currently, most national "child labor" policies are based on the ILO Minimum Age Convention (no. 138) as the international standard, that is, a blanket ban against the "employment or work" of all children below a legal minimum age set around adolescence. They should be revised to instead reflect the UNCRC and ILO Worst Forms of Child Labor Convention (no. 182) as the guiding international standards. Because its implementation has sometimes been shown to have harmed children whom it is supposed to protect, ILO Convention 138 should be suspended as the general standard, while people, organizations, and the ILO's tripartite membership should press for new debate on this issue and consider annulling ratification of Convention 138. By the same token, consideration should be given to changing or eliminating the second paragraph of UNCRC Article 32, which concerns implementation activities, to exclude its minimum-age provision, and perhaps to update the whole paragraph to reflect modern findings and experience about what actions best achieve the objectives laudably set forth in the first paragraph of this article.

Rather than prohibiting work, we should seek ways to strengthen the developmental and educational function of existing work and minimize the possibility of work-related harm. Attention should focus on ensuring that any work that children do is appropriate to their age, gender, and ability, respects their rights—particularly the right to education—and is properly rewarded. This requires cooperation of employers and communities as well as governments and organizations.

Protection of children from unambiguously harmful work should be a high priority and urgent task for both government and civil society. Among others, it must involve the communities of which children and youth are a part, as well as media, and educational, religious, cultural, and other institutions that help set and implement social values. Society needs to be broadly interested in guarding the welfare of its children who work, and that means publicizing and taking action against situations in which children are being seriously harmed in their work, including strong legal action such as through the use of criminal laws and penal sanctions where these are merited. Public interest is necessary because labor inspectors and police cannot do this job alone.

Judgments about what work is "harmful" need to be justified by well-founded information about the actual risks and effects of that work on children rather than reflect unfounded stereotypes and assumptions. The more loosely and widely "harmful" is defined, the less urgent, focused and effective interventions against it become. Implementers of ILO Convention 182 should be aware of this danger and maintain a keen sense of priority, focusing the most effort on the worst conditions and the most endangered children.

Before removing any children, particularly disadvantaged children, from work, the harm and benefits should be carefully weighed against each other and against available alternatives, in consultation with the children and the local communities. Before banning any kind of work, the winners and losers from such a ban need to be assessed. In some situations it surely will be necessary to separate children from jobs in which they are engaged, but that should be a last resort. In such a situation, it is the responsibility of intervening parties to ensure that children have viable alternatives beneficial to them. Children should never be removed from their work unless and until better alternatives are immediately available to them.

In Structuring Children's Work

Help families, employers, educational programs, and children themselves to organize and oversee work that is safe and that promotes learning both in work and beyond it. Where appropriate, facilitate the successful combination of part-time work with school.

Work should be available to children as an appropriate vehicle for developing skills, attitudes, and connections that will enrich their lives and future prospects. Work that consumes their time and energies without protecting them and providing them commensurate value in return is exploitative. As previous chapters have pointed out, most children's work does not have to be either unsafe or exploitative, and can be structured to ensure that it is helpful to them. Many people who set tasks for working children have not thought about this or are not informed about options to make work appropriate and beneficial for children. Governments, educational institutions, the media, child advocacy organizations, religious organizations, and various community-based groups can provide information to parents, employers, and others regarding how to organize and supervise children's work in such a way as to ensure that children will benefit from it. At the international level, UNICEF, ILO, child defense NGOS, and bilateral assistance programs can be very helpful in making available the technical, human, and financial resources necessary to backstop a broad educational effort to make work appropriate for children.

We have pointed to various successful approaches to combining schooling and work, not only to accommodate children's multiple responsibilities, but in many cases even to enrich their developmental opportunities. While school may be a good place to work, work may also be a good place (sometimes the best or only place) to learn. Furthermore, since experience suggests that children will in fact work if they need and want to, regardless of laws, it is more productive to facilitate good work that does not interfere with school than to attempt to restrain children from working. It also should be remembered that many children can remain in school only because their work enables them to pay for necessary fees and materials. School curricula and teachers need to take this into account and perhaps, as now occurs in various rich countries, even assist students in finding appropriate part-time jobs and making work part of their school education experience.

Related to this, the purchase of products of children working in dignified conditions and combined with schooling should be encouraged. Prohibitions by governments or boycotts by consumers on the sale of products made by children, without consideration of the conditions of work and the alternatives available to them, are not in the interests of children.

In Children's Participation Rights

Find more effective ways to give children voice and to exercise their participation rights, taking into account differences among children due to class, gender, different abilities, and "the evolving capacities of the child."

Channels should be structured to provide working children on a regular basis with voice and influence in their own protection and interests. Working children's voices have been heard primarily through *ad hoc* events and local projects, but they need to be heard regularly and continuously through properly established channels for the purpose. Ordinarily, the most likely venue for worker action would be through existing or self-organized trade unions, but, as described earlier, children have been systematically excluded from them, by both government and union policies, under the guise of not being workers at all when they are under the legal minimum age. Internationally, the ILO and UNICEF should take the lead in revising existing codes and practice to provide for legal recognition of child workers and channels of access for them into institutions such as trade unions and worker insurance schemes that provide them voice and protection.

It is important to find more ways for children to be heard effectively and to exercise their participation rights. These must take into account differences among children due to class, gender, ability, and "the evolving capacities of the child." Children must have a say in their spaces for participation.

In Assessment

All policies relating to working children, including policies on minimum ages for employment, should be assessed according to their impact on children.

Assessment of projects must aim to establish how far and in what ways they have improved the lives of children: this question is not answered by statistics on changing numbers of children in the labor force. In general, this will require projects to collect baseline data on targeted children, in order for a reasonable before-and-after comparison to be made. Such initial data is important for projects in any case, so project teams understand how working children think their lives could be improved. Assessors also need to understand why things work as they do: how different factors in children's lives and work interrelate. This task is especially appropriate for independent researchers, such as many in academia, who have the requisite social science skills and no vested interests to impede their objectivity. Some of the sources we have cited for their particularly valuable assessments of policy and program impact on children are anthropologists, sociologists, psychologists, or other trained social scientists working independently. Studies of this type are badly needed and can make major contributions to the improvement of policies and programs governing the work of children.

In his recent book *Respecting Childhood*, Professor of Education Tim Loreman defines respect for childhood as: "to provide children with the basic necessities of life outlined in the UN Declaration on the Rights of the Child (1959) and the UN Convention on the Rights of the Child (1989); to value children's time, especially the present; to value children's enjoyment of childhood; to value children's relationships with others; to value children's contributions to family and society; to value children's individuality and diversity; [and] to value and accept children's abilities and capacities" (2009, 3). In this book, we have shown the importance for children of such principles of respect and understanding, rather than mindless adherence to unfounded dogmas, in addressing both the rights and the wrongs of children's work. We hope that this book will stimulate reflection and debate that promote children's best interests.

NOTES

CHAPTER 1   RAISING QUESTIONS, QUESTIONING THE ANSWERS

1. The statement in the heading came from a fourteen-year-old girl dismissed from a garment factory in Méknès, Morocco (Zalami, et al., 1998, 29). The Méknès case used here is summarized and paraphrased from this work.

2. Convention 138 of 1973 is ILO's general convention on the Minimum Age for Admission to Employment, which receives critical discussion in chapter 3 and throughout the book.

3. This is implied, for example, in the slogan of the international "Stop Child Labour" campaign: "Stop child labour. School is the best place to work!" See http://www .stopchildlabour.net/news.php (accessed June 9, 2009). We consider this slogan in chapter 6.

4. See http://www.guardian.co.uk/business/2008/jun/23/primark.children (accessed February 28, 2009).

5. The importance of understanding issues from the perspective of street children is well illustrated by Gigengack (2006). The different problems are presented with respect to Zimbabwe by Bourdillon (2001). For a more general exposition of how to focus on the problems of street children see Ennew (1994a).

6. Electronic text in possession of Michael Bourdillon.

7. As recalled in translation by Ben White and Bill Myers, who were present.

8. http://www.mvfindia.in/faqs.htm (accessed July 21, 2009).

9. Such ethnocentric thinking is fundamentally flawed, but remains embedded in much thinking and policy concerning children and work (Cunningham and Stromquist, 2005, 56–57).

10. Lieten, Karan, and Satpathy (2005, 159) state that the best decisions are those taken by adults, after children have been consulted. See also Burra (2003, 82).

11. For a fuller discussion of this terminology, see Myers (2001, 27–29) and Bourdillon (2006b, 1209–1213).

12. Weston and Teerink (2005) make a strong case for the use of the language of rights to stimulate action against abuses of children in the workplace. Their discourse on the abolition of "child labor" as a right, however, can mislead people into thinking that children have a right to be free of work.

13. They explained this as wanting adequate sources of income at home in their villages, so they would not have to go to the cities to find work. The rights and information about the movement can be found on http://eja.enda.sn (accessed July 23, 2009).

14. For a full list of reservations, see http://www.unhchr.ch/html/menu3/b/treaty15_asp.htm (accessed October 8, 2007).

15. The Charter was accepted by the Assembly of Heads of State and Government of the Organisation of African Unity in July 1990. It broadly follows the UNCRC in matters of rights, but with some variations (see Gose, 2002).

16. UNCRC Article 32, 2 suggests ways of providing such protection, including an unspecified minimum age or ages for entry into employment: this was a necessary consequence of the CRC's obligation to respect existing UN Conventions, including in this case the ILO's Convention 138 on Minimum Age for Admission to Employment. The inclusion of this clause, however, involves the Convention in a confusion of defining the problem as one of harmful or exploitative work (article 31, 1) with defining it as any work below a certain age (31,2).

17. For an overview of these efforts, see Hindman (2009a, xxx–xxxi).

CHAPTER 2   WORK THAT CHILDREN DO

1. E.g., Hindman (2009b, xxv). Such a notion of societies going through similar stages of development or "modernization" is problematic. For a critique of this thinking with respect to children's work, see Cunningham and Stromquist (2005, 55–58).

2. Some argue that children are being abused at work and that the law needs to be enforced (e.g., Lavalette, 2000; Landrigan, 1993; for a discussion of the dangers of deregulation with respect to Britain, see Lavalette, 2005). Others argue that the law is not enforceable and that the strategy needs to be modified (e.g., Whitney, 1999, 242–244). Neither of these approaches attends to improving the protection of children in their work.

3. However, a recent publication from the ILO (Guarcello, Lyon, et al., 2007) suggests that "children's non-market activities" (meaning largely reproductive work) be included in labor measurement.

4. The ILO, which sets the official international definitions of "work," "employment,' and similar terms, defines "economic activity" as "labour for the production of economic goods and services as defined by the United Nations System of National Accounts and Balances." According to the International Conference of Labour Statisticians, "economic activity" includes all production and services for the market and production for consumption. The only work excluded is schoolwork and services not connected to the market—that is, domestic work in one's own home. (Resolution concerning statistics of the economically active population, employment, unemployment, and underemployment, adopted by the Thirteenth International Conference of Labour Statisticians [October 1982], section 5.) In 2008, the 18th International Conference of Labour Statisticians adopted a new definition of child labor in Resolution II, which concerns statistics on child labor. The term is defined to encompass both economic activity ("children's employment") and household chores ("unpaid household services"). It thus includes the "worst forms of child labour" (see chapter 8), employment below the age of fifteen, and "hazardous unpaid household services, including household chores performed for long hours, in an unhealthy environment, in dangerous locations, and involving unsafe equipment or heavy loads" (see UNICEF, 2009, 16).

5. For the U.S.A., see Dodson and Dickert, and Lee et al. (2004) and Lee (2003). For Tanzania, see Akabayashi and Psacharopoulos (1999). On the relevance of

girls' domestic work to schooling, see Levison, et al. (2001) and Assaad et al. (2007, 2010).

6. In such rare cases, children are unlikely to have access to schooling and issues of development are more urgent than issues of work.

7. This comes from unpublished survey material in the possession of author William Myers. See also Kabeer et al. (2003, 362).

8. http://www.rb.se/NR/rdonlyres/F69FDA7D-6418–4DF6-A3C6-BB818A2A4EF3/0/ WorkingchildrenFinalDeclarationBerlin2004.pdf (accessed June 16, 2008).

CHAPTER 3   CHILDREN'S WORK IN HISTORICAL AND COMPARATIVE PERSPECTIVE

1. The genesis of this view is presented by Cunningham (1991, chapter 2, 8–17.) The *Child Labor Public Education Project* links child labor with industrialization, and reform with legislation and regulation: see http://www.continuetolearn.uiowa.edu/laborctr/ child_labor/about/us_history.html (accessed April 4, 2008).

2. *Chimney Sweeps Act* 1834; *Chimney Sweeps Act* 1840.

3. *Factory Act* 1974; *Factory and Workshop Act* 1891, 1901.

4. For example, Fyfe and Jankanish of the ILO claim that, historically, legislation is the most important response to child labor (1997, 17). Nardinelli (1990), an academic historian, argues in contrast that it was economic forces that produced the changes, which often started taking place before legislation was in place. For an overview, see Humphries (2003).

5. On the U.S.A., see Hindman (2002); on the Netherlands, White (1994).

6. McKechnie and Hobbs (1999: 92); see also Lavalette (1994, 65–67). Recent studies in Denmark showed 59 percent of fifteen-year-olds having some employment (Frederiksen, 1999); and in a Dutch school, 75 percent of pupils aged twelve to seventeen experienced paid employment (Huijsmans, 2004: 4).

7. These statistics are from the *NIBUD Scholierenonderzoek*, an annual survey of children's incomes, employment and spending carried out by the National Institute for Budget Research (www.nibud.nl).

8. Howieson, et al. (2006, 227). This does not necessarily amount to a recommendation of formal recognition of part-time work in the school system, which could have advantages but which could also change and damage the work experience, besides putting pressure on those who do not wish to work. The discussion on this point is summarized in Howieson, et al. (2006, 230–231).

9. This section draws on more detailed analysis by White (2004; 2009).

10. Their contemporary operation is discussed in chapter 6.

11. See Sachikonye (1991). For accounts of children's work in a variety of situations in the 1990s, see the essays in Bourdillon (2000b).

12. http://www.unicef.org/infobycountry/zimbabwe_statistics.html#46 (accessed May 14, 2008).

13. For this history see White (2005) and Dahlén (2007, chapters 4–10).

14. A lower age of fourteen is allowed, as a temporary measure, in countries where the economy and educational facilities are insufficiently developed. Recommendation 146 (article 7.1) accompanying this convention sets sixteen as the ideal minimum age to which all countries should aim.

15. Report IV (1) & (2) Minimum Age for Admission to Employment, International Labour Conference, 57th Session, Geneva 1972. This is a background document of a type known as a "grey report" in ILO parlance.

16. Some further background to the "worst forms" Convention is given by White (1999; 2005) and Fyfe (2007, 25–27).

17. Only one of the eleven countries participating in the ILO's IPEC program at the time had ratified Convention 138 (Fyfe, 2007, 26).

18. "During the debate on the draft . . . Convention . . . delegations competed in phrasing the criteria for the 'worst' kinds of children's work as broadly as possible, in the erroneous belief that this would help the greatest number of children" (Liebel, 2004, 212).

19. The ILO however seems still to have a rather limited view of the role of NGOs in the worldwide movement against exploitation of children, suggesting that a focus for NGO efforts with respect to child labor in the coming years could be "active participation in the ILO's ratification campaign" (of ILO Convention 138)! (Fyfe, 2007, 93).

20. http://www.stopchildlabour.eu/stopchildlabour/English/How-we-work/Our-mission (May 4, 2009).

21. Among the "non-negotiables" of the MV Foundation, Hyderabad, India (http://www .mvfindia.in/index.asp, accessed June 10, 2009).

22. http://www.streetkids.org/who_we_are/philosophy.htm (accessed August 1, 2009).

23. While noting that it was largely the internationalization of organized labor that led (in the latter half of the nineteenth century) to internationalization of debates about child labor (2007, 7), Fyfe's book devotes surprisingly little attention to the role of the ILO's social partners in the international Trade Union movement (such as the World Confederation of and the International Confederation of Free Trade Unions) or the employers' organizations (such as the International Organization of Employers). These organizations are mentioned only briefly (pp. 30–31).

CHAPTER 4   CHILD WORK AND POVERTY

1. Hulme and Mosley (1996, 105–108) discuss the debate about defining poverty. Narayan et al. (2000) explore poor people's definitions of poverty.

2. Manacorda and Rosati (2007, 3) cite a number of studies that arrive at this conclusion.

3. Author's observation. Deborah Levison, January 2008.

4. In addition, the study showed that household work to reduce expenditure increased when the household was short on income.

5. The World Health Organization (2004) reports alcohol dependence among adult populations for many countries. The percentage of males with a "sense of compulsion to take alcohol" (p. 29) ranges from close to zero in Muslim countries such as Egypt to 17.1 percent (Brazil) and 27.6 percent (South Africa). While these percentages seem high, and indeed are much lower for women, they indicate that many children are contending with difficult situations and may need to provide for themselves even when living with their parents.

6. For example, Beegle et al. (2006) write about the loss of crops or livestock in Tanzania; Dillon (2008) analyzes the effects of illness or related expenses in Mali; de Janvry et al. (2006) consider a variety of collective shocks in Mexico; Guarcello et al. (2003) analyze both collective and family-specific shocks in Guatemala; and Umaña Aponte (2003) looks at the effect of macroeconomic recession in Colombia.

7. For example, see Ray (2000b) regarding water storage and sewage disposal.

8. There is a theoretical literature in economics that addresses children's labor-force work and its interactions with adult work. Basu (2000), for example, works through possible effects of an increase in the adult minimum wage on child work, concluding that it may lead to an increase in children's market work.

9. PROGRESA stands for Programa de Educación, Salud y Alimentación—the Education, Health and Nutrition Program. Reports evaluating the PROGRESA program can be found on the website of the International Food Policy Institute, IFPRI: http://www.ifpri.org/themes/progresa.htm.

10. There is little reason to believe that this can provide a panacea to eliminate "child labor" on a worldwide basis, as suggested in an ILO report (2004).

11. This might also be argued with respect to household work, but it is rarely mentioned. Without adequate justification, household work is generally assumed to be compatible with acquiring formal education, and labor-force work is assumed to be incompatible.

12. Personal communication from Richard Carothers, Ottawa, May 2009.

CHAPTER 5   WORK IN CHILDREN'S DEVELOPMENT

1. It is clear that payment for work is integral to this experience. It is not therefore possible to distinguish work as benefiting child development from the value of work as a source of income (Harwood and Mull, 2002, 35).

2. The term "resilience," which implies "bouncing back," is but a common metaphor with such scarce scientific roots that specialists cannot even demonstrate that it exists other than as a concept dependent on a particular way of looking at adversity. But because it is so ubiquitous in the literature, and because recent neurobiological research may be finding evidence for something akin to it, we include it, but skeptically.

CHAPTER 6   EDUCATION, SCHOOL, AND WORK

1. This is the slogan of the "Stop child labour campaign" jointly undertaken by Alliance 2015, a partnership of nongovernment organizations in six European countries working in the field of development cooperation, and coordinated by Hivos in The Netherlands (see http://www.stopchildlabour.eu, accessed June 2, 2009).

2. See, e.g., Universal Declaration of Human Rights (1948), article 26 (1); UNCRC (1989), article 28 (1a); Charter on the Rights and Welfare of the African Child (1990), article 11 (3a).

3. See the "non-negotiable principle" of the MV Foundation in India, "All Children must attend full-time formal day schools" (http://www.mvfindia.in/index.asp, accessed October 8, 2007).

4. *World Declaration on Education for All: Meeting Basic Learning Needs* (1990). http://www.unesco.org/education/efa/ed_for_all/background/jomtien_declaration.shtml (accessed June 29, 2009).

5. http://web.worldbank.org/WBSITE/EXTERNAL/TOPICS/EXTEDUCATION/EXTDATAS-TATISTICS/EXTEDSTATS/0,,contentMDK:21528857~menuPK:4324013~pagePK:641684 45~piPK:64168309~theSitePK:3232764,00.html (accessed February 26, 2009).

6. Usually around thirty hours a week. The precise number of hours varies, depending on such factors as the situation of the children, the flexibility of the school system, and the kind of work.

7. For overviews and critical assessment of such statistical work, see Edmonds (2008, 3619–3625) and Dorman (2008, 1–28).

8. For example, Peter Dorman's review (2008) of research starts by trying to "identify the ways in which child labor influences educational outcomes," although he recognizes that school and labor-force work affect each other in complex ways. Guarcello, Lyon and Rosati (2006, 6–9) and Ray (2009) argue for a causal link and assume the conventional wisdom on its direction.

9. The authors state at the end of the article, without evidence or argument, that in the long term schooling would prove more rewarding. They do not provide information, however, on whether the particular children who stopped school early were likely to perform well enough at school to reap high rewards later in life in the local labor market.

10. The Young Lives Research Project (http://www.younglives.org.uk/) has been tracing the development of children from infancy in several countries and will eventually produce valuable and comparable data on their development.

11. Many research papers and books arising out of the study are listed on the web page of the Life Course Center, Department of Sociology, University of Minnesota: http://www .soc.umn.edu/research/lcc/pubpaper.html (accessed August 23, 2007).

12. These are summarized as four "myths" in Mortimer (2007, 119–121). We have rearranged the order in which to present them.

13. Post's large-scale study of the U.S.A. comparison of test scores in mathematics and science indicated that work of over twenty hours a week had an adverse effect on grades (Post and Pong, 2009, 115).

14. Thus Heady points out that it is easier to combine work and school in Ghana than in the slums of Bangladesh (2000, 12).

15. For examples and a discussion, see Delap (2004) and Winrock International (2008, 93–94).

CHAPTER 7   CHILDREN ACTING FOR THEMSELVES

1. The teachers at her school joined together to pay crèche fees for the two-year-old brother.

2. Typically, quantitative analyses rely on general purpose household surveys or labor-force surveys, such as the World Bank's Living Standards Measurement Surveys (LSMS), Demographic and Health Surveys (DHS), or surveys produced by a country's statistical office. Even child labor surveys funded by the ILO do not get into issues of agency. Usually such surveys include a question asking why a child stopped attending school, or why a child started working, but even this information is not collected carefully enough to be reliable.

3. See UNDP statistics at http://www.un.org/esa/population/meetings/EGMPopAge/1_ UNPD_Trends.pdf (accessed November 28, 2007).

4. Population Reference Bureau, 2008 World Population Data Sheet. PRB: Washington, D.C. www.prb.org/Publications/Datasheets/2008/2008wpds.aspx (accessed July 13, 2009).

5. Baker (1996, 182) suggested that for some street children, stress relates precisely to a lack of control over their lives.

6. Good illustrations of the wide variety of situations and responses of children on the streets of Mexico City, and the inadequacy of support, are found in Gigengack's work (2000; 2006). See also Ebigbo (2003).

7. Abuse of street children by officials is widespread. See, e.g., Human Rights Watch at http://www.hrw.org/children/street.htm (accessed April 4, 2008). For graphic accounts of all kinds of violence on street children in Haiti and how children cope, see Kovats-Bernat (2006).

8. The authors suggested this was due to lower levels of intense physical activity, more varied diet, and better access to medical care for street children. For similar results elsewhere, see Panter-Brick (2000, 84–88).

9. Padre Oberón ran a chain of shelters for street children and was dedicated to helping them (Gigengack, 2006, 144). See also Ennew (2000b, 178).

10. Studies in Bangladesh, Karnataka (India), Ghana, and Burkina Faso showed small numbers traveling due to lack of care or ill treatment: 10 percent or less (Whitehead, et al., 2007, 12).

11. *Protocol to Prevent, Suppress and Punish Trafficking in Persons, especially Women and Children* (2000), which came into force in December 2003 and by September 2007 had been ratified by 115 states (Bastick and Grimm, 2007).

12. The term "exploitation" is stated to include "at a minimum, the exploitation of the prostitution of others or other forms of sexual exploitation, forced labour or services, slavery or practices similar to slavery, servitude or the removal of organs" (article 3a). But it is not defined, and is open to a variety of interpretations.

13. See report in *Deccan Herald*, November 16, 2004. http://www.deccanherald.com/archives/nov162004/spt5.asp (accessed February 20, 2008).

14. Report to Save the Children, Norway, by Julian Kramer on a visit to Concerned for Working Children, October 26 to November 2, 2003.

15. Bourdillon (2005); also http://www.gossner-mission.de/nepalnewsarchiv.html (accessed November 30, 2007).

16. E.g., ILO (2002, 99). For a critique of child participation in this movement see Invernizzi and Milne (2002, 410).

17. Points raised in this and subsequent paragraphs arise largely from our experience with meetings of working children. See Bourdillon (2008).

18. Psychologist Roger Hart formulated a "ladder of participation" from manipulation and tokenism, through informing and consulting children, to "full participation" in which children take the initiative (1992). While this was useful in distinguishing different forms of participation and has been widely influential, the metaphor of the ladder can be misleading: appropriate forms of participation depend on the situation and usually require negotiation between children and adults.

19. For recent discussion of principles involved, see Lansdown (2001) and Thomas (2007).

20. For an analysis of the link in Norway between "child participation" and "participation" in sustainable community development see Kjørholt (2002).

21. For a summary of seven such initiatives in different countries, see Black (2004).

22. For an example of such a program in the Philippines, see Rialp (2005).

23. James et al. point out that opinions of children may be suppressed in formal reports to protect their confidence and relations with parents (2004, 197).

24. For a critique of participation as an overriding demand in development programs generally, see the collection of essays in Cooke and Kothari (2001).

CHAPTER 8   ASSESSING HARM AGAINST BENEFITS

1. For a fuller discussion, see Bourdillon (2009).

2. Domestic work is often the easiest kind of work for girls to find, especially when they suffer discrimination in other kinds of employment. A study in Latin America showed that very high proportions of employed girls aged ten to seventeen were in domestic service—often over 30 percent (Argentina, Brazil, Colombia, Costa Rica—Levison and Langer, 2009).

3. http://hrw.org/english/docs/2006/10/04/india14264.htm (accessed July 1, 2009).

4. Butterflies and Human Rights Law Network (2006, 13). A study in Karnataka state showed that hotels and restaurants provided a major opportunity for child migrants seeking to improve their situation. See Iversen (2002, 820).

5. For similar practices in other African countries, see Alber (2004); Langeni (1999); and Whitehead et al. (2007, 9–10).

6. Working children have objected that these refer to criminal activities, which clearly need to be stopped but which should not be associated with their work. See Dakar Declaration (1998) of International Movement of Working Children. http://www .workingchild.org/prota2.htm (accessed July 10, 2009).

7. A good starting point on this topic is Dottridge's studies (2004; 2008). For a recent report on West Africa, see http://www.truthout.org/071209X (accessed July 13, 2009).

8. In India, the practice was made illegal by *The Children (Pledging of Labour) Act* of 1933. The practice remains widespread in the country.

9. It is possible that in some trades, such as weaving, children may be bonded in order to provide an entry into the trade and a skill for the future (see Human Rights Watch, 2003, 31).

10. For overviews of children in armed conflict, see Wessells (2006) and Honwana (2006).

11. For a brief critique of the contemporary exclusion of children from armed conflict, see Rosen (2007).

12. Compare this with 467 minors killed in conflicts between Israel and Palestine in the occupied territories in the same period (Dowdney, 2003, 172).

13. For a fuller discussion of this topic, see Liebel (2004, 194–215, chapter 8).

14. The recent publication by UNICEF (2005) uses the term "exploitation" frequently without ever defining it. There are very few references in this document to low wages, and none to profit or surplus value.

15. The UNCRC allows employment under certain conditions, and therefore gives some other meaning to "exploitation."

16. The official explanation for this age-based wage discrimination is revealing, referring to assumed productivity differences, increasing young people's chances in the labor market, the lower needs of young people compared to adults, and the need not to make work more attractive than school to young people (Ministerie van Sociale Zaken, 2009c).

17. http://www.hmrc.gov.uk/nmw/ (accessed August 24, 2009).

CHAPTER 9   THE POLITICS OF INTERNATIONAL INTERVENTION

1. Interview by William Myers with Farook Sobhan, President, Bangladesh Enterprise Institute, June 2002. Mr. Sobhan was Foreign Secretary to the Government of Bangladesh during the period under discussion.

2. This was mentioned also in focus groups in a 2002 study of children who had worked in the garment industry. Sexual harassment in the factories was reported to be rare, but it was a worrying factor for females having to walk between home and work.

3. The study was sponsored by the ILO and UNICEF. The results were not published.

4. Even though quoted pay rates were clearly higher in the garment industry according to the literature, study respondents have regularly complained that many dishonest firms cheated them out of pay owed them.

5. A brief summary of the findings was published in Boyden and Myers (1995).

6. Bachman was connected to Santa Clara University at the time, and not only was a recognized writer on child labor and globalization issues, but also had substantial Bangladesh experience and Bangla language skills. Her research, supported by UNICEF, included a full review of the United States literature and media around the Harkin Bill and its Bangladesh impact, plus interviews with some fifteen of the United States individuals and organizations most involved. She produced a detailed report (2002). It is the most complete narrative of United States events leading toward the MOU (see below). The authors thank Sarah Bachman for the use of this unpublished material, and hope it will some day find its way to much merited publication.

7. Bachman looked for evidence of hidden commercial motives in documents and her interviews with a variety of Americans involved in the Harkin Bill and the campaign in Bangladesh. She did not find it, which result perhaps could be attributed to reluctance by her informants to be fully forthcoming about a potentially embarrassing matter. Farooq Sobhan, the Bangladesh Foreign Secretary during the period under discussion, said in a June 2002 interview with William Myers that he and the Bangladesh government at first took the Harkin Bill language at face value, but gradually became convinced from American behavior that it was at least in part intended to disguise a commercial motive of protecting the interests of American manufacturers and trade unions against even legitimate developing country competition. Various observers from foreign child advocacy organizations working in Bangladesh at the time arrived at the same conclusion.

8. See Bissell (2000). Also interview by William Myers with representatives of Bangladesh Garment Manufacturers and Exporters Association (BGMEA), 2002.

9. AAFLI is an organization funded by American trade unions and the United States government to promote free trade unions in Asia.

10. Interviews by William Myers with Bangladesh Rural Advancement Committee (BRAC), Gonoshahajjo Sangstha (GSS), Nari Uddyag Kendra, Christian Action Research and Education (CARE), Save the Children Alliance, and the Bangladesh Women Lawyers Association, May–July 2002.

11. National and international press reports of large numbers of former garment workers turning to prostitution were wildly exaggerated. However, documented cases proved the problem did exist.

12. Conducted by MRC-Mode for UNICEF in 2002. The authors thank Susan Bissell of UNICEF for her valuable assistance in making this and related information available to us.

13. For a variety of reasons, neither the Government of Bangladesh nor the *Asian-American Free Labor Institute* (AAFLI) participated in these negotiations, but they were at least officially supportive.

14. ILO: *BGMEA/ILO/UNICEF Project Bangladesh: Facts and Figures*, Dhaka, n.d.

15. Myers heard these repeated criticisms of the UNICEF role in confidential conversations with staff from some of the most prominent national and international NGOs working on child rights issues in Dhaka, and even from within UNICEF itself. For obvious reasons, these were not recorded.

16. Further details about information contained in this section will be forthcoming from the PPIC-W project.

CHAPTER 10   POLICIES AND INTERVENTIONS

1. See, e.g., http://www.unesco.org/education/efa/global_co/working_group/presentation_india2.pps (accessed August 12, 2009).

2. Eric Edmonds (2008, 3694–3695) comments that empirical evidence on the effectiveness of general bans or restrictions on employment are not available for low-income countries, and that the most compelling evidence on the effectiveness of a general ban comes from the historical experience of developed countries (which, we pointed out in chapter 3, is not a universal experience). He argues that it appears that child labor laws made a small marginal contribution to the decline in child labor in the U.S.A.

3. The ILO study, *Investing in Every Child* (2004), argues that ending child labor would result in a net economic benefit globally. Apart from problems with the supporting data, this does not appear relevant in cases where children's protection from harm is a matter of right, nor where children have a right to benefits from their work.

REFERENCES

Ainsworth, Martha 1992. *Economic aspects of child fostering in Côte d'Ivoire.* LSMS working paper, no. 92. Washington, D.C: World Bank.

Aitken, Stuart, Silvia López Estrada, Joel Jennings and Lina María Aguirre 2006. "Reproducing life and labour: Global processes and working children in Tijuana, Mexico." *Childhood.* 13:365–387.

Akabayashi, Hideo and George Psacharopoulos 1999. "The trade-off between child labour and human capital formation: a Tanzanian case study." *The Journal of Development Studies.* 35:120–140.

Akello, Grace, Annemiek Richters and Ria Reis 2006. "Reintegration of former child-soldiers in northern Uganda: Coming to terms with children's accountability." *Intervention.* 4:229–243.

Alber, Erdmute 2004. "Grandparents as foster-parents: Transformations in foster relations between grandparents and grandchildren in northern Benin." *Africa.* 74:28–45.

Alderman, Harold, Pierre-André Chiappori, Lawrence Haddad, John Hoddinott and Ravi Kanbur. 1995. "Unitary Versus Collective Models of the Household: Is It Time to Shift the Burden of Proof?" *World Bank Research Observer.* 10:1–19.

Alderson, Priscilla 1994. "Researching children's rights to integrity." In Mayall, B. (ed.), *Children's Childhoods: Observed and experienced.* London and Washington: Farmer Press. 45–62.

Aldrich, Richard 1999. "The apprentice in history." In Ainley, P. and H. Rainbird (eds.), *Apprenticeship: Towards a New Paradigm of Learning.* London: Kogan Page. 14–24.

Allais, Federico Blanco and Frank Hagemann 2008. *Child labour and education: Evidence from SIMPOC surveys.* Working Paper. Geneva: ILO, IPEC, SIMPOC.

Alvim, Rosilene 2000. "Debates on poor children in Brazil: Between marginalisation and premature labour." In Schlemmer, B. (ed.), *The Exploited Child.* London and New York: Zed Books. 160–175.

Ambadekar, N. N., S .N. Wahab, S. P. Zodpey and D. W. Khandait 1999. "Effect of child labour on growth of children." *Public Health.* 113:303–306.

Amigó, María Florencia 2005. *Children's Work: Chasing Money in Rural Lombok,* Ph.D. Thesis, Department of Anthropology, University of Sydney. Amin, Sajeda, Ian Diamond, Ruchira T. Naved and Margaret Newby 1998. "Transition to Adulthood of Female Garment-factory Workers in Bangladesh." *Studies in Family Planning.* 29:185–200.

Anarfi, John, Saskia Gent, Iman M. Hashim, Vegard Iversen, Sumaiya Khair, Stephen Kwankye, Cynthia Addoquaye Tagoe, Dorte Thorsen and Ann Whitehead 2006. *Voices of Child Migrants: "A Better Understanding of How Life Is."* Development Research Centre on Migration, Globalisation and Poverty, Brighton. http://www.migrationdrc.org/publications/other_publications/Voices_of_Children.pdf (17 December 2007).

Andvig, Jens Chr. 1998. "Child labour in Sub-Saharan Africa: An exploration." *Forum for Development Studies.* 2:327–362.

—— 2001. *Family-controlled child labour in Sub-Saharan Africa: A survey of research.* Social Protection Discussion Paper Series. Washington, D.C.: The World Bank.

Anker, Richard, M. E. Khan and R. B. Gupta 1988. *Women's Participation in the Labour Force: A Methods Test in India for Improving Its Measurement.* Geneva: ILO.

Anker, Richard and Helma Melkas 1995. *Income Replacement and Substitution Activities Intended to Eliminate or Reduce Child Labour.* Geneva: ILO.

Anonymous 1998. *Children Working in Small and Micro Enterprises.* Cairo: Egyptian Small and Micro Enterprise Association.

Apel, Robert, Raymond Paternoster, Shawn D. Bushway and Robert Brame 2006. "A job isn't just a job: The differential impact of formal versus informal work on adolescent problem behaviour." *Crime and Delinquency.* 52:333–369.

Aptekar, L. 1989. "Characteristics of the street children of Colombia." *Child Abuse and Neglect.* 13:427–437.

Archard, David 2004. *Children: Rights and Childhood (2nd edition).* London & New York: Routledge.

Asghar, Syed Mehmood, Sabir Farhat and Shereen Niaz 2005. *Camel Jockeys of Rahimyar Khan: Findings of a participatory research on life and situation of child camel jockeys.* Peshawar, Pakistan: Save the Children Sweden, Pakistan Programme.

Assaad, Ragui, Deborah Levison and Nadia Zibani 2007. *The Effect of Child Work on Schooling: Evidence from Egypt.* Minnesota: Minnesota Population Center, University of Minnesota.

—— 2010. "The Effect of Domestic Work on Girls' Schooling: Evidence from Egypt." *Feminist Economics.* 16.

Babugura, Agnes A. 2008. "Vulnerability of Children and Youth in Drought Disasters: A Case Study of Botswana." *Children, Youth and Environments.* 18:126–157.

Bachman, Sarah L. 2000. "The Political Economy of Child Labor and Its Impacts on International Business." *Business Economics.* 30–41.

—— 2002. *Narrative: Development of the Harkin Bill and the garment industry MOU as seen by United States actors.*

Baker, Rachel 1998. "Runaway Street Children in Nepal: Social Competence Away From Home." In Hutchby, I. and J. Moran-Ellis (eds.), *Children and Social Competence: Arenas of Action.* London: Falmer Press. 46–63.

Baker, Rachel, Catherine Panter-Brick and Alison Todd 1996. "Methods used in research with street children in Nepal." *Childhood.* 3: 171–194.

Banpasirichote, Chantana 2000. "Rapid economic growth: The social exclusion of children in Thailand." In Schlemmer, B. (ed.), *The Exploited Child.* London and New York: Zed Books. 135–145.

Barnes-September, Rose, Ingrid Brown-Adam, Anne Mayne, Danielle Kowen and Geraldine Dyason 2000. *Commercial Sexual Exploitation of Children: An explorative study conducted with child victims of prostitution in the Western Cape.* Bellville: Institute for Child and Family Development, University of the Western Cape.

Barros, Ricardo Paes de, Rosane Mendonça and Tatiana Velazco 1994. *Is Poverty the Main Cause of Child Work in Urban Brazil?* Série Seminários, 13/94. Rio de Janeiro: Diretoría de Pesquisa, Instituto de Pesquisa Econômica Aplicada.

Bass, Loretta E. 1996. "Beyond homework: Children's incorporation into market-based work in urban areas of Senegal." *Anthropology of Work Review.* 17:19–24.

—— 2004. *Child Labour in Sub-Saharan Africa.* Boulder & London: Lynne Reiner.

Bastick, Megan and Karin Grimm 2007. *Security Sector Responses to Trafficking in Human Beings.* Policy Paper no. 21. Geneva: Geneva Centre for the Democratic Control of Armed Forces.

Basu, Kaushik 2000. "The Intriguing Relation between Adult Minimum Wage and Child Labour." *The Economic Journal.* 110:C50-C61.

Baufumé, Isabel 2001. "Working in the streets: A lesson for life." In Liebel, M., B. Overwien and A. Rechnagel (eds.), *Working Children's Protagonism: Social Movements and empowerment in Latin America, Africa and India.* Frankfurt and London: Verlag für Interkulturelle Kommunikation. 295–305.

Beegle, Kathleen, Rajeev Dehejia and Roberta Gatti 2005. *Why Should We Care about Child Labor? The Education, Labor Market, and Health Consequences of Child Labor?* Policy research Working Paper 3479. World Bank.

—— 2006. "Child Labor and Agricultural Shocks." *Journal of Development Economics.* 81:80–96.

Begg, I. 2004. "Participation rights in Norway." In Crimmens, D. and A. West (eds.), *Having Their Say: Young People and Participation: European Experiences.* Lyme Regis: Russell House.

Ben-Porath, Yoram 1980. "The F-Connection: Families, Friends, and Firms and the Organization of Exchange." *Population and Development Review* 6:1–30.

Benería, Lourdes 1992. "The Mexican Debt Crisis: Restructuring the Economy and the Household." In Benería, L. and S. Felman (eds.), *Unequal Burden: Economic Crisis, Persistent Poverty and Women's Work.* Boulder: Westview Press.

Bequele, Assefa and William Myers 1995. *First Things First in Child Labour.* Geneva: International Labour Organisation.

Berlan, Amanda 2009. "Child labour and cocoa: whose voices prevail?" *International Journal of Sociology and Social Policy* 29:141–151.

Betcherman, Gordon, Jean Fares, Amy Luinstra, and Robert Prouty 2004. "Child Labour, Education, and Children's Rights." World Bank Social Protection Discussion Paper No. 0412. Washington, D.C.: The World Bank.

Bey, Marguerite 2003. "The Mexican child: from work with the family to paid employment." *Childhood.* 10:287–299.

Bhalotra, Sonia 2003. *Child Labour in Africa.* OECD Social, Employment and Migration Working Papers. Paris: Organisation for Economic Co-operation and Development.

Bhalotra, Sonia and Christopher Heady 2003. "Child farm labor: The wealth paradox." *World Bank Economic Review.* 17:197–227.

Bhalotra, Sonia and Zafaris Tzannatos 2003. "Child labor: What have we learnt?" World Bank Social Protection Paper No. 0317. Washington, D.C.: The World Bank. September.

Bhima Sanga 2005. *Submission to the Commission of the United Nations Secretary General on Violence Against Children.* Save the Children Alliance.

Bissell, Susan 2000. *Manufacturing Childhood: The Lives and Livelihoods of Children in Dhaka's Slums,* Ph. D. Melbourne: Anthropology, University of Melbourne.

—— 2004. "Incentives to education and child labour elimination: a case study of Bangladesh." In Lieten, G. K., R. Srivastava and S. Thorat (eds.), *Small Hands in South Asia: Child Labour in Perspective.* New Delhi: Manohar. 269–289.

—— 2005. "Earning and learning: tensions and compatability." In Weston, B. (ed.), *Child Labor and Human Rights.* Boulder & London: Lynne Reiner. 377–399.

Black, Maggie 1995. *In the Twilight Zone: Child workers in the hotel, tourism and catering industry.* Geneva: International Labour Office.

—— 2002. *Child Domestic Workers: Finding a Voice. A Handbook on Advocacy.* London: Anti-Slavery International.

Bissell, Susan 2004. *Opening Minds, Opening Up Opportunities: Children's participation in action for working children*. London: Save the Children.

Blagbrough, Johnathan 1995. *Child Domestic Work in Indonesia: A preliminary situation analysis*. Geneva: ILO-IPEC.

—— 2009. "Child domestic labor." In Hindman, H. D. (ed.), *The World of Child Labor: A Reference Encyclopedia*. New York: M.E. Sharpe. 86–90.

Blanchet, Thérèse 1996. *Lost Innocence, Stolen Childhoods*. Dhaka: The University Press Limited.

—— 2004. *Slavery revisited: Adopting a child to secure a servant: Palok meye, palok chele*. Dhakar: Save the Children, Sweden—Denmark.

Blanchet, Thérèse 2005. *"Slave for a Season": The Dulabhangas and other Cheap Labour in the Bangladesh Dry Fish Industry*. Dhaka: Save the Children, Sweden-Denmark.

Blanchet, Thérèse and Anisa Zaman 2004. *Slavery revisited: Child domestic servants*. Dakar: Save the Children, Sweden and Denmark.

Blattman, Christopher and Jeannie Annan 2007. *The Consequences of Child Soldiering*. 22. Falmer: Institute of Development Studies, University of Sussex.

—— forthcoming. "On the Nature and Causes of LRA Abduction: What the Abductees Say." In Allen, T. and K. Vlassenroot (eds.), *The Lord's Resistance Army: War, Peace and Reconciliation in Northern Uganda*. Oxford: James Currey.

Bolin, Inge 2006. *Growing up in a Culture of Respect: Child Rearing in Highland Peru*. Austin: University of Texas Press.

Bonnet, Michel 2000. "Introduction: Child labour in the light of bonded labour." In Schlemmer, B. (ed.), *The Exploited Child*. London and New York: Zed Books. 179–191.

Boomgaard, Peter 1989. *Children of the Colonial State: Population Growth and Economic Development in Java 1795–1880*. Amsterdam: Free University Press.

Bourdillon, Michael F. C. 1987. *Shona Peoples: An Ethnography of the Contemporary Shona with Special Reference to their Religion*. Gweru: Mambo Press.

—— 1994. "Street children in Harare." *Africa*. 64:134–152.

—— 2000a. "Children at Work on Tea and Coffee Estates." In Bourdillon, M. (ed.), *Earning a Life*. Harare: Weaver Press. 147–172.

—— 2001. "The children on our streets." *CYC-online: Reading for Child and Youth Care Workers*. (35). http://www.cyc-net.org/cyc-online/cycol-1201-bourdillon-1.html (Oct 8, 2007).

—— 2005. *Experiences with Working Children of Save the Children Norway—Zimbabwe*. Harare: Save the Children, Norway—Zimbabwe.

—— 2006a. *Child Domestic Workers in Zimbabwe*. Harare: Weaver Press.

—— 2006b. "Children and work: a review of current literature and debates." *Development and Change*. 37:1201–1226.

—— 2008. "Children and supporting adults in child-led organisations: experiences in southern Africa." In van der Geest, S. (ed.), *Generations in Africa: Connections and Conflicts*. Beyruth: LIT Verlag. 323–347.

—— 2009. "Children as domestic employees: Problems and promises." *Journal of Children and Poverty*. 15:1–18.

—— (ed.) 2000b. *Earning a Life: Working children in Zimbabwe*. Harare: Weaver Press.

Bourdillon, Michael F. C. and Rumbidzai Rurevo 2003. *Girls on the Street*. Harare: Weaver Press.

Bourdillon, Michael F. C., William E. Myers and Ben White 2009. "Reassessing working children and minimum-age standards." *International Journal of Sociology and Social Policy* 29:106–117.

Boyden, Jo 1997. "Childhood and policy makers: a comparative perspective on the globali-
sation of childhood." In James, A. and A. Prout (eds.), *Constructing and Reconstructing Childhood (2nd edition)*. London: Falmer Press. 190–229.

—— Forthcoming. "Risk and Capability in the Context of Adversity: Children's Contributions to Household Livelihoods in Ethiopia."

Boyden, Jo, Birgitta Ling and William Myers 1998. *What Works for Working Children*. Stockholm: Rädda Barnen & UNICEF.

Boyden, Jo and William Myers 1995. *Exploring alternative approaches to combatting child labour: Case studies from developing countries*. Innocenti Occasional Papers, Florence: UNICEF.

Brewer, Lara 2004. *Youth at risk: The role of skills development in facilitating the transition to work*. FP/SKILLS—InFocus Programme on Skills, Knowledge and Employability.

Bunn, Stephanie 1999. "The nomad's apprentice: Different kinds of 'apprenticeship' among Kyrgyz nomads in Central Asia." In Ainley, P. and H. Rainbird (eds.), *Apprenticeship: Towards a New Paradigm of Learning*. London: Kogan Page. 74–85.

Burman, Erica 2008a. *Deconstructing Developmental Psychology (2nd edition)*. London: Routledge.

—— 2008b. *Developments: Child, Image, Nation*. London: Routledge.

Burr, Rachel 2004. "Children's rights: International policy and lived practice." In Kehily, M. J. (ed.), *An Introduction to Childhood Studies*. Maidenhead: Open University Press. 145–159.

—— 2006. *Vietnam's Children in a Changing World*. New Brunswick: Rutgers University Press.

Burra, Neera 1995. *Born To Work: Child Labour in India*. Oxford: Oxford University Press.

—— 2003. "Rights versus needs: Is it in the 'best interest of the child'?" In Kabeer, N., G. B. Nambissan and R. Subrahmanian (eds.), *Child Labour and the Right to Education in South Asia*. New Delhi: Sage. 73–94.

Busza, Joanna, Sarah Castle and Aisse Diarra 2004. "Trafficking and health." *British Medical Journal*. 328:1369–1371.

Butterflies and Human Rights Law Network 2006. *Plan of Action for Working Children in Delhi*. Delhi: Butterflies and Human rights Law Network.

Bwibo, N.O and Philista Onyango 1987. *Final report of the Child Labour and Health research*. Nairobi: University of Nairobi.

Caldwell, Melissa S., Karen D. Rudolph, Wendy Troop-Gordon and Do-Yeong Kim 2004. "Reciprocal influences among relational self-views, social disengagement, and peer stress during early adolescence." *Child Development*. 4:1140–1154.

Call, Kathleen T. 1996. "The Implications of Helpfulness for Possible Selves." In Mortimer, J. T. and M. D. Finch (eds.), *Adolescents, Work, and Family: An Intergenerational Developmental Analysis*. Thousand Oaks, London, New Delhi: Sage Publications. 63–96.

Camacho, Agnes Zenaida V 1999. "Family, child labour and migration: Child domestic workers in Metro Manila." *Childhood*. 6:57–73.

Campos, R. M., W. Raffaelli, M. Ude, A. Greco, J. Ruff, C. M. Rolf, N. Antunes, D. Hlsey and Greco and the Street Youth Study Group 1994. "Social Networks and Daily Activities of Street Youth in Belo Horizonte, Brazil." *Child Development*. 65:319–330.

Chakraborty, Sudip and G.K. Lieten 2004. "What do child labourers do? Details of a rural district in Northeast India." In Lieten, G. K. (ed.), *Working Children Around the World*. Amsterdam & New Delhi: IREWOC Foundation & Institute for Human Development. 140–157.

Chandra, Vinod 2007. "Negotiating gender identities: Domestic work of Indian children in Britain and in India." In Hungerland, B., M. Liebel, B. Milne and A. Wihstutz (eds.),

Working to be Someone: Child Focused Research and Practice with Working Children. London and Philadelphia: Jessica Kingsley. 67–75.

Chandra, Vinod 2008. *Children's Domestic Work: Children speak out for themselves.* New Delhi: Manak.

Chaudhury, Nazmul, Jeff Hammer, Michael Kremer, Karthik Muraldhiran and Halsey Rogers 2006. "Missing in Action: Teacher and Health Worker Absence in Developing Countries." *Journal of Economic Perspectives.* 20:91–116.

Che, Hie-Joang 1995. "Children in the Examination War in South Korea: A Cultural Analysis." In Stephens, S. (ed.), *Children and the Politics of Culture.* Princeton, NJ: Princeton University Press. 141–158.

Child Workers in Nepal Concerned Centre 2003. *A situational Analysis of Child Sex Tourism in Nepal (Kathmandu Valley and Pokhara).* Kathmandu: CWIN.

Children of Balkur Panchayat 1999. *Work We Can and Cannot Do.* Bangalore: The Concerned for Working Children.

Childs, Michael J. 1992. *Labour's Apprentices: Working-Class Lads in Late Victorian and Edwardian England.* Montreal: McGill-Queen's University Press.

Chotikapanich, Duangkamon, D. S. Prasada Rao, William E. Griffiths and Vicar Valencia 2007. *Global Inequality: Recent evidence and trends.* Research Paper, 2007/01. United Nations University. World Institute for Development Economics Research.

Chowdhury, A. Mushtaque R. 2003. "Filling a critical gap in basic education in Bangladesh." In Kabeer, N., G. B. Nambissan and R. Subrahmanian (eds.), *Child Labour and the Right to Education in South Asia.* New Delhi: Sage. 292–303.

CIDA 2007. *Impacts of Microfinance Initiatives on Children: Overview of the study report.* Ottawa: Children's Rights and Protection Unit in the Human Rights and Participation: Canadian International Development Agency.

Cigno, Alessandro and Furio C. Rosati 2005. *The Economics of Child Labour.* Oxford: Oxford University Press.

CINI-ASHA 2003. "Family adjustments for mainstreaming child labourers into formal schools in Calcutta: the experience of CINI-ASHA." In Kabeer, N., G. B. Nambissan and R. Subrahmanian (eds.), *Child Labour and the Right to Education in South Asia.* New Delhi: Sage. 335–348.

Clacherty, Glynis 2002. *Report on a Children's Participation Process: Towards a South African Child Labour Programme.* Pretoria: Department of Labour.

Clacherty, Glynis and Joahanna Kistner 2001. "Evaluating the Zimisileni researchers' project: participatory research as intervention with "hard-to-reach" boys." *PLA Notes.* 29–33.

Connolly, Mark and Judith Ennew 1996a. "Introduction: children out of place." *Childhood.* 3:131–146.

Connolly, Mark and Judith Ennew (ed.) 1996b. *Children Out of Place—Working and Street Children. Special issue of Childhood, Volume 3, number 2.* London: Sage.

Cook, S. 1986. "The 'managerial' vs. the 'labor' function, capital accumulation, and the dynamics of simple commodity production in rural Oaxaca, Mexico." In Strickon, A. and S. M. Greenfield (eds.), *Entrepreneurship and Social Change.* Lanham, Maryland: University Press of America.

Cook, S. and L. Binford 1990. *Obliging Need: Rural Petty Industry in Mexican Capitalism.* Austin: University of Texas Press.

Cooke, Bill and Uma Kothari (ed.) 2001. *Participation. The New Tyranny.* London: Zed Books.

Crossen, Cynthia 1994. *Tainted Truth: The Manipulation of Fact in America.* New York: Simon & Schuster.

Cunnien, Keith A., Nicole Martin Rogers and Jeylan T. Mortimer 2009. "Adolescent work experience and self efficacy." *International Journal of Sociology and Social Policy* 29:164–175.

Cunningham, Hugh 1990. "The employment and unemployment of children in England c. 1680–1851." *Past & Present*. 126:115–149.

—— 1991. *The Children of the Poor: Representations of childhood since the seventeenth century*. Oxford: Blackwell.

—— 1995. *Children and Childhood in Western Society since 1500*. Studies in Modern History. London: Longman.

Cunningham, Hugh and Shelton Stromquist 2005. "Child labor and the rights of children: historical patterns of decline and persistence." In Weston, B. (ed.), *Child Labor and Human Rights*. Boulder & London: Lynne Reiner. 55–83.

Dahlén, Marianne 2007. *The Negotiable Child: The ILO Child Labour Campaign 1919–1973*, Doctor of Laws. Uppsala: Department of Law, Uppsala University.

Davies, Matthew 2008. "A Childish Culture?: Shared understandings, agency and intervention: an anthropological study of street children in northwest Kenya." *Childhood*. 15:309–330.

Davin, Anna 1996. *Growing up Poor: Home, School and Street in London 1870–1914*. London: Rivers Oram Press.

de Kat Angelino, P. 1929. *Vorstenlandsche Tabaksenquete. Publicatie No. 5 van het Kantoor van Arbeid*. Weltevreden: Landsdrukkerij.

Dearden, Chris and Saul Becker 1999. "The experience of young carers in the United Kingdom: The mental health issues." *Mental Health Care*. 21:273–276.

—— 2004. *Young Carers in the UK: the 2004 Report*. London: Carers UK.

Delap, Emily 2000. "Urban children's work during and after the 1998 floods in Bangladesh." *Development in Practice*. 10:662–673.

—— 2001. "Economic and cultural forces in the child labour debate: evidence from urban Bangladesh." *The Journal of Development Studies*. 37:1–22.

—— 2004. *Planning Working Children's Education: A guide for education sector planners*. London: Save the Children.

den Berge, Marten van 2004. "Child agency in Bolivia." In Lieten, G. K. (ed.), *Working Children around the World*. Amsterdam & New Delhi: REWOC Foundation & Institute for Human Development. 109–128.

Diamond, Charles and Tammy Fayed 1998. "Evidence on Substitutability of Adult and Child Labour." *Journal of Development Studies*. 34:62–70.

Dillon, Andrew 2008. *Child Labor and Schooling Responses to Production and Health Shocks in Northern Mali*. IFPRI Discussion Paper 00755. Washington, D.C.: International Food Policy Research Institute.

Dodson, L. and K. Dickert 2004. "Girls' Family Labor in Low-Income Households: A Decade of Qualitative Research." *Journal of Marriage and Family*. 66: 318–332. 66: 318–332.

Dorman, Peter 2008. *Child Labor, Education and Health: A Review of the Literature*. Geneva: International Labor Organization.

Dottridge, Mike 2004. *Kids as Commodities? Child trafficking and what to do about it*. Lausanne: Terre des Hommes Foundation.

—— 2008. *Kids Abroad: Ignore them, Abuse them or Protect them?* Geneva: Terre des Hommes Internation Federation.

Douglas, Mary 1966. *Purity and Danger: An Analysis of Concepts of Pollution and Taboo*. London: Routledge.

Dowdney, Luke 2003. *Children of the Drug Trade: a Case Study of Children in Organised Armed Violence in Rio de Janeiro*. Rio de Janeiro: Viveiros de Castro Editora Ltda.

Dréze, Jean and Amartya Sen 2002. *India: Development and Participation*. New Delhi: Oxford University Press.

Droz, Yvan 2006. "Street children and the work ethic: New policy for an old moral, Nairobi (Kenya)." *Childhood*. 13:349–363.

Duryea, Suzanne, David Lam and Deborah Levison 2007. "Effects of economic shocks on children's employment and schooling in Brazil." *Journal of Development Economics*. 84:188–214.

Ebigbo, P.O. 2003. "Street Children the Core of Child Abuse and Neglect in Nigeria." 13(1), Spring." *Children, Youth and Environments* 13.:Retrieved July 25, 2003, from http://cye .colorado.edu.

Edmonds, Eric V. 2005. "Does child labor decline with improving economic status?" *Journal of Economic Perspectives*. 18:77–99.

—— 2006. "Child labour and schooling responses to anticipated income in South Africa." *Journal of Development Economics*. 81:386–414.

—— 2008. "Child labor." In Schultz, T. P. and J. Strauss (eds.), *Handbook of Development Economics*. Amsterdam: Elsevier Science.

Edmonds, Eric V. and Carrie Turk 2004. "Child labor in transition in Vietnam." In Glewwe, P., N. Agrawal and D. Dollar (eds.), *Economic Growth, Poverty, and Household Welfare in Vietnam*. Washington, DC: The World Bank. 505–550.

Edmonds, Eric V. and Nina Pavcnik 2005a. "Child Labor in the Global Economy." *Journal of Economic Perspectives*. 18:199–220.

Edmonds, Eric V. and Nina Pavcnik 2005b. "The Effect of Trade Liberalization on Child Labor." *Journal of International Economics*. 65:401–419.

Eekelaar, John 1994. "The interests of the child and the child's wishes: the role of dynamic self-determinism." *International Journal of Law and the Family*. 8:42–61.

Elson, Robert 1994. *Village Java under the Cultivation System 1830–1870*. Sydney: Allen & Unwin.

Emerson, Patrick M. 2009. "The economic view of child labor." In Hindman, H. D. (ed.), *The World of Child Labor: A Reference Encyclopedia*. New York: M.E. Sharpe. 3–9.

Emerson, Patrick M. and André Portela Souza 2007. *Is child labour harmful? The impact of working earlier in life on adult earnings*. http://oregonstate.edu/~emersonp/ (accessed 23 August 2009): Electronic manuscript.

Ennew, Judith 1994a. *Street and working children : a guide to planning*. London: Save the Children.

—— 1994b. "Parentless friends: A cross-cultural examination of networks among street children and street youth." In Nestmann, F. and K. Hurrelmann (eds.), *Social Networks and Social Support in Childhood and Adolescence*. Berlin: Walter de Gruyter. 409–426.

—— 2000a. "How can we define citizenship in childhood." In Rajani, R. (ed.), *The Political Participation of Children*. Cambridge, MA: Harvard Center for Population and Development Studies.

—— 2000b. "Why the Convention is not about street children." In Fottrell, D. (ed.), *Revisiting Children's Rights: 10 Years of the UN Convention on the Rights of the Child*. The Hague: Kluwer Law International. 169–182.

—— 2008. "Children as 'Citizens' of the United Nations (UN)." In Invernizzi, A. and J. Williams (eds.), *Children and Citizenship*. Los Angeles, London: Sage. 66–78.

Ennew, Judith and Jill Swart-Kruger 2003. "Introduction: Homes, Places and Spaces in the Construction of Street Children and Street Youth." *Children, Youth and Environments*. 13.:Retrieved 22/08/2003 from http://cye.colorado.edu.

Ennew, Judith, William Myers and Dominique Pierre Plateau 2005. "Defining child labor as if human rights really matter." In Weston, B. (ed.), *Child Labor and Human Rights*. Boulder & London: Lynne Reiner. 27–54.

Equations 2003. *A Situational Analysis of Child Sex Tourism in India (Kerala and Goa).* Equations.

Fassa, Anaclaudia F. and David H. Wegman 2009. "Special Health Risks of Child Labour." In Hindman, H. D. (ed.), *The World of Child Labor: A Reference Encylopedia.* New York: M.E. Sharpe. 127–130.

Felsman, Kirk J. 1984. "Abandoned children: a reconsideration." *Children Today.* 3:13–18.

Field, Norma 1995. "The Child as Laborer and Consumer: The Disappearance of Childhood in Contemporary Japan." In Stephens, S. (ed.), *Children and the Politics of Culture.* Princeton, NJ: Princeton University Press. 51–78.

Fithen, Caspar and Paul Richards 2005. "Making war, crafting peace." In Richards, P. (ed.), *No Peace, No War: An Anthropology of Contemporary Armed Conflicts.* Oxford: James Currey. 117–136.

Forastieri, Valentina 2002. *Children at Work: Health and Safety Risks.* Geneva: ILO.

Frederiksen, Lisa 1999. "Child and youth employment in Denmark: Comments on children's work from their own perspective." *Childhood.* 6:101–112.

Freeman, Michael 1997. *The Moral Status of Children: Essays on the Rights of the Child.* The Hague: Luwer Law International.

Freije, Samuel and Luis F. Lopez-Calva 2000. *Child Labor, School Attendance, and Poverty in Mexico and Venezuela,"* manuscript. I searched Google-Scholar—this doesn't seem to have been published. I have emailed the author.

Fyfe, Alec 2007. *The Worldwide Movement Against Child Labour: Progress and Future Directions.* Geneva: International Labour Office.

Fyfe, Alec and M. Jankanish 1997. *Trade Unions and Child Labour: A guide to Action.* Geneva: International Labour Organisation.

Gamlin, Jennie and Maria Eugena Pastor 2009. "Child labour in Latin America: theory, policy, practice." *International Journal of Sociology and Social Policy.* 29:118–129.

Garbarino, James, Frances M. Stott and Faculty of Erikson Institute 1992. *What Children Can Tell Us: Eliciting, interpreting and evaluating critical information from children.* San Francisco: Jossey-Bass Publishers.

Gibbs, S. 1994. "Post-war Social Reconstruction in Mozambique: Re-framing Children's Experience of Trauma and Healing." *Disasters.* 18:268–276.

Gigengack, Roy 2000. "*Populacho* and *Callejeros:* Stories about street children and other urban poor in Mexico City." *Medische Antropologie.* 12:71–102.

—— 2006. *Young, Damned and Banda: The World of Young Street People in Mexico City, 1990–1997,* Amsterdam: School for Social Science Research, University of Amsterdam.

Glasinovich, Walter A. 1995. "Trabajar o estudiar: un falso dilema." *Entr calles y plazas el trabajo de los ninos en lima.* Peru: IEP, UNICEF and ADEC/ATC.

Glewwe, Paul 1996. "The Relevance of Standard Estimates of Rates of Return to Schooling for Education Policy: A Critical Assessment." *Journal of Development Economics.* 51:267–290.

—— 2004. "An Investigation of the Determinants of School Progress and Academic Achievement in Vietnam." In Glewwe, P., D. Dollar and N. Agrawal (eds.), *Economic Growth, Poverty, and Household Welfare in Vietnam.* Washington, DC: The World Bank. 40–46.

Glewwe, Paul and Michael Kremer 2006. "Schools, teachers, and education outcomes in developing countries." In Hanushek, E. A. and F. Welch (eds.), *Handbook of the Economics of Education, volume 2.* New York: Elsevier. 945–1017.

Gose, Michael 2002. *The African Charter on the Rights and Welfare of the Child: an assessment of the legal value of its substantive provisions by means of a direct comparison to the Convention on the Rights of the Child.* Cape Town: Community Law Centre, University of Western Cape.

Goulart, Pedro and Arjun S. Bedi 2007. "Child labour and educational success in Portugal." *Economics of Education Review*. doi:10.1016/j.econedurev.2007.07.002.

Green, Duncan 1999. "Child workers of the Americas." *Nacla Report on the Americas*. 32:21–27.

Greenberger, Ellen and Laurence Steinberg 1985. *When Teen-agers Work: The Psychological and Social Costs of Adolescent Employment*. New York: Basic Books.

Grier, Beverley C. 2005. *Invisible Hands: Child Labour and the State in Colonial Zimbabwe*. Social History of Africa. Portsmouth, N.H.: Heinemann.

Grimsrud, Bjorne 2002. "Too much work at too early an age." In Grimsrud, B. (ed.), *The Next Steps: Experiences and Analysis of How to Eradicate Child Labour*. Oslo: Fafo. 9–23.

Grootaert, Christiaan 1999. "Child Labor in Côte d'Ivoire." In Grootaert, C. and H. A. Patrinos (eds.), *The Policy Analysis of Child Labor: A Comparative Study*. London: Macmillan. 23–62.

Grootaert, Christiaan and Harry Anthony Patrinos (ed.) 1999. *The Policy Analysis of Child Labor: A Comparative Study*. London: Macmillan.

Groves, Leslie 2003a. *Implementation of I.L.O. Child Labour Convention 182: Lessons from Bangladesh*. London: Save the Children UK.

—— 2003b. *Finding the Right Tools for the Job: Lessons learned on the application of I.L.O. Convention 182 on the worst forms of child labour*. London: Save the Children UK.

—— 2003c. *Good Practice in Working Children's Participation: A Case Study from Brazil*. International Save the Children Alliance.

Guarcello, Lorenzo, Fabrizia Mealli and Furio Rosati 2003. *Household Vulnerability and Child Labor: The Effect of Shocks, Credit Rationing and Insurance*. Understanding Children's Work Working Paper, Rome: Centre for International Studies on Economic Growth (CEIS), University of Rome "Tor Vergata."

Guarcello, Lorenzo, Furio Rosati, Scott Lyon and Cristina Valdivia 2005. *Impact of Children's Work on School Attendance and Performance: A Review of School Survey Evidence from Five Countries*. Understanding Children's Work: An inter-agency research co-operative. Geneva: International Labour Organisation, UNICEF, World Bank.

Guarcello, Lorenzo, Scott Lyon and Furio Rosati 2006. *Child Labour and Education for All: an issue paper*. Understanding Children's Work: An inter-agency research co-operative. Rome: University of Rome "Tor Vergata."

Guarcello, Lorenzo, I. Kovrova and Furio C. Rosati 2007. *Child labor as a response to shocks: evidence from Cambodian villages," UCW working paper, June*. Understanding Children's Work Project, Rome.

Guarcello, Lorenzo, Scott Lyon, Furio Rosati and Cristina Valdivia 2007. *Children's Non-Market Activities and Child Labour Measurement: A Discussion based on Household Survey Data*. Geneva: ILO.

Guldberg, Helene 2009. *Reclaiming Childhood: Freedom and Play in an Age of Fear*. Abingdon, New York: Routledge.

Gulrajani, Mohini 2000. "Child labour and the export sector in the Indian carpet industry." In Schlemmer, B. (ed.), *The Exploited Child*. London and New York: Zed Books. 51–66.

Gunn, S. E. and Z. Ostos 1992. "Dilemmas in tackling child labour: the case of scavenger children in the Philippines." *International Labour Review*. 131:629–646.

Gustafsson, I. 1987. *Schools and the Transformation of Work: A Comparative Study of Four Productive Work Programmes in Southern Africa*. Stockholm: Institute of International Education, University of Stockholm.

Hallack, Jacques and Muriel Poisson 2007. *Corrupt Schools, Corrupt Universities: What Can be Done?* Paris: International Institute for Educational Planning.

Hansen, David M., Jeylan T. Mortimer and Helga Krüger 2001. "Adolescent part-time employment in the United States and Germany: Diverse outcomes, contexts and pathways."

In Mizen, P., C. Pole and A. Bollton (eds.), *Hidden Hands: International Perspectives on Children's Work and Labour.* London: Routledge Farmer. 121–138.

Hansen, Hal 2004. "Apprenticeship." In Fass, P. S. (ed.), *Encyclopedia of Children and Childhood in History and Society.* New York: Thomson. 64–66.

Hanson, Karl and A. Vandaele 2003. "Working children and international labour law: A critical analysis." *International Journal of Children's Rights.* 11:73–146.

Hanssen, Einar 1996. "Finding care on the street: processes in the careers of Sri Lankan street boys." *Childhood.* 3:247–259.

Hanushek, Eric A., Victor Lavy and Kohtaro Hitomi 2006. *Do students care about school quality? Determinants of dropout behavior in developing countries.* Working Paper 12737. Cambridge, MA: National Bureau of Economic Research.

Harber, Clive 2004. *Schooling as Violence: How schools harm pupils and societies.* London & New York: RoutledgeFalmer.

Hart, Roger 1992. *Children's Participation: From Tokenism to Citizenship.* Innocenti Research Centre Publications. Florence: UNICEF.

—— 1997. *Children's Participation: The Theory and Practice of Involving Young Citizens in Community Development and Environmental Care.* London: Earthscan Publications.

Harwood, Bill and L. Dianne Mull 2002. *Education to Combat Abusive Child Labor: Planning Educational Response Strategies for Working Children in Honduras.* Washington, DC: Creative Associates International, for US Agency for International Development.

Hashim, Iman M. 2004. *Working with Working Children: Child Labour and the Barriers to Education in Rural Northeastern Ghana* D.Phil. Brighton: University of Sussex.

—— 2006. *The Positives and Negatives of Children's Independent Migration: Assessing the Evidence and the Debates.* Working Paper T16. Brighton: Development Research Centre on Migration, Globalisation and Poverty, University of Sussex.

Hazarika, Gautam and Arjun S. Bedi 2003. "Schooling costs and child work in rural Pakistan." *Journal of Development Studies.* 39:29–64.

Heady, Christopher 2000. *What is the effect of child labour on learning achievement? Evidence from Ghana.* Innocenti working papers. Florence: UNICEF, Innocenti Research Centre.

Hemrica, Jantine and Freida Heyting 2004. "Tacit notions of childhood: An analysis of discourse about child participation in decision-making regarding arrangements in case of parental divorce." *Childhood.* 11:449–468.

Hendrick, Harry 2003. *Child Welfare: Historical Dimensions, Contemporary Debate.* Bristol: Polity Press.

Heywood, Colin 2001. *A History of Childhood.* Cambridge: Polity.

Hindman, Hugh D. 2002. *Child Labor: An American History.* Armonk, NY and London: M.E. Sharpe.

—— 2009a. "Editor's note: Measuring child labor." In Hindman, H. D. (ed.), *The World of Child Labor: A Reference Encyclopedia.* New York: M.E. Sharpe. xxix-xxxii.

—— 2009b. "Editor's introduction: Child labor in global and historical perspective." In Hindman, H. D. (ed.), *The World of Child Labor: A Reference Encyclopedia.* New York: M.E. Sharpe. xxv–xxvii.

Holmes, Larry E. 1991. *The Kremlin and the Schoolhouse: Reforming Education in Soviet Russia, 1917–1931.* Bloomington: Indiana University Press.

Honwana, Alcinda 2006. *Child Soldiers in Africa.* Philadelphia: University of Pennsylvania Press.

Howieson, Cathy, Jim McKechnie and Shiela Semple 2006. *The Nature and Implications of the Part-Time Employment of Secondary School Pupils.* Scottish Executive Social Research, The

Department of Enterprise, Transport and Lifelong Learning. www.scotland.gov.uk/socialresearch (9 Feb 2007).

Huijsmans, Roy 2004. *Listening to Working School-Youth: Child-Centered Case Study of Employment Experiences of HAVO-Students in Rural Eastern Netherlands.*, Master's Dissertation. The Hague: Institute of Social Studies.

—— 2007. "Children working beyond their localities: Lao children working in Thailand." *Childhood.* 15:331–354.

Hulme, David and Paul Mosley 1996. *Fighting Against Poverty.* New York: Routledge.

Human Rights Watch 2001. *Borderline Slavery: Child Trafficking in Togo.* Human Rights Watch. New York: Human Rights Watch.

—— 2003. *Small Change: Bonded Child Labor in India's Silk Industry.* Human Rights Watch. New York: Human Rights Watch.

—— 2005. *Inside the Home, Outside the Law: Abuse of Child Domestic Workers in Morocco.* Human Rights Watch. New York: Human Rights Watch.

—— 2009. *Workers in the Shadows: Abuse and Exploitation of Child Domestic Workers in Indonesia.* New York: Human Rights Watch.

Humbert, Franziska 2009. *The Challenge of Child Labour in International Law.* Cambridge: Cambridge University Press.

Humphries, Jane 2003. "Child labor: lessons from the historical experience of today's industrial economies." *The World Bank Economic Review.* 17:175–196.

Hungerland, Beatrice 2007. "Work—a way to participative autonomy for children." In Hungerland, B., M. Liebel, B. Milne and A. Wihstutz (eds.), *Working to be Someone: Child Focused Research and Practice with Working Children.* London and Philadelphia: Jessica Kingsley. 167–175.

Hungerland, Beatrice, Manfred Liebel, Anja Liesecke and Anne Wihstutz 2007. "Paths to participatory autonomy: The meanings of work for children in Germany." *Childhood.* 14:257–277.

Ide, Lisa S. R. and David L. Parker 2005. "Hazardous Child Labor: Lead and Neurocognitive Development." *Public Health Reports.* 120:607–612.

Ilahi, Nadeem, Peter F. Orazem and Guilherme Sedlacek 2005. *How Does Working as a Child Affect Wage, Income and Poverty as an Adult?* Social Protection Discussion Paper Series, no. 0514. Washington, D.C.: The World Bank.

Ingenhorst, Heinz 2001. "Child labour in the Federal Republic of Germany." In Mizen, P., C. Pole and A. Bollton (eds.), *Hidden Hands: International Perspectives on Children's Work and Labour.* London: RoutledgeFarmer. 139–148.

International Labour Office 2002. *A Future without Child Labour: Global Report.* Geneva: ILO.

—— 2002a. *In-Depth Analysis of the Situation of Working Street Children in Moscow 2001.* Moscow: IPEC.

—— 2002b. *In-Depth Analysis of the Situation of Working Street Children in the Leningrad Region 2001.* St. Petersburg: IPEC.

—— 2004. *Investing In Every Child: An Economic Study of the Costs and Benefits of Eliminating Child Labour.* Geneva: IPEC.

—— 2005. *Combating Child Labour in Asia and the Pacific: Progress and Challenges.* Bankok: ILO/IPEC.

—— 2006. *The end of child labour: Within reach. Global Report under the follow-up to the ILO Declaration on Fundamental Principles and Rights at Work.* International Labour Conference, 95th Session 2006. Report I (B). Geneva: ILO.

—— 2007. *Child Labour, Wages and Productivity: Results from Demand-Side Surveys.* Geneva: International Labour Organisation.

International Working Group on Child Labour 1997. *Have We Asked the Children?* Bangalore & Amsterdam: International Working Group on Child Labour.

Invernizzi, Antonella 2001. "The work of children is not only work." In Liebel, M., B. Overwien and A. Rechnagel (eds.), *Working Children's Protagonism: Social Movements and empowerment in Latin America, Africa and India.* Frankfurt and London: Verlag für Interkulturelle Kommunikation. 31–51.

—— 2003. "Street-working children and adolescents in Lima: Work as an agent of socialization." *Childhood.* 10:319–341.

—— 2007. "Children's work as 'participation': thoughts on ethnographic data in Lima and the Algarve." In Hungerland, B., M. Liebel, B. Milne and A. Wihstutz (eds.), *Working to be Someone: Child Focused Research and Practice with Working Children.* London and Philadelphia: Jessica Kingsley. 135–144.

Invernizzi, Antonella and Brian Milne 2002. "Are children entitled to contribute to international policy making? A critical view of children's participation in the international campaign for the elimination of child labour." *International Journal of Children's Rights.* 10:403–431.

IPEC 2002. *Combatting Child Labour: A Handbook for Labour Inspectors.* Geneva: International Labour Office, International Programme for the Elimination of Child Labour.

Irwanto, S. et al. 1995. *Pekerja anak di tiga kota besar: Jakarta, Surabaya, Medan (Child workers in three large cities: Jakarta, Surabaya and Medan).* Jakarta: Pusat Penelitian Unika Atma Jaya.

Ivanova, Slavyanka, Antoaneta Getova and Diana Zheleva 2007. *Children Speak Out: Trafficking Risk and Resilience in Southeast Europe. Bulgaria Report.* Sofia: Animus Association Foundation with Save the Children.

Iversen, Vegard 2002. "Autonomy in child labor migrants." *World Development.* 9:817–834.

Iyer, Lalitha 2001. "Promoting child-centered community development through participatory evaluation." *PLA Notes.* 45–47.

Jacquemin, Mélanie 2004. "Children's domestic work in Abidjan, Côte d'Ivoire: The petites bonnes have the floor." *Childhood.* 11:383–397.

—— 2006. "Can the language of rights get hold of the complex realities of child domestic work? The case of young domestic workers in Abidjan, Ivory Coast." *Childhood.* 13:389–406.

James, Adrian L., Allison James and Sally McNamee 2004. "Turn down the volume?—not hearing children in family proceedings." *Child and Family Law Quarterly.* 16:189–202.

James, Allison, Chris Jenks and Allan Prout 1998. *Theorizing Childhood.* New York: Teachers College Press, Columbia University.

Janvry, Alain de, Frederico Finan, Elisabeth Sadoulet and Renos Vakis 2006. "Can Conditional Cash Transfer Programs Serve as Safety Nets in Keeping Children at School and from Working when Exposed to Shocks?" *Journal of Development Economics.* 79:349–373.

Johnson, Victoria, Joanna Hill and Edda Ivan-Smith 1995. *Listening to Smaller Voices: Children in an environment of change.* Chard, Somerset: Actionaid.

Kabeer, Naila 2001. *Bangladeshi Women Workers and Labour Market Decisions: The Power to Choose.* Dhaka: University Press Limited.

—— 2003. "Deprivation, discrimination and delivery: competing explanations for child labour and educational failure in South Asia." In Kabeer, N., G. B. Nambissan and R. Subrahmanian (eds.), *Child Labour and the Right to Education in South Asia.* New Delhi: Sage. 351–393.

Kabeer, Naila, Geetha B. Nambissan and Ramya Subrahmanian (ed.) 2003. *Child Labour and the Right to Education in South Asia: Needs versus Rights.* New Delhi: Sage.

4000242

REFERENCES

Kamal, Gulam Mustafa, Pratima Paul-Majunder and M. Khalilur Rahman 1993. *Economically Active Children in Bangladesh*. Publication # 40. Dhaka: Associates for Community and Population Research.

Kanbargi, Ramesh and P.M. Kulkarni 1991. "Child work, schooling and fertility in rural Karnataka, India." In Kanbargi, R. (ed.), *Child Labour in the Indian Subcontinent*. London: Sage. 125–163.

Karunan, Victor 2005. "Working children as change makers: perspectives from the South." In Weston, B. (ed.), *Child Labor and Human Rights*. Boulder and London: Lynne Rienner. 293–317.

Kassouf, Ana Lúcia 1999. "Trabalho Infantil e Rendimentos." *Qualidade de Vida*. 1:1–4.

Katz, Cindi 1996. "Introduction." *Anthropology of Work Review*. 17:3–8.

—— 2004. *Growing Up Global: Economic Restructuring and Children's Everyday Lives*. Minneapolis: University of Minnesota Press.

Keenean, Thomas and Subhadra Evans 2009. *An Introduction to Child Development (2nd edition)*. Los Angeles: Sage.

Khan, Ali 2007. *Representing Children: Power, Policy, and the Discourse on Child Labour in the Football Manufacturing Industry of Pakistan*. Karachi: Oxford University Press.

Kielland, Anne and Maurizia Tovo 2006. *Children at Work: Child labor practices in Africa*. Boulder & London: Lynne Rienner.

Kirby, Perpetua and Sara Bryson 2002. *Measuring the Magic? Evaluating and researching young people's participation in public decision making*. London: Carnegie Young People Initiative.

Kirby, Peter 2003. *Child Labour in Britain, 1750–1870*. Basingstoke: Palgrave Macmillan.

Kjørholt, Anne Trine 2002. "Small is powerful: discourses on "children and participation" in Norway." *Childhood*. 9:63–82.

Knaul, Felicia Marie 1998. *Learning and Earning: The impact of early entry into the labour force on earnings in Colombia*. Mexico City: Documento de Trabajo, Centro de Investigacion y Docencia Económicas.

Kombarakaran, Francis A. 2004. "Street children of Bombay: their stresses and strategies of coping." *Children and Youth Services Review*. 26:857–75.

Kovačević, Atana and Verica Mirović 2007. *Children Speak Out: Trafficking Risk and Resilience in Southeast Europe. Montenegro Report*. Podgorika: Save the Children in Montenegro.

Kovats-Bernat, J. Christopher 2006. *Sleeping Rough in Port-au-Prince: An Ethnography of Street Children and Violence in Haiti*. Gainsville: Florida University Press.

Krishna, Sumi 1996. *Restoring Childhood*. Delhi: Konark.

Lancy, David F. 2008. *The Anthropology of Childhood: Cherubs, Chattel, Changelings*. Cambridge: Cambridge University Press.

Landrigan, Philip J. 1993. "Child labor: a re-emergent threat." *American Journal of Industrial Medicine*. 24:267–268.

Lane, Robert 1991. *The Market Experience*. Cambridge: Cambridge University Press.

Langeni, T. 1999. "Child out-fostering and other factors influencing reproductive behaviour in Botswana's changing society." *Botswana Notes and Records*. 31:135–142.

Lansdown, Gerison 2001. *Promoting Children's Participation In Democratic Decision-Making*. Florence: UNICEF.

—— 2005. *The evolving capacities of the child*. Florence: UNICEF, Save the Children.

Larson, R. and M.H. Richards 1994. *Divergent Realities: The emotional lives of mothers, fathers, and adolescents*. New York: Basic Books.

Lavalette, Michael 1994. *Child Employment in the Capitalist Labour Market*. Aldershot: Avebury.

—— 2000. "Child employment in a capitalist labour market: The British case." In Schlemmer, B. (ed.), *The Exploited Child*. London and New York: Zed Books. 214–230.

——— 2005. "'In defence of childhood': against the neo-liberal assault on social life." In Qvortrup, J. (ed.), *Studies in Modern Childhood: Society, Agency, Culture*. Basingstoke: Palgrave Macmillan. 147–166.

Lavalette, Michael, Sandy Hobbs, S. Lindsay and Jim McKechnie 1995. "Child employment in Britain: Policy, myth and reality." *Youth and Policy*. 45:1–15.

Leach, Fiona, Vivian Fiscian, Esme Kadzamira, Eve Lemani and Pamela Machakanja 2003. *An Investigative Study of the Abuse of Girls in African Schools*. Educational Papers. Sevenoaks: Department for International Development.

Lee, Yun-Suk, Barbara Schneider and Linda J. Waite 2003. "Children and housework: some unanswered questions." *Sociological Studies of Children and Youth*. 9:105–125.

Lee-Wright, Peter 1990. *Child Slaves*. London: Earthscan Publications.

Legault, L., M. Anawati and R. Flynn 2006. "Factors favoring psychological resilience among fostered young people." *Children and Youth Services Review*. 28:1024–1038.

Lehohla, Pali 2001. *Survey of activities of young people in South Africa 1999: Tables on children's work-related activities*.

Leonard, Madeleine 2004. "Children's views on children's right to work: reflections from Belfast." *Childhood*. 11:45–61.

——— 2007. "Child work, child employment: addressing myths, confronting realities." In Engwall, K. and I. Soderlind (eds.), *Children's Work in Everyday Life*. Stockholm: Institute for Futures Studies. 151–165.

Levine, David 1987. *Reproducing Families*. Cambridge: Cambridge University Press.

Levine, Robert A. and Merry I. White 1986. *Human Conditions: The Cultural Basis of Educational Development*. London & New York: Routledge & Kegan Paul.

Levine, Robert A. and Rebecca S. New (ed.) 2008. *Anthropology and Child Development: A Cross-Cultural Reader*. Malden: Blackwell.

Levine, Susan 1999. "Bittersweet harvest—Children, work and the global march against child labour in the post-apartheid state." *Critique of Anthropology*. 19:139–155.

Levison, Deborah 2000. "Children as economic agents." *Feminist Economics*. 6:125–134.

Levison, Deborah, Richard Anker, Shahid Ashraf and Sandhya Barge 1998. "Is Child Labour Really Necessary in India's Carpet Industry?" In Anker, R., S. Barge, S. Rajagopal and M. P. Joseph (eds.), *Economics of Child Labour In Hazardous Industries of India*. New Delhi: Hindustan Publishing. 94–134.

Levison, Deborah, Karine S. Moe and Felicia Marie Knaul 2001. "Youth education and work in Mexico." *World Development*. 29:167–188.

Levison, Deborah and Marta Murray-Close 2005. "Challenges in Determining How Child Work Affects Child Health." *Public Health Reports*. 120:1–12.

Levison, Deborah, Jasper Hoek, David Lam and Suzanne Duryea 2007. "Intermittent Child Employment and Its Implications for Estimates of Child Labour." *International Labour Review*. 146:217–251.

Levison, Deborah and Anna Langer 2009. *Counting Cinderellas: Numbers and Trends of Child Domestic Servants*. Detroit.

Liebel, Manfred 2001a. "A right to work for children? Experiences from the 'Third World' for the 'First World.'" In Liebel, M., B. Overwien and A. Rechnagel (eds.), *Working Children's Protagonism: Social Movements and empowerment in Latin America, Africa and India*. Frankfurt and London: Verlag für Interkulturelle Kommunikation. 221–232.

——— 2001b. "The dignity of the working child: What children in Nicaragua, El Salvador and Guatemala think about their work." In Liebel, M., B. Overwien and A. Rechnagel (eds.), *Working Children's Protagonism: Social Movements and empowerment in Latin America, Africa and India*. Frankfurt and London: Verlag für Interkulturelle Kommunikation. 53–66.

Liebel, Manfred 2003. "Working children as social subjects: the contribution of working children's organisations to social transformations." *Childhood*. 10:265–285.

—— 2004. *A Will of their Own: Cross-Cultural Perspectives on Working Children*. London & New York: Zed Books.

Lieten, G. Kristoffel 2000. "Children, Work and Education." *Economic and Political Weekly*. 35:2037–2043, 2171–2178.

—— 2009. "Toward an Integrative Theory of Child Labor." In Hindman, H. D. (ed.), *The World of Child Labor: A Reference Encylopedia*. New York: M.E. Sharpe. 26–32.

Lieten, G. K., Anup K. Karan and Anoop K. Satpathy 2005. *Children, School and Work: Glimpses from India*. Amsterdam and New Delhi: IREWOC and Institute for Human Development.

Lister, Ruth 2008. "Unpacking children's citizenship." In Invernizzi, A. and J. Williams (eds.), *Children and Citizenship*. Los Angeles, London: Sage. 9–19.

Loreman, Tim 2009. *Respecting Childhood.* . London & New York: Continuum.

Madsian, Carla 2004. "Not for bread alone: peanut vendors in Brazil." In Lieten, G. K. (ed.), *Working Children Around the World*. Amsterdam & New Delhi: IREWOC Foundation & Institute for Human Development. 128–139.

Malhotra, Rajeev, Arvinder S. Sachdeva and S. V. Ramana Murthy 2003. "Child labour in India: nature and policy options." In Lieten, G. K., R. Srivastava and S. Thorat (eds.), *Small Hands in South Asia: Child Labour in Perspective*. New Delhi: Manohar. 127–145.

Manacorda, M. and Furio Rosati 2007. *Local labor demand and child labor*. Rome: Understanding Children's Work (UCW) Project.

Manning, Wendy D. 1990. "Parenting employed teenagers." *Youth and Society*. 22:184–220.

Mansurov, Valery 2001. "Child labour in Russia." In Mizen, P., C. Pole and A. Bollton (eds.), *Hidden Hands: International Perspectives on Children's Work and Labour*. London: Routledge-Farmer. 149–166.

Mantle, Greg, Jane Leslie, Sarah Parsons, Jackie Plenty and Ray Shaffer 2006. "Establishing children's wishes and feelings for family court reports: The significance attached to the age of the child." *Childhood*. 13:499–518.

Mason, Jan and Jan Falloon 2001. "Some Sydney children define abuse: implications for agency in childhood." In Mayall, B. (ed.), *Conceptualizing Child-Adult Relations*. London: Routledge/Falmer. 99–113.

McKechnie, Jim and Sandy Hobbs 1998. *Working Children: Reconsidering the Debates. Report of the International Working Group on Child Labour*. Amsterdam: Defence for Children International & International Society for the Prevention of Child Abuse and Neglect.

McKechnie, Jim and Sandy Hobbs 1999. "Child labour: The view from the North." *Childhood*. 6:89–100.

McKechnie, Jim, Seonaid Anderson and Sandy Hobbes 2005. *Cumbria's Working Youngsters: A 2004 Update*. Cumbria County Council.

Medick, Hans 1976. "The proto-industrial family economy: the structural function of household and family during the transition from peasant society to industrial capitalism." *Social History*. 2:291–315.

Miljeteig, Per 2001. "Establishing partnerships with working children and youth." In Lieten, G. K. and B. White (eds.), *Child Labour: Policy Options*. Amsterdam: Aksant. 117–129.

—— 2005. "Children's democratic rights: What we can learn from young workers organising themselves." In Mason, J. and T. Fattore (eds.), *Children Taken Seriously in Theory, Policy and Practice*. London and Philadelphia: Jessica Kingsley. 123–135.

Ministerie van Sociale Zaken 2009a. *Arbeid door Jongeren: Informatie voor Werkgevers*. The Hague: Ministerie van Sociale Zaken en Werkgelegenheid.

—— 2009b. *Vakantiewerk 2009*. The Hague: Ministerie van Sociale Zaken en Werkgelegenheid.

—— 2009c. *Minimumloon: informatie voor werknemers*. The Hague: Ministerie van Sociale Zaken en Werkgelegenheid.

Mizen, Philip, Angela Bolton and Christopher Pole 1999. "School age workers: the paid employment of children in Britain." *Work, Employment and Society.* 13:423–438.

Mizen, Philip, Christopher Pole and Angela Bollton 2001. "Why be a school age worker?" In Mizen, P., C. Pole and A. Bollton (eds.), *Hidden Hands: International Perspectives on Children's Work and Labour*. London: RoutledgeFarmer. 37–54.

MNNATSOP 1999. *Declaration By The National Movement Of Working Children And Adolescents Of Peru (Mnnatsop) On The New ILO Convention Concerning Child Labour.*

Montgomery, Heather 2001. *Modern Babylon? Prostituting Children in Thailand*. In Parkin, D. and S. Tremayne (eds.). Fertility, Reproduction and Sexuality. Oxford: Berghahn Books.

—— 2007. "Working with child prostitutes in Thailand: Problems of practice and interpretation." *Childhood.* 14:415–430.

—— 2009. "Are child prostitutes child workers? A case study." *International Journal of Sociology and Social Policy.* 29: 130–140.

Morice, Alain 1982. "Underpaid child labour and social reproduction: apprenticeship in Kaolack, Senegal." *Development and Change.'* 13:515–526.

Morley, Samuel A. and David Coady 2003. *From Social Assistance to Social Development: Targeted Education Subsidies in Developing Countries. IFPRI.* Washington, D.C.: International Food Policy Research Institute.

Morrow, Virginia 1994. "Responsible children? Aspect's of children's work and employment outside school in contemporary UK." In Mayall, B. (ed.), *Children's Childhoods: Observed and experienced*. London: Farmer Press. 128–143.

—— 1999. "'We are people too': Children's and young people's perspectives on children's rights and decision-making in England." *International Journal of Children's Rights.* 7:149–170.

—— 2005. "Social capital, community cohesion and participation in England: a space for children and young people?" In Milne, B. and A. Invernizzi (eds.), *Children's Citizenship: An Emergent Discourse on the Rights of the Child?* Delhi: Kamla-Raj. 58–69.

Mortimer, Jeylan T. 2003. *Work and Growing Up in America*. Cambridge, MA: Harvard University Press.

—— 2007. "Working and Growing Up in America: Myths and Realities." In Hungerland, B., M. Liebel, B. Milne and A. Wihstutz (eds.), *Working to be Someone: Child Focused Research and Practice with Working Children*. London and Philadelphia: Jessica Kingsley. 117–132.

Moser, Caroline O.N. 1996. *Confronting Crisis: A Comparative Study of Household Responses to Poverty and Vulnerability in Four Poor Urban Communities*. Environmentally Sustainable Development Studies and Monographs Series. Washington, D.C.: The World Bank.

Mudege, Netsayi N., Eliya Zulu and Chimaraoke Izugbara 2008. "How insecurity impacts on school attendance and school drop out among urban slum children in Nairobi." *International Journal of Conflict and Violence.* 2:98–112.

Mueller, Eva L. 1984. "The value and allocation of time in rural Botswana." *Journal of Development Economics.* 15:329–360.

Myers, William 1988. "Alternative Services for Street Children: The Brazilian Approach." In Bequele, A. and J. Boyden (eds.), *Combating Child Labour*. Geneva: ILO. 125–143.

—— 2001. "Valuing diverse approaches to child labour." In Lieten, G. K. and B. White (eds.), *Child Labour: Policy Options*. Amsterdam: Aksant. 27–48.

Myers, William 2001a. "The Right Rights? Child labor in a globalizing world." *Annals of the American Association of Political and Social Science.* 575:38–55.

—— 2001b. "Can children's work and education be reconciled." *International Journal of Educational Policy, Research and Practice.* 2:307–330.

—— 2009. "Organization of working children." In Hindman, H. D. (ed.), *The World of Child Labor: A Reference Encyclopedia.* New York: M.E. Sharpe, 153–157.

Myrstad, Geir 1999. "What can trade unions do to combat child labour?" *Childhood.* 6:75–88.

Naker, Dipak 2007. "From Rhetoric to Practice: Bridging the Gap between What We Believe and What We Do." *Children, Youth and Environments.* 17:146–158.

Nambissan, Geetha B. 2003. "Social exclusion, children's work and education: a view from the margins." In Kabeer, N., G. B. Nambissan and R. Subrahmanian (eds.), *Child Labour and the Right to Education in South Asia.* New Delhi: Sage. 109–142.

Nangia, Parveen and Nizamuddin Khan 2002. "Educational deprivation and employment status of children in rural areas of Andhra Pradesh, Madhya Pradesh and Orissa: Evidences from NHFS-2." In Ramachandran, N. and L. Massun (eds.), *Coming to Grips with Rural Child Work.* Institute for Human Development. 324–344.

Narayan, Deepa, Raj Patel, Kai Schafft, Anne Rademacher and Sarah Koch-Schulte 2000. *Voices of the Poor: Can Anyone Hear Us?* New York: Oxford University Press.

Nardinelli, Clark 1990. *Child Labour and the Industrial Revolution.* Bloomington: Indiana University Press.

Nasaw, David 1996. *Children of the City at Work and at Play.* New York: Oxford University Press.

Nieuwenhuijs, Olga 1998. "Global childhood and the politics of contempt." *Alternatives.* 23:267–289.

—— 1997. "The paradox of the competent child and the global childhood agenda." In Fardon, R., W. v. Binsbergen and R. v. Dijk (eds.), Leiden and London: EIDOS. 33–48.

—— 2000. "The household economy in the commercial exploitation of children's work: The case of Kerala." In Schlemmer, B. (ed.), *The Exploited Child.* London and New York: Zed Books. 278–291.

—— 2005. "The wealth of children: reconsidering the child labour debate." In Qvortrup, J. (ed.), *Studies in Modern Childhood: Society, Agency, Culture.* Basingstoke: Palgrave Macmillan. 167–183.

Nilsen, Ann C. E. 2002. *Negotiating Children's Work: A Comparative Study of Children's Work in Norway and Zimbabwe,* M.Sc. Dissertation. Bergen: Department of Sociology, University of Bergen.

Nyambedha, Erick Otieno and Jens Aagaard-Hansen 2003. "Changing place, changing position: orphans' movements in a community with high HIV/AIDS in Western Kenya." In Olwig, K. F. and E. Gulløv (eds.), *Children's Places.* London, New York: Routledge. 162–176.

O'Callaghan, Marion 1977. *Southern Rhodesia: The Effects of a Conquest Society on Education, Culture and Information.* Paris: UNESCO.

O'Connell Davidson, Julia 2001. *Children in the Sex Trade in China.* Stockholm: Save the Children, Sweden.

—— 2005. *Children in the Global Sex Trade.* Cambridge: Polity Press.

O'Connell Davidson, Julia and Caitlin Farrow 2008. *Child Migration and the Construction of Vulnerability.* Stockholm: Save the Children, Sweden.

O'Donnell, Owen A., Eddy K. A. van Doorslaer and Furio C. Rosati 2002. *Child Labour and Health: Evidence and Research Issues.* Florence: ILO, UNICEF, World Bank.

O'Donnell, Owen A., Furio C. Rosati and Eddy van Doorslaer 2004. "Health effects of child work: Evidence from rural Vietnam." *Journal of Population Economics*. 18:437–467.

Obeng, Celia S. 2002. *"Home was uncomfortable; school was hell": A confessionalist-ethnographic account of traditional beliefs and socio-educational crises in the schooling of Ghanaian rural girls*. New York: Nova Science Publishers.

Oey-Gardiner, M. 2000. "Schooling in a Decentralized Indonesia: New Approaches to Access and Decision-making." *Bulletin of Indonesian Economic Studies*. 36:127–134.

Offit, Thomas A. 2008. *Conquistadores de la Calle: Child Street Labor in Guatemala City*. Austin: Texas University Press.

Oloko, Beatrice Adenike 1989. "Children's work in urban Nigeria: a case study of young Lagos street traders." In Myers, W. E. (ed.), *Protecting Working Children*. London: Zed Books. 11–23.

—— 1993. "Children's street work in urban Nigeria as adaptation and maladaptation to changing socioeconomic circumstances." *International Journal of Behavioural Development*. 16:465–482.

Omokhodion, F. O., S. I. Omokhodion and T. O. Odusote 2006. "Perceptions of child labour among working children in Ibadan, Nigeria." *Child: Care, Health & Development*. 32:281–286.

Orellana, Maarjorie Faulstich 2001. "The work kids do: Mexican and Central American immigrant children's contributions to households and schools in California." *Harvard Educational Review*. 71:366–389.

Oudenhoven, Nico van and Rekha Wazir 2006. *Newly Emerging Needs of Children: An Exploration*. Antwerp-Apeldoorn: Garant.

Ould, David, Claire Jordan, Rebecca Reynolds and Lacey Loftin 2004. *The Cocoa Industry in West Africa: A history of exploitation*. London: Anti-Slavery International.

Overwien, Bernd 2001. "Informal learning, social movements and the acquisition of competence for self-determined working and living." In Liebel, M., B. Overwien and A. Rechnagel (eds.), *Working Children's Protagonism: Social Movements and empowerment in Latin America, Africa and India*. Frankfurt and London: Verlag für Interkulturelle Kommunikation. 247–267.

Oyaide, Omolara Dakore 2000. *Child Domestic Labour in Lusaka: A Gender Perspective*. Lusaka: Department of Gender Studies, University of Zambia.

Panter-Brick, Catherine 2000. "Street children and their peers: perspectives on homelessness, poverty, and health." In Fottrell, D. (ed.), *Revisiting Children's Rights: 10 Years of the UN Convention on the Rights of the Child*. The Hague: Kluwer Law International. 83–97.

Parker, David forthcoming. "The Health Effects of Child Labour." In Fassa, A., D. Parker and T. Scanlon (eds.), *Child Labour and Public Health (tentative title)*. Oxford.

Paul-Majunder, Pratima and Jamil H. Chowdhury 1993. *Child Workers in the Garment Industry in Bangladesh, unpublished paper, ACPR, n.d. (but known to be released November 1993)*. Dhaka: Associates for Community and Research.

Paul-Majunder, Pratima and Sharifa Begum 1997. *Upward Occupational Mobility Among Female Workers in the Garment Industry of Bangladesh, Dhaka: BIDS, October 1997*. Dhaka: Bangladesh Institute of Development Studies.

Pearl, Judea 2000. *Causality: Models, Reasoning, and Inference*. Cambridge: Cambridge University Press.

Pelto, Bert 1997. *Daily Lives of Working Children: Case Studies from Bangladesh*. Dhaka: UNICEF.

Percy-Smith, Barry and Karen Malone 2001. "Making children's participation in neighbourhood settings relevant to the everyday lives of young people." *PLA Notes*. 18–22.

Pieterse, Jan Nederveen 2002. "Global inequality: bringing politics back in." *Third World Quarterly.* 23:1023–1046.

Pineda, Gustavo and Bertha Rosa Guerra 1998. *How Children See Their World: An Exploratory Study.* Managua: Redd Barna.

Pinheiro, Paulo Sérgio 2006. *World Report on Violence Against Children.* Geneva: United Nations.

Pole, Christopher 2007. "Vocabularies, motives and meanings—school-age workers in Britain: Towards a synthesis?" In Hungerland, B., M. Liebel, B. Milne and A. Wihstutz (eds.), *Working to be Someone: Child Focused Research and Practice with Working Children.* London and Philadelphia: Jessica Kingsley. 151–160.

Post, David 2001. *Children's Work, Schooling, and Welfare in Latin America.* Boulder CO: Westview Press.

Post, David and Suet-ling Pong 2009. "Student labour and academic proficiency in international perspective." *International Labour Review.* 148:93–122.

Powell, Steve 2007. *Children Speak Out: What Influences Child Trafficking in Southeast Europe. Bosnia and Herzegovina—short report.* Sarajevo: Save the Children Norway South East Europe Regional Office.

Prakash, Aseem 2002. "Food insecurity and children in Madya Pradesh: A need for structural change." In Ramachandran, N. and L. Massün (eds.), *Coming to grips with Rural child work.* New Delhi: Institute for Human Development and UN World Food Programme. 260–277.

Psacharopoulos, George 1997. "Child labour versus educational attainment: Some evidence from Latin America." *Journal of Population Economics.* 10:377–386.

Punch, Samantha 2001. "Household division of labour: Generation, gender, age, birth order and sibling composition." *Work, Employment and Society.* 15:803–823.

Quashigah, E. K. 1998. "Religious freedom and vestal virgins: the 'trokosi' practice in Ghana." *African Journal of International and Comparative Law.* 10:193–215.

Qvortrup, Jens 2001. "School-work, paid work and the changing obligations of childhood." In Mizen, P., C. Pole and A. Bolton (eds.), *Hidden Hands: International Perspectives on Children's Work and Labour.* London: Routledge Farmer. 91–107.

Raffles, Stanford 1817. *The History of Java.* London.

Rahman, Wahidur no date. *Feasibility of an Educational Programm for the Working Girls of the Garment Industries and a Prototype Model, unpublished draft report prepared for the ILO.* Dhaka: Underprivileged Children's Educational Programs.

Rajagopal, Shobhita 2003. "Operationalising the right to education: the Lok Jumbish experience in Rjasthan." In Kabeer, N., G. B. Nambissan and R. Subrahmanian (eds.), *Child Labour and the Right to Education in South Asia.* New Delhi: Sage. 304–320.

Rani, D. Lakshmi and Manabendranath Roy (ed.) 2005. *Child Domestic Work: A Violation of Human Rights: Issues, causes and consequences in West Bengal.* Kolkata: Save the Children, UK.

Ratna, Kavita 2000. *Documenting Bhima Sangha's process.* Oxford.

Ravallion, Martin and Quentin Wodon 2000. "Does child labour displace schooling? Evidence on behavioural responses to an enrolment subsidy." *The Economic Journal.* C158–C175.

Ravololomanga, Bernard and Bernard Schlemmer 2000. "'Unexploited' labour: Social transition in Madagascar." In Schlemmer, B. (ed.), *The Exploited Child.* London and New York: Zed Books. 300–314.

Ray, Manabendranath and Asha N. Iyer 2006. *Abuse among Child Domestic Workers: A Research Study in West Bengal.* Calcutta: Save the Children, U.K.

Ray, Ranjan 2000a. "Child Labor, Child Schooling, and Their Interaction with Adult Labor: Empirical Evidence for Peru and Pakistan." *World Bank Economic Review.* 14:347–367.

—— 2000b. "Analysis of child labor in Peru and Pakistan: A comparative study." *Journal of Population Economics.* 13:3–19.

—— 2009. "Education and child labor: a global perspective." In Hindman, H. D. (ed.), *The World of Child Labor: A Reference Encyclopedia.* New York: M.E. Sharpe.

Reddy, B. S. 2000. *IDS Project: Background Note on Andhra Pradesh.* (mimeo). Hyderabad: Osmania University, Hyderabad.

Reddy, Nandana and Kavita Ratna 2002. *A Journey in Children's Participation.* Bangalore: Concerned for Working Children.

Rende Taylor, Lisa 2005. "Dangerous trade-offs: The behavioural ecology of child-labor and prostitution in rural northern Thailand." *Current Anthropology.* 46:411–431.

Rialp, Victoria V. 2005. "Combatting child labor in the Philippines: Listening to the children." In Weston, B. (ed.), *Child Labor and Human Rights.* Boulder and London: Lynne Reinner. 187–208.

Riisøen, Kari Hauge, Anne Hatløy and Lise Bjerkan 2004. *Travel to Uncertainty: A study of child relocation in Burkina Faso, Ghana and Mali.* Fafo-report 440. Oslo: Fafo.

Robson, Elsbeth 2004. "Children at work in rural Nigeria: patterns of age, space and gender." *Journal of Rural Studies.* 20:193–210.

Rodda, Michela Da 2007. *Participation and Protagonism: The Working Children's Movement in Venezuela,* The Hague: Institute of Social Studies.

Rogoff, Barbara 1990. *Apprenticeship in Thinking: cognitive development in social context.* New York: Oxford University Press.

—— 2003. *The Cultural Nature of Human Development.* New York: Oxford University Press.

Rosen, David M. 2007. "Child soldiers, international humanitarian law, and the globalisation of childhood." *American Anthropologist.* 109:296–306.

Sabo, Kim 2001. "The benefits of participatory evaluation for children and youth." *PLA Notes.* 48–51.

Sachikonye, Lloyd M. 1991. *Child Labour in Hazardous Employment: The Case of Zimbabwe.* Consultancy Report Series. Harare: Zimbabwe Institute of Development Studies.

Salazar, Marìa Cristina and Walter A. Glasinovich (ed.) 1998. *Child Work and Education: Five case studies from Latin America.* Florence: UNICEF.

Sanon, Chandragupt S. 1998. *Working Children: A Sociological Analysis.* New Delhi: APH Publishing.

Sastre, Béatrice S. Céspides and María-Isabel Zarama V. Meyer 2000. "Living and working conditions: child labour in the coal mines of Colombia." In Schlemmer, B. (ed.), *The Exploited Child.* London and New York: Zed Books. 83–92.

Save the Children Alliance 2007. *Children and Work: Save the Children's position on children and work.* London: Save the Children Alliance.

Save the Children Sweden 2001. *The Commercial and Sexual Exploitation of Children in St Petersburg and Northwest Russia.* Stockholm: Save the Children Sweden.

Save the Children U.K. 1997. *Stitching Footballs: Voices of Children in Sialkot, Pakistan.* London: Save the Children Fund.

—— 2000. *A Situational Analysis of Children in the Informal Mining Sector in Mutorashanga and Shamva.* Harare: Save the Children U.K.

—— 2005. *Children's views and definitions of harmful work: implications for policies and practice.* Dhaka, Bangladesh: Save the Children UK.

Schlemmer, Bernard 2000. "General introduction." In Schlemmer, B. (ed.), *The Exploited Child.* London & New York: Zed Books. 1–18.

Schultz, T. Paul 2004. "School Subsidies for the Poor: Evaluating the Mexican PROGRESA Poverty Program." *Journal of Development Economics.* 74:199–250.

Shady, Norbert R. 2002. *The (Positive) Effect of Macroeconomic Crises on the Schooling and Employment Decisions of Children in a Middle-Income Country.* World Bank Policy Research Working Paper, No. 2762. Washington, DC: World Bank.

Sharp, Lesley A. 1996. "The work ideology of Malagasy children: Schooling and survival in urban Madagascar." *Anthropology of Work Review.* 17:36–42.

Shepler, S. 2004. *The Social and Cultural Context of Child Soldiering in Sierra Leone.* Oslo.

Sinclair, Ruth 2004. "Participation in practice: Making it meaningful, effective and sustainable." *Children & Society.* 18:106–118.

Sinclair, Ruth, K. Cronin, L. Lanyon, V. Stone and A. Hulsi 2002. *Aim High Stay Real: Outcomes for Children and Young People: The Views of Children, Parents and Professionals.* London: Children and Young People's Unit.

Sinha, Santha 2003. "Schools as institutions for the elimination of child labour. The experience of the MV Foundation in the Ranga Reddy District." In Kabeer, N., G. B. Nambissan and R. Subrahmanian (eds.), *Child Labour and the Right to Education in South Asia.* New Delhi: Sage. 321–334.

Skoufias, Emmanuel 1994. "Market Wages, Family Composition and the Time Allocation of Children in Agricultural Households." *Journal of Development Studies.* 30:335–360.

Skoufias, Emmanuel and Susan W. Parker 2009. "The Impact of PROGRESA on Child Labor and Schooling. In , eds. Palgrave Macmillan." In Orazem, P., G. Sedlacek and Z. Tzannatos (eds.), *Child Labor and Education in Latin America: An Economic Perspective.* Basingstoke: Palgrave Macmillan. 167–185.

Smidt, Sandra 2006. *The Developing Child in the 21st Century: A Global Perspective on Child Development.* London: Routledge.

Smucker, Glenn R. and Gerald F. Murray 2004. *The Uses of Children: A Study of Trafficking in Haitian Children.* Port-au-Prince: USAID, Haiti Mission.

Sommerfelt, Tone 2003a. "Petites Bonnes and Their Parents: Experiences and Motivational Factors." In Sommerfelt, T. (ed.), *Domestic Child Labour in Morocco: An analysis of the parties involved in relationships to "Petites Bonnes."* Oslo: Fafo Institute for Applied Social Science. 21–69.

Sommerfelt, Tone (ed.) 2003b. *Domestic Child Labour in Morocco: An analysis of the parties involved in relationships to "Petites Bonnes."* Fafo Report 370.oslo: Fafo Institute for Applied Social Science.

Song, M. 1999. *Helping Out: Children's Labor in Ethnic Business.* Philadelphia: Temple University Press.

Spittler, G. 2001. *Work: anthropological aspects.* Amsterdam: Elsevier.

Stack, Niamh and Jim McKechnie 2002. "Working children." In Goldson, B., M. Lavalette and J. McKechnie (eds.), *Children, Welfare and the State.* London: Sage. 87–101.

Staff, Jeremy and Jeylan T. Mortimer 2007. "Educational and work strategies from adolescence to early adulthood: Consequences for educational attainment." *Social Forces.* 85:1169–1194.

Stafford, Anne, Ann Laybourn, Malcolm Hill and Moira Walker 2003. "'Having a say': Children and young people talk about consultation." *Children & Society.* 17:361–373.

Staunton, Irene (ed.) 2008. *Our Broken Dreams: Child Migration in Southern Africa.* Harare: Weaver Press.

Stearns, Peter N. 2006. *Childhood in World History.* New York and London: Routledge.

Strakova, Nadia and Pavel Vondra 2008. *Stop Child Labour Africa Tour: Final Integrated Report.* Stop Child Labour.

Super, C. and S. Harkness 1986. "The developmental niche: a conceptualisation at the interface of child and culture." *International Journal of Behavioural Development.* 9:545–569.

Swart, Jill 1989. *Malunde: The Street Children of Hillbrow.* Johannesburg: University of Witwatersrand Press.

Swift, Anthony 1999. *Working Children Get Organised.* London: International Save the Children Alliance.

Talib, Mohammad 2003. "Modes of learning-labour relations: educational strategies and child labour." In Kabeer, N., G. B. Nambissan and R. Subrahmanian (eds.), *Child Labour and the Right to Education in South Asia.* New Delhi: Sage. 143–163.

Taracena, Elvia 2003. "A schooling model for working children in Mexico: the case of children of Indian origin working as agricultural workers during the harvest." *Childhood.* 10:301–318.

Theis, Joachim 2001. "Participatory research with children in Vietnam." In Schwartzman, H. B. (ed.), *Children and Anthropology: Perspectives for the 21st Century.* London: Bergin and Garvey. 99–109.

Thomas, Nigel 2000. *Children, Family, and the State: Decision-Making and Child Participation.* London: MacMillan.

—— 2007. "Towards a theory of children's participation." *International Journal of Children's Rights.* 15:199–218.

Thorne, Barry 1987. "Re-visioning women and social change: where are the children?" *Gender and Society.* 1:85–109.

Thorsen, Dorte 2006. "Child migrants in transit. Strategies to assert new identities in rural Burkina Faso." In Christiansen, C., M. Utas and H. E. Vigh (eds.), *Navigating Youth, Generating Adulthood. Social Becoming in an African Context.* Uppsala: Nordiska Afrikainstitutet. 88–114.

Tjandraningsih, Indrasari and Popon Anarita 2002. *Pekerja Anak di Perkebunan Tembakau (Child workers in tobacco plantations).* Bandung: AKATIGA.

Tyldum, Guri, Marianne Tveit and Anette Brunovskis 2005. *Taking Stock: A review of the existing research on trafficking for exploitation.* Fafo report 493. Oslo: FAFO.

Umaña Aponte, Claudia Marcele 2003. "Child Labour and the Economic Recession of 1999 in Colombia." *Revista de Economía del Rosario.* 6:139–178.

UNICEF 1998a. *Child Domestic Workers.* Innocenti Digest, Issue No. 5. Florence: UNICEF.

—— 1998b. *Implementation Handbook for the Convention on the Rights of the Child.* New York: UNICEF.

—— 2005. *Child Labour Today.* London: UNICEF.

—— 2006. *Africa's Orphaned and Vulnerable Generations: Children Affected by AIDS.* UNICEF.

—— 2009. Progress for Children: A Report Card on Child Protection. New York: UNICEF.

UNICEF and ILO 2004. *Addressing Child Labour in the Bangladesh Garment Industry 1995–2001: A synthesis on UNICEF and ILO evaluation studies of the Bangladesh garment sector projects.* New York and Geneva: UNICEF and ILO.

Volpi, Elena 2003. "Street Children: Promising Practices and Approaches." *Children, Youth and Environments.* 13.

Waal, C. S. van der 1996. "Rural children and residential instability in the Northern Province of South Africa." *Social Dynamics.* 22:31–53.

Wal, S. 2006. *Child Labour in Various Industries.* Encyclopaedia of Child Development: Priorities for 21st Century. New Delhi: Sarap and Sons.

Weiner, Eric 2008. *The Geography of Bliss.* New York: TWELVE.

Weiner, Myron 1991. *The Child and the State in India: Child Labor and Education Policy in Comparative Perspective.* Princeton, NJ: Princeton University Press.

Wenger, Martha 2008. "Children's Work, Play and Relationships among the Giriama of Kenya." In Levine, R. A. and R. S. New (eds.), *Anthropology and Child Development: A Cross-Cultural Reader*. London: Blackwell. 287–306.

Werner, Emmy E. 1989. "Adolescents and work: A longitudinal perspective on gender and cultural variability." In Stern, D. and D. Eichorn (eds.), *Adolescence and Work: Influences of Social Structure, Labor markets. and Culture*. Hillside, New Jersey: Lawrence Erlbaum Associates.

Werner, Emmy E. and Ruth S. Smith 1982. *Vulnerable but Invincible: A Longitudinal Study of Resilient Children and Youth*. New York: McGraw-Hill.

Werner, Emmy E. and Ruth S. Smith 1992. *Overcoming the Odds: High Risk Children from Birth to Adulthood*. Ithaca: Cornell University Press.

Wessells, Michael 2006. *Child Soldiers: From Violence to Protection*. Cambridge, Mass.: Harvard University Press.

Weston, Burns H. 2005. "Bringing human rights to child labour: Guiding principles and call to action." In Weston, B. H. (ed.), *Child Labor and Human Rights:*. Boulder & London: Lynne Reiner. 427–436.

Weston, Burns H. and Mark B. Teerink 2005. "Rethinking child labor: a multidimensional human rights problem." In Weston, B. H. (ed.), *Child Labor and Human Rights*. Boulder & London: Lynne Reiner. 3–25.

White, Ben 1994. "Children, Work and Child Labour: Changing responses to the Employment of Children." *Development and Change*. 25:854–861.

—— 1996. "Globalization and the child labour problem." *Journal of International Development*. 8:829–839.

—— 1997. "Child labour in the international context." In McCloskey, S. (ed.), *No Time to Play: Local and Global Perspectives on Child Employment*. Belfast: One World Centre for Northern Ireland. 11–28.

—— 1999. "Defining the intolerable: Child work, global standards and cultural relativism." *Childhood*. 6:133–144.

—— 2004. "Constructing Child Labour: Attitudes to Juvenile work in Indonesia, 1900–2000." In Elmhirst, R. and R. Saptari (eds.), *Labour in Southeast Asia: Local Processes in a Globalised World*. London: Routledge. 77–105.

—— 2005. "Shifting positions on child labor: the views and practices of intergovernmental organizations." In Weston, B. (ed.), *Child Labor and Human Rights*. Boulder & London: Lynne Reiner. 319–342.

—— 2009. "Labour in childhood's global past: child work and colonial policies in Indonesia, 1800–1949." In Lieten, G. K. and E. v. Nederveen Meerkerk (eds.), *Child labour's global past, 1600–2000*. Bern: Peter Lang.

White, Ben and Indrasari Tjandraningsih 1998. *Child Workers in Indonesia*. Bandung: Akatiga.

White, Ben, Ugik Margiyatin, Lusia Peilouw and Atsushi Sano 2009. *Youth, Generation and Development: The Experience of Teenagers in Three Indonesian Regions*. Ottawa.

White, Sarah C. and Shyamol A. Choudhury 2007. "The Politics of Child Participation in International Development: The Dilemma of Agency." *The European Journal of Development Research*. 19:529–550.

Whitehead, Ann, Iman M. Hashim and Vegard Iversen 2007. *Child Migration, Child Agency and Inter-Generational Relations in Africa and South Asia*. Working Paper T24. Brighton: Development Research Centre on Migration, Globalisation and Poverty, University of Sussex.

Whitney, Ben 1999. "Unenforced or unenforceable? A view from the professions." In Lavalette, M. (ed.), *A Thing of the Past? Child Labour in Britain in the Nineteenth and Twentieth Centuries*. Liverpool: Liverpool University Press. 231–247.

Wihstutz, Anne 2007. "The significance of care and domestic work to children: a German portrayal." In Hungerland, B., M. Liebel, B. Milne and A. Wihstutz (eds.), *Working to be Someone: Child Focused Research and Practice with Working Children*. London and Philadelphia: Jessica Kingsley. 77–86.

Wilk, Valerie A. 1993. "Health hazards to children in agriculture." *American Journal of Industrial Medicine*. 24:283–290.

Winrock International 2008. *Best Practices in Preventing and Eliminating Child Labor through Education Drawn from the Global Circle Project*. Arlington VA: Winrock International.

Wolf, Joshua 2009. "What Makes us Happy?" *The Atlantic*. 303:36–53.

Woodhead, Martin 1998. *Children's Perceptions of Their Working Lives. A participatory study in Bangladesh, Ethiopia, the Philippines, Guatemala, El Salvador, and Nicaragua*. Stockholm: Save the Children, Sweden.

—— 1999. *Is There a Place for Work in Child Development?* Stockholm: Save the Children, Sweden.

—— 2001. "The value of work and school: A study of working children's perspectives." In Lieten, G. K. and B. White (eds.), *Child Labour: Policy Options*. Amsterdam: Aksant. 103–116.

—— 2004. "Psychosocial Impacts of Child Work: A Framework for Research, Monitoring and Intervention." *International Journal of Children's Rights*. 12:321–377.

Woods, Robert 1992. *The Population of Britain in the Nineteenth Century*. New Studies in Economic and Social History, no. 20. Cambridge: Cambridge University Press.

World Health Organization 2004. *Global Status Report on Alcohol 2004*. Geneva: WHO.

World Movement of Working Children. (2004). "Final Declaration of the 2nd Meeting of the World Movement of Working Children and Adolescents, Berlin, Germany, April 19 to May 2, 2004." Retrieved August 10, 2007, from http://www.rb.se/NR/rdonlyres/ F69FDA7D-6418-4DF6-A3C6-BB818A2A4EF3/0/WorkingchildrenFinalDeclaration Berlin2004.pdf.

Wyness, Michael 2005. "Regulating participation: The possibilities and limits of children and young people's councils." In Milne, B. and A. Invernizzi (eds.), *Children's Citizenship: An Emergent Discourse on the Rights of the Child?* Delhi: Kamla-Raj. 7–18.

Zalami, Fatima Badry, Nandana Reddy, Margaret A. Lynch and Clare Feinstein 1998. *Forgotten on the Pyjama Trail: A Case Study of Garment Workers in Méknès (Morocco) Dismissed from their Jobs Following Foreign Media Attention*. Amsterdam: Defence for Children International/ International Society for the Prevention of Child Abuse and Neglect.

Zaman, Anisa and Thérèse Blanchet 2003. *Literature Review: Slavery and slave-like conditions among children in Bangladesh*. Dhaka: Save the Children Sweden and Denmark.

ZARD and MAPODE 2001. *"Invisible Girls": The life circumstances and legal situation of female street children in Lusaka*. Lusaka: Zambia Association for Research and Development; Movement of Community Action for the Prevention and Protection of Young People against Poverty, Destitution, Diseases and Exploitation.

Žegarac, Nevenka 2007. *Children Speak Out: Trafficking Risk and Resilience in Southeast Europe. Serbia Report*. Belgrade: Save the Children UK.

Zelizer, Viviana A. 2002. "Kids and commerce." *Childhood*. 9:375–396.

Zhou, Xueguang and Liren Hou 1999. "Children of the Cultural revolution: The State and the Life Course in the People's Republic of China." *American Sociological Review*. 63:12–36.

Zimmermann, B. 2001. "Work and labor: History of the concept." In Smelser, N. J. and P. B. Baltes (eds.), *International Encyclopedia of the Social and Behavioral Sciences*. Amsterdam: Elsevier. 16:561–565.

Zohir, Salma Chaudhuri and Pratima Paul-Majunder 1996. *Garment Workers in Bangladesh: Economic, Social and Health Conditions.* Dhaka: Bangladesh Institute of Development Studies.

Zweegers, Sonja (ed.) 2005. *Studying Child Labour: Policy implications of child-centered research.* Amsterdam: International Research on Working Children.

INDEX

Note: References to end-note numbers are indicated by "n".
Note: References to tables are indicated by *italics*.

ABOUT THE AUTHORS

Michael Bourdillon was born in Zambia, studied Social Anthropology at Oxford University, and taught for over twenty-five years in the Department of Sociology, University of Zimbabwe, where he now holds the post of Emeritus Professor. He is an honorary fellow of the Royal Anthropological Institute of Great Britain. He has conducted and supervised field research on working children in Zimbabwe. He has been involved with support for street children in Harare for twenty years, and has worked with NGOs supporting working children and children's participation locally, regionally, and internationally.

Deborah Levison is a Professor at the University of Minnesota's Hubert H. Humphrey Institute of Public Affairs. She has a Ph.D. in Economics from the University of Michigan, where she also was trained in Population Studies. Much of her research focuses on children's work and schooling in the context of the household, with particular attention to gendered dimensions of work. Recent projects include analyses of microdata from surveys in urban Brazil and Egypt. Levison is one of the investigators on the IPUMS-International project, which collects and distributes census data from around the world.

William Myers is an associate in the Department of Human and Community Development, University of California, Davis. He received his Master of Public Administration and Doctor of Education degrees from Harvard University, where he explored education and training for rural development. Throughout his career, which includes stints with UNICEF and the International Labour Office (ILO), he has been interested in education-work linkages, especially in regards to children and youth, as well as the protection of working children. He is author or co-author of numerous publications, primarily on child labor issues.

Ben White is Professor of Rural Sociology at the Institute of Social Studies, The Hague, where he has taught rural development and childhood/youth studies for 30 years, and Professor in Social Sciences at the University of Amsterdam.

He has a B.A. from Oxford University, and a Ph.D. in Anthropology from Columbia University. Many of his publications focus on Indonesia, where he has been involved in research since the early 1970s. His research interests focus on processes of rural change and the anthropology and history of childhood and youth, particularly in the area of child work. From 1997 to 2009 he was Chair of the Editorial Board of the journal *Development & Change*.